DICTATES OF CONSCIENCE

Laurie Lee Hall

DICTATES OF CONSCIENCE

FROM MORMON HIGH PRIEST TO MY NEW LIFE AS A WOMAN

Laurie Lee Hall

SIGNATURE BOOKS | 2024 | SALT LAKE CITY

Printed in the USA using paper from sustainably harvested sources.

Join our mail list at www.signaturebooks.com for details on events and related titles we think you'll enjoy.

Design by Jason Francis

FIRST EDITION | 2024

LIBRARY OF CONGRESS CONTROL NUMBER: 2024945741

Hardback ISBN: 978-1-56085-479-1
Ebook ISBN: 978-1-56085-498-2

Contents

“We claim the privilege of worshiping Almighty God according to the dictates of our own conscience, and allow all men the same privilege.”

—Joseph Smith, Article of Faith 11 of the Church of Jesus Christ of Latter-day Saints

TO ALL WHO DARE TO FOLLOW
THE DICTATES OF THEIR CONSCIENCE AND,
IN SO DOING, DISCOVER THE AUDACITY
TO LIVE WITH AUTHENTICITY

Acknowledgments

This book owes its existence to my loving Nancy Beaman, who created the safe space where I could connect and organize my lived experiences, re-experience the trauma, find healing, and find the courage to use my voice. I also owe it to my editor and publisher, Barbara Jones Brown, who has tirelessly sought to understand my life as a transgender woman, encouraged me to tease out unexplored elements of my story, and helped make my expression understandable for all readers. And finally, I acknowledge all those trans and nonbinary people, past and present, who have lived visible, vulnerable lives, providing the world with the example to follow their conscience and live authentically.

Preface

Why Share My Story, and Why Now?

Many Mormons and Mormon-adjacent people know of me because of my work as an architect for the Church of Jesus Christ of Latter-day Saints on high-profile projects over two decades. I also served ecclesiastically as a bishop and stake president for fourteen years. In these capacities, I associated closely with senior church leaders and came to know them and their character well. Most were sincere in their efforts and service. Some I relied upon as colleagues and friends.

Regarding my life pre-transition, there might be many, including women, who would have relished the opportunity to serve ecclesiastically in the church as I did, and likely many architects who would have loved to work on a single temple or some other major church project, let alone lead in their design and construction over many years. I recognize that these life experiences in my chosen field and area of service could only have occurred in the time and place they did because I benefited from male privilege and divine blessings.

That privilege and the visibility of these experiences, together with the notoriety that came from my publicly coming out, transitioning, and being put out of the church, have given me a powerful story to share. Though I might prefer to live in peaceful obscurity and blend into the world of cisgender women, I feel an obligation to use my voice to speak out for change and a better world for my LGBTQ community.

I have studied the burgeoning queer community in the Weimar Republic of Germany a century ago, particularly the scientific, social, and legal support afforded to transgender and cisgender queer citizens at that time. Tragically, that progress ended in 1933 with the rise of Nazi Germany. Within weeks, soldiers confiscated the library of the Institute for Sexual Science, which housed the foremost research on sexuality and gender then in existence. They held a public book burning in Berlin's city center, destroying thousands of irreplaceable documents and scholarly works on human sexuality. By the end of the year, gay and trans social clubs were shuttered, and queer magazines were forced to fold.[1]

My great hope is that we never repeat these kinds of horrors and that we will be committed to kindness, acceptance, and protecting the rights and bodily autonomy of all. As humans, we should never be driven apart by false wedges while paying no heed to the suffering of those who are different from us.

Transgender author and lecturer Jennifer Finney Boylan recently warned about the current political animosity against the transgender community in a guest essay for the *New York Times*. "We have become a favorite political boogeyman," she wrote. Like abortion rights, trans rights are "issues that go to the core of what we mean by bodily autonomy, and what kinds of choices individuals get to make about our private, physical selves." She noted that since efforts to exploit abortion bans for electoral gain have largely failed, the same marginalizing and criminalizing tactics have been trained on transgender people, especially youth.[2]

At the time of this writing, hundreds of thousands of transgender youth and adults cannot obtain gender-affirming healthcare or protections in the states where they live. Similar numbers have become modern political refugees, leaving their homes for states that have declared themselves sanctuaries to those seeking to escape the repression and obtain health care. In many cases, this has led to the division of families, where one parent lives with a transgender child in a sanctuary state while the other holds down a job in their current state.[3]

A significant majority of federal judges, both liberal and conservative, have ruled against anti-trans bans and statutes, noting violations of the constitutional rights of individuals to equal protection under the law and unlawful discrimination based on sex, in addition to the harm that enforcement of these measures would bring upon transgender persons, especially youth.[4]

Meanwhile, the apprehension and trauma the current political environment inflicts on trans people is damaging and potentially life-threatening. "It's not just dangerous rhetoric. In 2023 alone, some 20 states banned or limited gender-affirming care for minors; similar legislation is being debated in a number of others," writes Boylan. "Conservatives began by claiming they were protecting children—despite protests from the American Academy of Pediatrics that trans children should 'have access to comprehensive, gender-affirming, and developmentally appropriate health care that is provided in a safe and inclusive clinical space.' But they're now even attempting to restrict care for adults."[5]

My purpose is to combat this politically and religiously charged tsunami by affirming, through my story, what I view as three essential truths:

1. Gender identity is real. Self-determination is the only way to know a person's gender identity and should be accepted and respected.
2. Gender dysphoria is a real medical and mental health condition. The distress resulting from suppressing or denying one's identity interrupts peace and only grows more arduous with time if left unrecognized and untreated.
3. There is strength, peace, and joy in owning the truth of self-determined gender identity, pursuing gender-affirming healthcare, and finding personal and societal acceptance.

I share my life experiences as I remember them and, in some instances, as I recorded them at the time or as I researched other primary sources. Some accounts may not be consistent with the memories of others present. I am solely responsible for what I have written and the interpretations I have drawn.

Though I use the actual names of public figures, I have changed most of the personal names of other individuals to protect their privacy. In the rare cases where I use the actual names of private citizens, I do so with their permission.

What I have to say has broader application than just for transgender and nonbinary people, for the Mormon/Mormon-adjacent LGBTQ community, or those struggling against the constraints of any high-demand religion. However, it does speak directly to all of those. I grew up in a dysfunctional family. I was a teen trying to find myself in a world not designed for her, with no safe pathway forward or answers to give. Struggling under expectations entirely contrary to my desires, I broke free from constriction and poverty to gain my education and excel in my field of choice. I once crushed and buried my inner truth to follow a religious path that predicted acceptance and success, and in time, I achieved it all. Then, squarely faced with the cost of all I appeared to be, I gave it away to hold my inner truth again, discover its beauty, and offer it life.

Laurie Lee Hall
September 12, 2024

Notes

1. Natasha Frost, "The Early 20th-Century ID Cards That Kept Trans People Safe from Harassment," *Atlas Obscura,* November 2, 2017.

2. Jennifer Finney Boylan, "Abortion Rights and Trans Rights Are Two Sides of the Same Coin," *New York Times,* October 10, 2021, and Jennifer Finney Boylan, "Why Do Conservatives Attack Abortion and Trans Rights the Same Ways?" *New York Times,* September 9, 2021.

3. Charles M. Blow, "L.G.B.T.Q. Americans Could Become a 'New Class of Political Refugees,'" *New York Times,* June 14, 2023.

4. Brendan Pierson, "US judge in Florida blocks enforcement of state ban on gender-affirming care," *Reuters,* June 6, 2023.

5. Boylan, "Why do Conservatives Attack?"; Lee Savio Beers, MD, FAAP "American Academy of Pediatrics Speaks Out Against Bills Harming Transgender Youth," *American Academy of Pediatrics,* March 16, 2021.

Introduction

Orientation to Gender Identity

Modern scholarship has come to differentiate between "gender" and "sex." Gender identity is the innate and immutable personal sense of being masculine or feminine, in between, or neither. Most people's gender identity aligns with societal expectations of the sex assigned at birth based on their visible genitalia, but in many cases, it does not. Current terminology places those whose gender identity is at variance from their sex assigned at birth under the umbrella term "transgender and gender diverse" (TGD). About 1.3 million adults and 300,000 children in the United States reportedly identify as transgender, though stigma may still contribute to significant underreporting of the actual number.[1]

Examination or testing cannot definitively determine gender identity. The most effective way to know a person's gender identity is to allow them to describe their internal sense of self. For this reason, I tirelessly champion the importance and validity of each person's self-determined gender identity.

The Diagnostic and Statistical Manual of Mental Disorders, Fifth Edition (DSM-5), is the American Psychiatric Association's publication for classifying mental disorders using a common language and standard criteria. Until 2013, the DSM-4 classified the sense of one's gender identity being incongruent with their sex assigned at birth as "gender identity disorder" (GID). Just as the DSM declassified homosexuality as a mental disorder in 1973, forty years later, the DSM-5 reclassified GID as "gender dysphoria," removing the stigma of "mental health disorder" and employing a positive mental health treatment model.[2]

I was initially diagnosed with GID when I began therapy in the fall of 2012. But in 2013, I joined the first class of people diagnosed with gender dysphoria rather than GID, consequentially receiving a positive pathway for my effective treatment. The change from having a diagnosed "mental disorder" to a treatable "mental health condition" bolstered my sense of hope and potential wellness.

Not all people who feel gender incongruence experience negative gender dysphoria (the unnerving conflict between identity and body). Some may only choose a path incorporating a specific gender presentation that fully represents their sense of self regardless of their assigned sex. For example, gender presentation may include any combination of hair, accessories, clothing style, makeup, nail polish, how one carries oneself, voice tone, and so forth, which conform or conflict with societal norms for gender. Others seek treatment to mitigate gender dysphoria through mental health counseling and medical or surgical interventions. These steps often successfully bring their emotional state or their physical body to be more congruent with their gender identity. Those who have done so frequently report a reduction of the dysphoric conflict between identity and body to a neutral condition or even bring feelings of gender euphoria. Social transition (living consistently full-time according to one's gender identity), legal name or gender marker changes on identification documents, and using correct pronouns can also be affirming and essential to the individual.

Modern biology sheds additional new light on gender and sex. Biologists now suggest that gender is not "binary" but "bimodal."[3] According to the binary model, only two gender categories exist, and all humans fit into one of those two categories. This model assumes all primary bodily traits (reproductive organs, genes, and chromosomes) match the binary sex (male or female) assigned to the person at birth. The binary model also says that when maturation begins, secondary bodily traits align with the initial sex assigned at birth, including hormone levels, height, weight distribution, muscle mass, fat mass, hair texture, facial hair, and so forth.[4]

In contrast, the bimodal model declares that these characteristics exist on a spectrum of differences rather than in only two categories. Each individual falls along the spectrum between the male end of the bimodal model and the female end. "The notion that sex is not strictly binary is not even scientifically controversial," explains Dr. Steven Novella, a clinical neurologist at Yale University and executive editor of *Science-Based Medicine.* "Among experts, it is a given, an unavoidable conclusion derived from actually understanding the biology of sex. It is more accurate to describe biological sex in humans as bimodal but not strictly binary. There is every conceivable type of overlap in the middle."[5]

Biologists and geneticists have long acknowledged that some persons are biologically or anatomically "intersex," meaning they possess any variety of reproductive or sexual anatomy, hormonal activity or sensitivity, or numerous combinations of so-called "sex" chromosomes different from the binary XY (male) or XX (female). Sexual differentiation analysis suggests that between one and two percent of people in the United States are born with reproductive or sexual anatomy that doesn't fit the typical definition of female or male, a spectrum of conditions categorized by the term "differences in sexual development" or DSD.[6] Although being intersex is dissimilar from experiencing gender dysphoria, there is likely overlap between the two groups. At the very least, the existence of 36,000 to 72,000 intersex children born each year (based on a US annual rate of 3.6 million live births) establishes a significant exception to any notion of gender determined solely by the sex assigned at birth.

Even now, the non-consensual treatment and surgeries performed due to intersex conditions on newborns and children may outweigh the consensual gender-affirming care given to transgender children. Some states and countries are now outlawing non-consensual treatment and surgeries on intersex children. Other states, however, have proposed or passed legislation to ban gender-affirming care for transgender children while including legislative exceptions to *maintain* non-consensual gender-mandating treatment for newborns and children.[7]

Built on decades of research and refinement, established standards of care are now available to guide transgender and gender-diverse people seeking treatment for gender dysphoria or gender-affirming healthcare. The World Professional Association of Transgender Health (WPATH), whose mission is to promote evidence-based care, education, research, public policy, and respect for transgender health, publishes its Standard of Care. Its eighth version (SOC 8) comprises the collective research of multidisciplinary teams. It provides "evidence-based standards for safe and effective gender-affirming health care, representing the most in-depth, evidence-based, consensus-based guidelines internationally." Those wishing to learn more about gender-affirming healthcare can study SOC 8 and other helpful materials at wpath.org.[8]

A significant challenge that transgender and gender-diverse (TGD) people face is the negativity attributed to gender nonconformity in many societies, particularly conservative communities. Diversity of gender identity and gender expression from established societal norms is often stigmatized and can lead to prejudice, discrimination, and being targeted for violence.[9]

"Transgender and gender nonconforming individuals experience higher rates of discrimination and victimization than cisgender individuals. In addition to external stresses, they are more likely to attempt suicide or report a history of suicidal ideation. Gender minorities may also experience internalized stigma because they may have to conceal their identity or true self," writes Dr. Alisha Powell, LCSW.

According to Alejandro Rodriguez, LMHC at The Center Orlando, "Minority Stress speaks to the added layers of stress that are felt by those of a marginalized group. These stressors are those felt on top of the everyday stressors felt by those of the larger community. An example of minority stress within the LGBTQ community would be the everyday stress of being in and navigating conflict within romantic relationships but added to this would be the isolation one may feel of not being able to seek support from friends and/or family for fear of judgment or ridicule for who you love."[10]

Given the complex realities of gender-affirming healthcare, the stigma and dangers associated with being TGD in many communities, and the real possibility of losing family, friends, employment, standing, and even life itself, one might ask, "Why come out at all and attempt to live this way? Why acknowledge you're transgender, ever?"

Best-selling author and transgender activist Jennifer Finney Boylan described the longing for one's yet unrealized expression of authentic, self-determined gender identity in this way: "I compare it to a sense of homesickness for a place you've never been.

The moment you stepped onto those supposedly unfamiliar shores, though, you'd have a sense of overwhelming gratitude, solace, and joy. Home, you might think. I'm *finally home*."[11]

What follows is my story of searching for my true home and living authentically as the woman I have always known myself to be.

Orientation to Mormonism

I spent most of my adult life ecclesiastically volunteering in and professionally working for the Church of Jesus Christ of Latter-day Saints. Hence, many chapters of this memoir specifically describe my experiences within the church context. I endeavor here to provide some introduction to the institution's hierarchy, culture, and terminology.

I'll point out first that current church leaders prefer that church members be referred to as "Latter-day Saints" rather than their nickname of "Mormons." But for most of my life, church members have been known as Mormons. To be true to the period this memoir covers, I use the term "Mormon" interchangeably with "Latter-day Saint" or "LDS." In doing so, I mean no disrespect. Similarly, I do not intend to build up nor destroy anyone's belief system. Instead, my focus is to share my journey of self-determined gender identity in the context of my Mormon identity.

The word Mormon comes from the Book of Mormon, a book of scripture accepted by the Latter-day Saints as "Another Testament of Jesus Christ," which church members believe is God's word in addition to the Holy Bible. The Bible and the Book of Mormon, along with the Doctrine and Covenants and the Pearl of Great Price—revelations and other teachings given through nineteenth- and twentieth-century church presidents—are accepted by the church as its canon of scripture.

A complex hierarchy of ordained priesthood leaders, all men, lead the church. Its top governing body consists of two principal quorums (committees) of the First Presidency (consisting of the church president and his two counselors) and the Quorum of the Twelve Apostles (including the quorum president and eleven others). These men have vast church leadership experience and serve for life. Consequently, these men are senior leaders, typically aged from their fifties through their nineties. These men are sustained (or recognized and accepted) by church members as "prophets, seers, and revelators," and are often referred to as "the Brethren." Church members covenant with God in the holy temples to not speak ill of their church leaders, who are considered the Lord's anointed. When a prophet speaks on behalf of the church, the membership accepts it as the mind, will, and word of God.[12]

The next top-ranking leaders, serving directly under the First Presidency and Quorum of the Twelve Apostles, are the General Authority Seventies, just over 100 of them at the time of this writing. General Authority Seventies, like the First Presidency and Quorum of the Twelve, are considered General Authorities and may serve anywhere in the world and as executive directors of administrative departments in the church. General Authorities bear the title of "Elder," as do, somewhat confusingly, all young male missionaries during their expected two-year, full-time missionary service. The fourth group of General Authorities is a group of three men, the Presiding Bishopric, who oversee the church's temporal affairs worldwide.

Serving under the direction of General Authorities are more than 300 Area Seventies, men who hold similar authority but only in one of the church's designated geographic areas. An Area Presidency oversees each geographic area of the world, including a president and two counselors. General Authority Seventies usually fill these positions. Area Presidencies direct the Area Seventies in their geographic regions, who in turn consult with and instruct "stake presidents"—local volunteer or "lay-leaders" of large, regional congregations called "stakes."

If you're reading this and having a hard time grasping this complex leadership hierarchy, don't worry. Most rank-and-file church members don't fully grasp it, either!

The church structure at the local level is also hierarchical but easier to understand. Stakes are comprised of several smaller congregations called wards, divided geographically. Wards are led by lay-leader bishops. Seven to fourteen wards make up a regional unit called a stake. Each stake is presided over by a stake president, assisted by his two counselors. Each lay minister is assigned or "called" to serve for several years. Before serving as a bishop or stake president, men must be ordained to the priesthood office of "high priest." I served five years as a bishop (1998–2003) and more than eight years as stake president (2004–2012).

Each local church leader "presides" over or directs the church's work within their stewardship and provides pastoral care to the individuals in their respective wards or stakes to the best of their untrained ability. All while holding full-time jobs and setting an example by providing for the needs of their marriage and family. Leaders are assisted by many other local members who help by serving in their responsibilities, or "callings," which their bishop or stake president assigns to them. Though presiding leaders are only male priesthood holders, women oversee the auxiliary organizations that teach and care for the children, teenage girls, and women in their respective wards and stakes.

Church members meet each Sunday for worship and instruction at the local ward meetinghouse, usually a nearby church-built and maintained building, and for activities at other times throughout the week. The church building becomes an active focal point of the family-centered, church-supported system now in place. On the other hand, the church's temples are considered the holiest places on earth, where individuals receive "higher ordinances" or religious rites associated with spiritual training and progression. Couples also attend the temple to be "sealed" in "eternal marriage," a rite that Latter-day Saints trust will bind their marriage relationship and their children to them in the afterlife. Attendance at the temple for one's ordinances occurs just once. However, Latter-day Saints are encouraged to return to the temples often to repeat the same rituals, acting as proxies for deceased individuals, especially their ancestors.

Although baptism and confirmation of membership within the church are received the same by all, the subsequent ordinances found in the temple are specifically gendered, either male or female, defined by one's sex assigned at birth. These separations by gender, male-only leadership authority, lesser potential for service on the part of girls and women, and the policies supported by current doctrines and teachings, create an environment rigidly cemented in the male/female gender binary, which forms the doctrinal anchor of many conservative religious institutions and social structures. Church members often refer to each other as "brother" or "sister."

The past seventy years have seen a significant shift within the church's dogmatic thought on LGBTQ issues. This history is documented in Gregory A. Prince's book, *Gay Rights and the Mormon Church: Intended Actions, Unintended Consequences.* In it, Prince describes the consternation of church leaders, their opposition to marriage equality, and the legal and political lengths they pursued to prevent same-sex marriage from becoming the law of the land in the US and beyond. This decades-long battle spawned the brief authoritative statement, "The Family: A Proclamation to the World" and the church's public affairs debacle when the politically neutral institution supported the 2008 Proposition 8: California Marriage Protection Act using coerced member donations of cash and volunteer hours, only to have a US District Court deem the measure unconstitutional. Ultimately the 2015 SCOTUS ruling in *Obergefell v. Hodges* ensured marriage equality throughout the United States.[13]

Understanding the church's direct involvement in these culture wars provides a much better understanding of the battle that the church (and many other conservative organizations and legislatures) continue to wage to protect their view of a binary, gender-normative society. These chapters will further explain how the church responded after *Obergefell* with what colloquially became the "Policy of Exclusion." What followed was a significantly heightened effort by the church, mostly away from the public eye, against transgender and nonbinary people by denying self-determined gender identity and establishing the manufactured doctrine that eternal gender is determined by sex assigned at birth. The timing of my transition and effort to live openly and publicly as a woman occurred concurrently with the peak of the church's opposition to gender identity. This is how I ran headlong into the perfect storm of conflict with the organization I spent my adult life serving.

Notes

1. Fransesca Paris, "Bans on Transition Care for Young People Spread Across US," *New York Times,* April 15, 2023.

2. Francine Russo, "Where Transgender Is No Longer a Diagnosis," *Scientific American*, January 6, 2017.

3. Goran Štrkalj and Nalini Pather, "Beyond the Sex Binary: Toward the Inclusive Anatomical Sciences Education," *National Library of Medicine*, September 4, 2020.

4. Fred P. Thieme and William J. Schull, "Sex Determination from the Skeleton," *Human Biology* 29: 3 (1957), 242–273.

5. Steven Novella, MD, "The Science of Biological Sex: What does the science say about biological sex?" *Science Based Medicine*, July 13, 2022.

6. Anne Fausto-Sterling, *Sexing the Body: Gender Politics and the Construction of Sexuality* (Seal Press, 2000).

7. Jojo Macaluso, "Where gender-affirming care for youth is banned, intersex surgery may be allowed," *National Public Radio*, April 11, 2023.

8. "Standards of Care Version 8," *World Professional Association for Transgender Health*, 2024.

9. Mayo Clinic Staff, "Transgender Facts," *Mayo Clinic*, February 14, 2023.

10. Alisha Powell, PhD, LCSW, "What Minority Stress Means for LGBTQ+, BIPOC, & More," *Choosing Therapy*, February 13, 2024.

11. Jennifer Finney Boylan, "To understand biological sex, look at the brain, not the body," *Washington Post*, May 1, 2023. See also, Gregory A. Prince, "Science vs. Dogma: Biology Challenges the LDS Paradigm," 2017 Sterling M. McMurrin Lecture, Tanner Humanities Center, University of Utah, September 27, 2017.

12. The Doctrine and Covenants of the Church of Jesus Christ of Latter-day Saints, section 1, verse 38.

13. Gregory A. Prince, *Gay Rights and the Mormon Church: Intended Actions, Unintended Consequences* (University of Utah Press, 2019).

1

The Church vs. Me

Marleen squirmed in her chair. I looked across the church waiting area at my wife of thirty-two years, who hadn't planned to accompany me but changed her mind at the last moment. The reality that we were now here for this purpose engulfed her in emotion. She avoided my gaze, and I understood that doing so kept her from being overwhelmed with panic. Marleen refused to believe her "forever family" could be nullified tonight. God wouldn't do that to her after all she had gone through. I felt sorry for her because I knew what she would soon witness.

In contrast, I was apathetic. I had attended hundreds of meetings in these offices, even presiding over most of them during my years as stake president—the leading clergyman responsible for this ecclesiastic area of Tooele Valley, Utah. Marleen and I had arrived early for the meeting. As we waited for the top of the hour, I distracted myself by surveying the foyer and its furnishings. I knew the woman who selected the upholstery for these couches and chairs. They were used throughout the worldwide church as part of the "meetinghouse standard floor plan program" I directed for many years. Plastic-lens, ceiling-mounted fluorescents provided a cold, dim light. Two table lamps sat useless, their warm incandescent light bulbs burnt out. Upon arriving here for meetings in the past, when I was the stake president, I always turned the lamps on. They created a soothing, welcoming feeling. Without them, the waiting area felt clinical and insensitive.

The impassivity I now felt was not due to a lack of concern for my membership in the church. I had devoted all my adult life to faithful church service. I was an employee of the institutional church for twenty years and fully believed I was doing the Lord's work.

My detachment stemmed from having already grieved the expected outcome of the disciplinary council now being convened "on my behalf." Three weeks earlier, my stake president—my priesthood leader—instructed me to write a letter to church headquarters to resign my church membership. When I told him I would not, he scheduled this meeting to accomplish the same result.

As a Latter-day Saint, I understood this council possessed the authority to not only remove my membership from the records of the church but also to cancel all blessings and sacred covenants I had made with God regarding my eternal salvation and my relationship with my family members in the afterlife.

At 7:00 P.M., the door of the stake high council room opened and Marleen and I were invited in. The rustle of wooden chair legs on the commercial carpet was familiar to me as all sixteen men of the council, each dressed in business suits, scooted back their chairs and rose to their feet as a gesture of respect. Upon entering, I smiled at these men, all of whom I knew well. Most looked pained or anxious.

They were seated in a conference room, around four large wooden tables forming a rectangle, almost filling the room. My mind wandered as I remembered how this table layout resulted from my first request as leader of this newly created stake. I decided to replace the standard, three-table "T" configuration, with the stake president and his two counselors seated at the head table and the twelve high councilors and clerks (all lay clergymen serving under the stake presidency) sitting along both sides of the stem of the T.

Before I became the stake president, I had often observed that the T-shape meant there were literally no seats at the table for the female leaders of the women's and children's "auxiliary" organizations who participated in the broader stake council meetings. Instead, the women leaders had sat in chairs lining the walls of the room, disconnected, facing the backs of the meetings' male participants. The new four-table rectangular arrangement and my invitation to the female leaders to sit in the chairs closest to me and my counselors in the stake presidency accomplished my goal of mitigating the patriarchal nature of stake council meetings. This gave women a significant voice in the planning and implementing of stake goals and ministry. Now, sixteen men would sit in judgment of me—a woman—around the same table where I once empowered women to lead in our local congregations.

Marleen and I took our seats to the right of the stake presidency as directed. I continued to consider the men around the table, all friends and close neighbors. I served in the church alongside nearly all of them. Under my authority as stake president, I ordained most of these men to priesthood offices or gave them priesthood blessings as they began various church-service assignments or "callings." I twice called the current stake president to serve as a bishop of smaller congregations, called wards, within the stake. Later, I called him as one of my two counselors in the stake presidency. When top-ranking church leaders released me from my calling as stake president almost five years earlier, I recommended him as my successor.

Being in this room with these friends again for the first time in years should have been a reason to rejoice, but I was painfully jolted back into the moment when the stake president announced the purpose of the meeting.

"Brother David Bruce Hall Jr.," he addressed me, even though I'd had this name rendered obsolete by Utah's Third District Court nine months earlier. In a moment of feigned sensitivity, he looked into his lap and explained he needed to refer to me by the name appearing on my church record. We both knew that he had refused my repeated requests to change my records to reflect my legal name and gender markers, even though church policy allowed for name changes. Even worse, he had required each bishop to instruct their ward members never to call me by my chosen, affirming name, Laurie Lee, or as Sister Hall.

I silently noted his hypocrisy as symbolic of the more significant contention surrounding this night's council. The church was on record in documents, submitted as amicus briefs to the United States Supreme Court, linking fundamental church doctrines and teachings to the widely held assumption that gender is only equivalent to an individual's assigned sex at birth. This official position eliminated any possibility of a person's right to define their gender identity, should it differ from their birth sex assignment.

My lived experience, from my earliest memories, included the persistent reality that my female gender identity conflicted with my male sex assignment. After more than fifty years, the time had finally come when my "eternal gender identity" could no longer tolerate living the falsehood of my male presentation. With the light of personal revelation supporting my journey, I was now living a self-determined life authentically as a woman.

The bias of the institution that I believed held the keys of my eternal salvation now conflicted with my right to live my mortal life according to my truth. As my wife and I now sat at the high council table, I knew what was about to happen.

2

Learning To Pee "Like a Boy"

"Because your body is different from mine or your sisters', see how you can stand right here and pee into the toilet like all boys do?" Mom exclaimed, unable to restrain her heightened level of angst.

We were in the only bathroom of our house. I was standing with my back to the sink and looking straight up at Mom because, at age five, I was still pretty small. Then in her mid-twenties, Mom was tall and thin with long, blonde hair. She was facing the toilet as she spoke to me. What caught my attention was that she told me my body was different from hers and my sisters'. Mom was trying to train me to be a boy!

Neither of us understood then that I had been born with hypospadias, a Difference in Sexual Development (DSD) condition in which the urethra tube exits from the underside instead of the tip of the penis, often accompanied by a smaller-than-average penis. Despite Mom's instructions I received that day, standing to pee did not work well, nor did it ever feel right to me. What was medically referred to as "intersex" is now classified as a DSD. Infants born with this type of DSD often undergo non-consensual surgery to "correct" their genitalia to correlate with a binary sex assignment.[1]

Beyond this outward, physical manifestation, inside I knew I was a girl and I never felt right being singled out as different from other girls. Before this incident, I had never imagined that Mom thought I was different from my sisters or that I was a boy. But what persisted within me from that point forward was the damaging and unavoidable knowledge that I was physically unlike other girls in my family in one specific part of my body, even though I felt the same as them. It left me confused and frustrated that Mom designated me as some sort of other thing. I thought unhappy thoughts about it often.

Though it was impossible for my young mind to understand, the doctor who attended my delivery assigned me as male at birth, based on my genitalia. I became the first-born son, named after my dad, destined to carry his name followed by the suffix, "Jr." Regardless of how I felt inside, like the heir to a throne, I was born into a role I did not choose and that never sat well with me.

Through my more than sixty years of life, I have managed to hold onto only a handful of memories from my childhood. I have realized that these first memories fall into a few types. The earliest has to do with the arrival or parting of a loved one.

Before the use of seat belts was required in passenger automobiles, free-range children bounced all over car interiors. I preferred to ride lying down on the shelf behind the back seat, watching everything outside sail past through the panoramic luxury of a large, curved back window. That's where I was riding when I went with my mother's parents to the same hospital where I was born, where Mom had just given birth to my younger sister. I waited with my maternal grandmother, whom I called Gram, in the car while Grandpa went inside to identify which room Mom was in and to let her know we were in the parking lot. When Grandpa returned, he showed us which room window was Mom's. I gazed at it until she appeared there, holding a tiny baby wrapped in a blanket. For the first time, I saw my little sister Debora. It was May 1964, five weeks before my third birthday.

My following two memories are from the other end of someone's life journey. Granny Morlock was my great-grandmother, my mother's grandmother. Born Ragna Thorkildsen Larsen, she came to America alone as a teenager from Norway in the 1890s, finding work as a house servant on a prosperous dairy farm in the central Massachusetts hill country my family still called home. She stood six feet tall and slender, with long, wavy hair knotted into a bun and a square jaw always set a certain way, giving her a determined appearance. In

Granny Ragna Margaret Morlock (seated) with an unidentified female companion, ca. 1930. Courtesy Laurie Lee Hall.

time, she married the heir of the farm, himself a mere five-feet-two. Upon his untimely passing due to complications of gallbladder surgery, Ragna took full possession of the farm at a young age. She ran it with a formidable hand for decades, when property ownership and business proprietorship were still uncommon for single or widowed women, and long before women generally had sole and equitable access to financial instruments like credit. Granny eventually yielded the farm operations to her daughter's three sons.

I have a photo of Granny at the height of her power. She is sitting erect in an armchair, holding a book. Her posture, broad shoulders, and direct gaze speak to her strength as a woman in a man's world and of *her* definition of gender in a society not yet ready for her. Standing close behind her is another woman, more demure and feminine. I do not know who that woman was, but have always felt that she might have been Granny's life companion.

Mom lived as a child on the farm in one of the many small cottages lining the main road across from the big house. Those homes were reserved for grown children of the owner's family or, when available, for farm staff and their families. A trove of black and white photographs depicts Mom in little cotton dresses with bright blonde curls, chasing the dogs who herded the cows through the fields, or riding high upon the hay wagon with her several boy cousins, looking like the Little Rascals. Mom's life on the farm appeared idyllic, but those boys were dressed to learn farmwork. Over time, those cousins grew into the men who ran the farm.

Mom had special memories of being a young girl on the farm. She told stories of her Granny Morlock waking before the men who milked the cows each day, preparing enormous spreads of breakfast foods and baked goods to feed the hungry men who came in after their morning chores. Granny often gifted Mom more than her fair share of homemade pastries from her pantry, unbeknownst to Mom's parents. Mom was always spoiled, being the only little girl on the farm during the 1940s.

My only visual memory of Granny was when I accompanied Mom and Gram to the farm on a crisp winter's day. The snow crunched under our boots as we walked onto the broad wrap-around porch leading to the main foyer entrance. We found Granny in her bed in the front room of the big farmhouse she once commanded. As her health waned, her family moved her downstairs so they could better attend to her.

While Mom and her mother Gram visited with Granny, I sat across the floor near the door, playing quietly, taking in their conversation. I thought with childish curiosity how, even in her old age and poor health, she must have been the tallest woman I had ever seen, or the longest, since she was lying down. She became my reference point when my sister Debbie and I grew six feet tall as teenagers.

Granny died a few weeks later. I remember sitting on the kitchen floor playing when Mom took the call on the white, rotary-dial phone attached to the wall of our bright pink kitchen. She broke into sobs, hung up the phone, then turned and told me the sad news. Deflated, she collapsed toward the kitchen table and into a chair to cry a while longer. I felt emotions for Mom that were new to me and seemed perhaps to belong only to someone older than me. Even at my young age, it felt important that I had met Granny and witnessed the news of her passing, though I didn't know why. I was four when Granny Morlock died in March 1966.

Another category of my early memories, beginning with being taught to pee while standing, pertains to what is now called "gender socialization," which also had a powerful impact on my young life. For the longest time, the simple act of being taught to pee while standing was all I thought that memory meant. I don't know for sure what precipitated that conversation in the bathroom. But now I sense that Mom's angst-filled instruction was deliberate reinforcement for some other reason, probably because I had insisted to Mom that I was a girl, like my sisters, and she was determined to do something to prove to me otherwise. That is how Mom dealt with such things. Once explained, her expectation was, "That was that." I knew I was a girl, but for some reason, everyone felt it was essential to make me a boy. It was my first time experiencing gender conflict, but it certainly wasn't the last.[2]

In the summer of 1966, Dad ran a gas station on the town square of our hometown, Westminster, Massachusetts. Positioned at the intersection of the state roads east to Boston and south to Worcester, it was a great business location until the following year, when a bypass highway was completed, taking all the traffic off the old town streets and forcing the station to close.

Mom remained determined to fulfill her duty to teach me to act like a boy. She discovered a boy my age, Chuck, who lived in the apartment house just behind the gas station. It gave her the idea to help me get to know a boy, so she set a play date with Chuck's mom.

It was a bright day; dappled sunlight shone through the leaves of the hardwood tree overhanging the dirt driveway in Chuck's front yard. He dressed and looked poor, like he spent the majority of the summer right there in the driveway. Mom and his mom left us out there to play while they retreated into the kitchen to relax with a coffee and chat. Excited to have a playmate, Chuck produced a pile of olive-green plastic army men and proposed we stage a war right there in the dirt. He was unprepared for the conflict his suggestion would ignite!

The war in Vietnam was being waged every night on our black-and-white TV screen, complete with grueling footage of struggle and carnage. My thoughts were haunted by the awareness that because everyone labeled me a boy, in time, I would be forced to go to war, fight, and die just like those guys I saw on the news. It scared me to death as I tried to fall asleep each night. I had never seen toy army men, but immediately knew I wanted no part of it and told Chuck so.

He tried coaxing me to play, but I was determined not to. I'm sure I caused a scene, arms folded, heels dug in, refusing to send the army men to battle. The commotion brought the moms rushing back to the screen door. Under their interrogation, I explained that I did not want to play war. Instead of attempting to see if there was something else we could both enjoy playing, Mom lectured me on how I needed to be a good guest and to do what my host wanted to do.

I refused to yield, and the play date was over faster than it began. Appalled at my behavior, Mom never brought me back. Chuck's family moved away by the time first grade started a year later. I walked past their driveway on my route to school every day, self-satisfied that I had never engaged in war. Mom never arranged another playdate for me, either.

The back room of the attic of our 1828 farmhouse was used as storage. Its only access was from the dormer bedroom I shared with my sisters. The backroom's contents included Mom's wardrobe from her teen years, easily retrievable for dress-up play.

Middle sister Sandra possessed the dominant personality, so she created all the situations and roles for our dress-ups. With her fertile imagination, the plots changed daily. We might be three neighbor ladies, three sisters, or three generations of a family, but we were always three female characters. We were "dressed to the nines" in fifties-era skirts, blouses, or dancing dresses, ready for shopping, meeting for coffee, or tending to affairs in the house or at school. I don't remember Sandra ever suggesting that I take a male role. Perhaps I had protested if she ever did. So long as all the clothes were returned to storage before bedtime, we could play like this most evenings after supper. This continued for several years.

In the same way, when Barbies became the thing in our house, Mom made sure we each owned one, and again, the play was between three female characters. I never even knew Barbie had male friends. I wouldn't have wanted a Ken anyway, or heaven forbid, a GI Joe!

In contrast to how I refused to play army, I enthusiastically enjoyed this pretend play with my sisters. I knew what I wanted to do and what didn't work for me. Playing female characters with my sisters was a safe space to explore feeling like *me.* I didn't have to deal with the discomfort of gender conflict because no one was telling me to be a boy. Nevertheless, I felt shame, somehow sensing that I was wrong to play with dress-up clothes or Barbies. I don't remember being taught why it was inappropriate, but I do remember being vigilant to make sure Dad never saw me in ladies' clothes or playing with dolls. And yet, my desire to pretend-play in these female roles outweighed all feelings of fear and shame I harbored. To me, it was worth the risk.

Once most children learn the basics of gender recognition in themselves and family members, the next major step of gender socialization (learning about the social expectations, attitudes, and behaviors associated with boys and girls) occurs upon leaving home and siblings to attend school with peers. For children who experience gender conflict, being socially expected to act a certain way in public, which feels contrary to one's nature, becomes stressful and detrimental. Fortunately, not all my memories involving gender were negative.

A few months into Ms. Deloise's first-grade class, we were allowed to pair our desks with a friend of our choice, which did not go as successfully as our young teacher hoped. I paired with a kind, gregarious boy named Keith, whose family owned Bailey's Dairy Bar in the center of town. Everyone knew Bailey's for its ice cream, shakes, and malts. One of two available lunch counters long before the emergence of fast-food joints, Bailey's was the place to hang out for kids on bikes after school and teens in cars in the evenings.

Keith inherited all the Bailey family charm. I was quiet and shy, especially around boys, but Keith was as bubbly as his family's soda fountains. He made me feel liked, and we couldn't stop talking during class. It turned out we weren't the only ones chatting too much. The day came when Ms. Deloise had had enough and called out Keith, me, and the two girls in front of us, Caren and Lena. I didn't notice their conversations, having been caught up in our own.

Ms. Deloise thought she had a sure-fire fix. She attempted to use our gender against us by swapping Keith and Lena so we were now paired girl/boy, boy/girl. The new arrangement suited me just fine. Lena was soft-spoken and artistic like me. The other two seemed unfazed by the unique pairing as well. Now, Ms. Deloise had a bigger problem on her hands. Caren and Keith, the more outgoing of the bunch anyway, now turned around and talked with us, causing four-way conversations to erupt. Gender weaponization had failed!

In another memory, I was flying through the air, my long, light brown hair sunlit, flowing in the breeze, and my white dress fluttering well past my feet as it trailed behind me. I glided from place to place, feeling joyful, light, and free!

"Wake up for school, DB!" Mom called up the stairs, jarring me back to the open attic room where I slept. I opened my eyes, and the dim glow of the light from the living room downstairs created distorted shadows across the sloped ceiling. In my dream, I was free to fly and, most importantly, free to be me. I heard the rain falling hard on the roof outside my window. It was still dark outside, and my sleeping area was cold even though the steam radiator across the room was hissing and knocking. I knew I would also be cold and wet at school after walking through town in the rain to get there. Living in a world that told me I was a boy, I got dressed in my plaid shirt and corduroy pants.

Somehow, I had been chosen as one of six members of our third-grade student council. I don't remember offering to run or even if there was an election. The fact that I was there proved that it wasn't a popularity contest. I entrenched myself in a quiet and shy persona. Perhaps it felt safer for me to withhold myself and limit interactions with others. I suspect the teachers selected one boy and one girl from each class who always seemed to complete their work way ahead of the others and thus had extra time which needed to be used constructively. We were sent from our classrooms one afternoon a week to walk to the school library, where our council meetings were held with one of the school's administrators.

Mary Catherine was the (other) girl selected from my class to serve on the council. I had known her all my life. We were christened on the same day as babies and attended the same children's Sunday School classes that Mom taught. She was bright and outspoken. If eight-year-old girls could look like spinster librarians,

Mary Catherine did, with pale skin and small, thick-lensed oval glasses. She wore her copious long red hair pulled back and secured high on each side with acrylic-bobbled elastic bands, with the back hair left to hang loose between. Mom adored the look, named it the "Mary Catherine," and coaxed my sisters to wear it in her honor as often as possible. Debbie wasn't going for it and eventually got a pixie cut, which suited her much better. But Sandra loved the style and wore it for years until she discovered curling irons and hairspray. Whenever Mom asked Sandra if she wanted a Mary Catherine, it felt like a needle inserted permanently into my skin. Why couldn't *I* have thick, long hair and a pretty style named after me? Or at least the long hair so I could do the doo, too?

Mary Catherine excelled at everything she did. In our church children's choir she sang the solos and played guitar, while I was tone-deaf and sat on the back row playing the kazoo. Mary Catherine became a cheerleader, our high school valedictorian, and a Harvard-educated attorney. This all started when our best wisdom was required to adjudicate, with the utmost fairness, the thorny problems facing our third-grade student council.

One issue of overriding importance was the question of girls' snow pants. We lived in a time when girls were required to wear skirts or dresses to school everyday, even when our New England winters doled out temperatures well below zero and deep or blowing snow. Moms would send their daughters to school in snow pants with their skirts tucked into them as best possible. This was true for my sisters, who walked with me to school each day.

The problem with the bulky snow pants was finding space to store them during the day. School hallways were already crowded with snow boots (lined with Wonder Bread bags for water tightness), gloves, and hats piled up outside each classroom. The bulk of fifteen or more pairs of snow pants per classroom was surely a fire hazard, so boys, who already wore regular pants, weren't permitted to wear them at all. Who better prepared than six, experienced third graders to resolve the crisis once and for all? There was serious debate amongst five of those young council members, but I, too afraid to speak up, felt like a spectator of this gradeschool exercise in self-government. There was a discussion over how to address the storage problem. Someone even asked if girls should be allowed to wear snow pants to school at all.

Then, a resolution was proposed and put to a vote by secret ballot: Girls should be allowed to wear snow pants, and better coat hooks were needed along the hallway to organize and improve the storage capacity. It passed five to one in the affirmative. It was soon discovered I was the dissenting vote. So much for confidentiality! Mary Catherine, each of my colleagues, and even the shocked advisor questioned why on earth I voted against girls wearing snow pants. What was the matter with me? But no one paused to listen to why I voted against the measure.

My young mind had uncovered what I felt was a fatal flaw in the measure. "Why create a rule that applies only to girls and not everyone?" I thought. I believed there needed to be gender equity regarding the wearing of snow pants. I was confident I alone could see the issue from both sides. I thought myself to be a girl. I would have loved to wear a skirt every day to school if I had been permitted to, even at minus twenty degrees, until my bare legs turned eggplant purple. But as a walker, even dressed as a boy, I was exposed to the daily elements. My own experience consisted of corduroy pants, often wet up to the knee and frozen stiff by the time I reached school, only to thaw out on me through the day, smelling something like a wet dog. I thought snow pants were a good idea for *all*, not just those fortunate enough to be girls!

Not understanding the council process, I assumed we would still have time to discuss and modify the proposal for the greater good. I expected to be able to stand up and defend the virtue of gender equity and snow pants for all. It didn't happen; time was up, and the resolution passed without me or my revolutionary egalitarian ideas ever being presented. My walk of shame back to the classroom with the future Assistant District Attorney for the Commonwealth of Massachusetts was lonely. I felt I had discovered an independent and reasonable alternate opinion which fear caused me to suppress when I should have spoken up. The news was soon whispered abroad, meaning my unexpressed hope for gender equity backfired, resulting in my scorn as the pariah who, in 1969, was against women's rights.

My paternal grandmother was born seventy-two years before

Laurie Lee, Debbie, Grandma Emma Laurie Hall, and Sandra, ca. 1966. Courtesy Laurie Lee Hall.

me in the same small town where I would grow up. She raised six children and lived twenty-four years as a widow. Her given names were Emma Laurie Rita, but I knew her as Gramma Hall, and she seemed to me to be very kind and gentle, possessing a sharp wit and a vibrant sense of humor.

Just before I turned eight, I attended her eightieth birthday party in her home with most of her children and grandchildren. Long folding tables covered in white linen spanned the entire width of the living room's hardwood floor, from the stairs leading up to the bedrooms on the left, to the enormous upright piano she had once played with all her children surrounding her singing old Irish songs across the room on the right. Around the tables were folding chairs filled with aunts, uncles, and cousins I barely knew.

Gramma was in the center of the long table, her back to the big console color TV tuned to a muted Red Sox ballgame. In front of her was a giant horseshoe-shaped eightieth birthday cake, with white frosting trimmed with yellow roses and bows. I suppose it may have been the only family dessert any of us ever enjoyed which hadn't been made by her hands.

She was the master of baked goods, with none more delicious and even more spectacular to look upon than her freshly squeezed lemon meringue pie. The sweet, fluffy white topping was so light it stood a good three inches above the lemon filling, so tart your glands ached upon tasting it. Gramma's baking was all done the old-fashioned way, without electric appliances. Her ultra-light meringue was only ever whipped by hand with a wooden spoon.

The festivities of the day included Gramma receiving a beautiful cuckoo clock. I made sure to be in the picture of her holding it proudly. Later on, when the adults, young adults, and teens all paired off, Sandra, Debbie, and I, along with our nine-year-old cousin Laurie, found playful refuge out on the back screened-in porch.

At one point in the evening, Mom came to the porch to check on us. Something prompted her to tell me there that if I had been born a girl, my parents would have named me Laurie, too—one of my dad's favorite names and the name of the grand lady whose birthday we were celebrating. My full first-name would have been Laurie Lee, partly to distinguish me from my cousin sitting next to me and to follow the naming convention in my family, my mom's first name being Linda Lee. We even had aunts named Lois and Lois Lee.

I felt a pang of jealousy towards my cousin. She was lucky enough to be allowed to be a girl and named after this dear grandmother we both adored, but I was not. The feeling was fleeting as I realized that, more importantly, Mom had just given me an essential bit of knowledge. I now knew my real name, the name that belonged to my true identity. I kept both secret, deep inside me, for decades.

I was a girl, and I was Laurie Lee!

Notes

1. Claire Ainsworth, "Sex Redefined: The Idea of 2 Sexes is Overly Simplistic," *Nature Magazine,* October 22, 2018, accessed at scientificamerican.com.

2. For more on the early establishment and development of gender identity in young children, see Dr. Jason Rafferty, "Gender Identity Development in Young Children," healthychildren.org, May 7, 2024.

3

A Clip-on Bow Tie

"Why were you praying?" Sandra asked with equal parts of mocking and curiosity.

"I wasn't!" I retorted through my tears. But soon, the Polaroid Land Camera spit out the evidence. Mom captured the three of us at the kids' table, my sisters Sandra and Debbie ready to devour their plates of cake, and me, with head bowed and eyes closed. Sandra and Debbie were wearing the Easter dresses they'd gotten the previous Sunday, while I was wearing a white shirt and clip-on bow tie—accessories that distinguished me as a boy.

It was the evening of my kindergarten graduation family party. I lived in a time and place where free, public kindergarten was not available. My mother's generous cousin Jane, who had purchased a full living room set for my parents so they would have furniture, offered to pay for me to attend the only private kindergarten option in town. It was a half-day session at the local Baptist Church on Main Street. I don't know how many Baptist families were in town. But I did know almost all the kids in my kindergarten class from the children's Sunday classes at the Congregational Church my family attended, further down Main Street on the village square.

Our kindergarten was taught by Ms. Matthews, a young single lady who lived in a small apartment above Westminster's Rexall drug store diagonally across the street from the church where she taught. My most prominent memory of the school year was the last-day picnic. Held on the lawn behind the church, there was a small ceremony, diplomas awarded, games, and food. Mom came, along with my sisters. There, I learned that Ms. Matthews received a full-time teaching job in the fall in Maine and would be moving over the summer.

Towards the end of the picnic, my sisters were getting fussy, so Mom packed us all up and we headed back to the house. We held our own, smaller party in our kitchen that evening, with my grandparents attending. With the kitchen table full of adults, we three kids sat at the kids' table set up by the front door. What I was feeling in the moment was enough to keep the memory forever a part of me.

Contrary to what Sandra had thought, I had not been praying. Our family did not practice praying at mealtime and certainly not over party cake. The real reason I bowed my head was I had just realized that since Ms. Matthews was moving to Maine, I wouldn't ever see her again. In the rush to leave earlier, I had not said goodbye to her or thanked her for being my teacher.

The thought continued to upset me all evening. After going to bed, my not-quite-six-year-old mind was still troubled. In tears, I came downstairs and found my parents outside, enjoying the last hour of summer twilight in peace. I needed a good reason to go downstairs after bedtime, or my sad tears would have been given "a real reason to cry," and I would be jettisoned right back upstairs to the attic. I explained my predicament before my judge and jury and pleaded to be taken to Ms. Matthews' apartment above the drugstore to tell her goodbye.

Before my birth, Mom, as a local telephone operator, went around the county teaching folks how to use that radical rotary dial telephone. Putting those skills to work, she found Ms. Matthews's phone number. I held the massive receiver to my little ear and heard my teacher's voice again. The conversation may have lasted a minute, but with my farewell and gratitude offered, and I suppose a teacher's heart touched forever, I hung up the phone and, satisfied, returned to bed.

But oh, there was still the pang of my sisters' Easter dresses. Before our annual egg hunt on the previous Easter morning, Mom had unveiled those lovely, matching, chiffon dresses for my sisters to wear to church. Sandra's was pastel yellow, Debbie's pastel violet. They had identical embroidered flower petals gracing the waistline, forming loops for the chiffon tie to pass through. The dresses had puffy sleeves and lacy trim. I wished for a pastel green or blue one

Debbie, Sandra, and Laurie Lee, Easter Sunday, April 10, 1966. Courtesy Laurie Lee Hall.

in my size. I hated always being left out that way. Instead, I was given yet another of my Uncle Bill's hand-me-down, clip-on bow ties, almost as if an afterthought. After church, Mom lined us up by age, as always, on the front porch step and took our picture. In this snapshot, too, I look as though I am about to cry. I felt that bow tie would better represent me if it were on my head. I often wanted to clip my bow ties into my hair instead of around my neck. But Mom kept my hair in a crew cut, so there was nothing to attach bows to.

I can see me as a child, learning to express myself, likely standing out for doing so, and being misunderstood or poorly treated because I was different. Often that became awkward; occasionally it was truly frightening.

When I entered first grade, no one in charge at Westminster Elementary School apparently saw any harm having all six grades on the playground for recess at the same time. One day near the end of the morning recess period, a group of sixth-grade boys singled me out for a bit of "fun." Our school playground had several wood and metal contraptions, which I remember as old even when I was there in the mid-1960s. All of these would, in time, be judged as hazardous to young children, much like the forest-green lead paint slathered on them every summer in an attempt to maintain those relics.

One such piece of equipment was the merry-go-round, with a heavy-gauge, galvanized pipe frame and thick wooden planks built into an octagonal shape. The weight of the whole thing bore on one stout center bearing. The bearing was well-worn because the merry-go-round listed a bit off-level depending upon how it was loaded. It took the strength of several kids holding onto it and running in circles on the paved perimeter to get the enormous thing spinning. Even empty, it was a chore to get going, but loaded with kids it required the efforts of an entire gang.

The older boys decided their solemn duty was to put some little kid under the merry-go-round and make it spin as fast as possible. I was the first grader they chose for this stunt. I cannot imagine why I was singled out from among the sixty or so of my peers outside that day. What did I say, how did I look, what were they thinking about me?

I never saw it coming. They grabbed me from behind, flipped me onto my back, and stuffed me between the plank and frame above and the pavement below, a slot just tall enough to fit a skinny kid through. My eyes were shut tight as this happened. When I opened them, I found myself on my back in the dirt, looking up at the underside of the spinning planks sailing just above my nose. I heard the boys above celebrating as they ran around, pushing the merry-go-round to go faster and faster.

The contraption was anchored in this spot to the old dirt playground. Though the area around it had been paved with about three inches of asphalt, underneath where I found myself, there was a bit more space. The slot to crawl out looked far thinner from where I was trapped than it did from on the playground, especially with the merry-go-round spinning so fast. If someone suddenly jumped on board, it would have tipped and eliminated what little space I had.

Terrified, I kept still until I heard the school bells signaling the end of recess. My captors put in their final pushes, as if hoping the merry-go-round might still be spinning when they came out for the lunch recess. Peering through the slot, I saw the children run to the back of the school to assemble by classes. Teachers came out, organized the kids, and escorted them all inside. But the merry-go-round continued to spin.

Ms. Deloise must not have missed me as she brought our class back inside. The playground fell silent, leaving me alone to sort this out. I decided I could not attempt my escape until the thing stopped spinning; otherwise, I would risk getting beat up by the fast-moving pipes beneath the planks. I knew little of the physics of momentum at the time, but I knew enough about this beast from the topside to know one skinny kid alone could do nothing to stop its turning. All I could do was to remain as still as I could and wait for it to stop.

Once it finally did, I slithered out to freedom. Covered in dirt and badly scuffed up, I went back to my classroom, where it was impossible for my arrival to go unnoticed. Ms. Deloise asked me to rehearse the whole affair for the entire class. Though I remember the traumatic event on the playground with remarkable visual clarity, I have no recollection of what happened after that.

Occasionally, Florence, the lady who lived in the apartment on the other side of our duplex, would come over for coffee with Mom. I would watch them as they talked, then imitate them in my role-play with my sisters. Once, Mom decided to go over to Florence's place, and we came along. Though we rarely went there, the other half of our duplex intrigued me partly because it was fascinating to see how the old house had been divided into two. While in the kitchen, I nosily went into the pantry storage room off the back of Florence's kitchen and looked at the shelves of food and other things stored there, not knowing that I would end up sleeping in that little room over the next many years.

When I was about seven, our Sunday School class was asked to draw a picture of any Biblical story we learned about that year. I was a budding artist and an accomplished cartoonist at a young age. My Uncle Bill, a professional artist, always assured me of my potential. Our drawings were handed to the teachers, and those of us who could write our names signed them on the back. At the end of class, we were to assemble in the central area of the church basement, where we would hold up our drawings for our parents when they came to take us home. My teacher handed me a picture.

"This isn't mine," I said, looking at the colorful scrawling.

"It doesn't matter," came my teacher's hurried reply as she indiscriminately passed out drawings to all the children. It did matter. It mattered to me a lot. I did not want to be seen as someone who was only capable of scrawling. I was embarrassed and hurt that it didn't matter to the teacher.

I don't remember enjoying much about second grade. My only remaining memory occurred just before Christmas when our teacher asked us to each draw a picture of what we most wanted to receive as a gift. We were then asked to show the class our picture and describe why we wanted it more than anything. Most of the boys who went before me showed various indiscernible drawings they claimed were model railroads or slot car setups. The girls shared somewhat better pictures of their next doll or doll accessories.

I would have been happy with either of the gifts the boys and girls described, as I was fond of all those things. But thinking independently, I drew something I hoped for more than anything—a drawing pad of paper. The drawing pad I drew was proportioned correctly, its notably thick stack of pages in accurate perspective. I had learned how to do this from my copy of *Learn to Draw* by John Gnagy, which came in a drawing kit I received for my sixth birthday.

I told the class how much I loved to draw, and without a fresh supply of drawing paper, I had been drawing on whatever scraps I could pull from the rubbish. The explanation didn't seem to matter, and it may not have been heard by most since, upon realizing my fondest wish was for a simple pad of blank sheets, most of the class began to laugh and tease me. I remember slinking into my chair, wondering why I chose to share my true feelings when it brought so much ridicule.

I never had braces growing up. My family struggled financially, so I don't recall even seeing a dentist until I was ten or so. Fortunately, my teeth came in pretty straight, with one exception. The second upper tooth on the right is in a crossbite with the tooth below it. One day, as our third-grade class returned from an assembly, I paused to get a drink from the water bubbler in the hallway. As I bent my head to drink, a hand slammed down hard against the back of my head, causing my teeth to collide with the chrome water spigot. In shock, I jumped back and turned to see the boy did that to me.

Back in the classroom, I knew it was bleeding; I shut my mouth and occasionally swallowed the blood until it stopped. I never told on the person who did this, perhaps out of embarrassment or maybe out of fear of retribution. I don't know. The tooth that took the brunt of the blow was a baby tooth that wedged so tight that the adult tooth had no place to go once it came in. My smile permanently wears the mark of being bullied.

I became marked in another way beginning that year. Everyone was IQ tested, and from then on, teachers treated me oddly. My fourth-grade teacher rode me incessantly. In fifth grade, the teacher sent a note home to Mom telling her to encourage me to find a different best friend since mine was "beneath" me. Confused, Mom contacted the teacher, who told her that the school's proficiency testing had showed I possessed the highest IQ in the class, in fact, higher than they had ever seen. Mom sought to reason with me by telling me the test results, falling in with the teacher by saying I should pick the most intelligent and capable friends. The idea of having to have a social reason to choose a friend troubled me for years. My only solace came from the thought that I scored higher than everyone else and higher than even Ms. Mary Catherine Pinkerton!

At church, most of the kids participated in the children's "Cardinal Choir." We wore red robes and practiced Christian songs after school until we were ready to present them to the parents in the main chapel. I liked performing in the choir. I loved wearing the splendid choir robes, and presenting in the chapel was a treat over Sunday classes in the basement. Unfortunately, my time in the choir was cut short when the choir leader, Ms. Phillips, told me after practice one afternoon I was no longer welcome in the choir because I could not sing in tune. My schoolgirl's heart was broken. When Mom learned I'd been kicked out, she pulled Sandra from the choir and our whole family stopped attending the Congregational church.

For a couple of my elementary school years, two brothers close to my age lived with their family in a rented house across the open field from my house. Whenever they saw me outside with my sisters, they would cross the field to see if I would play. My sisters didn't like them and would disappear inside when they came. Harlan Jr., who went by "Skippy," was tall and wiry and a year ahead of me in school. His brother Mitchell, short and heavy-set, was a year behind me. Both were scrappy and foul-mouthed. Skippy liked to wrestle when he wasn't punching Mitchell. He would often take me down and, depending upon the season, hold my face to the grass or the snow until I gave up—and then a little longer, just for emphasis. It made me wary of ever being seen outside.

Dad supported our family by working at several different auto repair shops. He took me to the garage on weekends when he was free to do personal projects. I had started going to the garage as a young child, and whenever there was a loud noise like a compressed air impact wrench, I would cover my ears and scamper off to the farthest location in the building to wait it out in safety. The mechanics were a rowdy and vocal bunch and often made fun of me for that. The guys always called me "Little Dave." I didn't like the moniker at all, especially once I surpassed my dad in height at age twelve.

As a kid, I liked soft, pastel-colored clothing and Mom obliged by buying me what I wanted. One afternoon, I was wearing pink and lavender Bermuda shorts when I went with Dad to the garage. A younger mechanic I had considered a friend said my shorts looked like girls' shorts and teasingly asked why I was wearing them. Soon, everyone, including my dad, was in on the joke. I felt embarrassed and devastated. Upon returning home, I took those shorts off and vowed never to wear them again. I stopped wearing shorts altogether. More than forty years would pass before I wore a pair of shorts again in public, and yes, by then, they were girl's shorts!

If either of my sisters or any other girl our age had been wearing those shorts, of course there would never have been any comments made, let alone ongoing mockery. I knew my situation was unique. I was a girl who was expected to dress, look, and act like a boy all the time, whether I wanted to or not.

If I had only been allowed to be the girl I felt I was inside, would I have been stuffed under the merry-go-round? Would a mean boy have slammed my head into a water bubbler and, if he did, would I have felt okay to tell on him? Would the neighbor boy have tackled me and held my head to the ground?

Wanting to wear an Easter dress and pastel-colored shorts wasn't a weird fetish for an item of clothing; it was about being seen and recognized for who I really was. *I* knew who I was, and couldn't understand why no one else could see me. It did not seem fair to be taunted for just being me.

Nevertheless, to avoid disparagement and abuse, I consciously chose to fit in and be safe instead of doing what made me feel whole or right. By the time I was a teenager, I no longer wanted to be seen as my authentic self.

4

Tied To a Tree

In good weather, I would play as a young child right outside the front door of our house, in the shade of an old apple tree that had long-since ceased producing decent fruit. Instead, it made scores of hard green apples the size of grapes that pelted me as I played beneath its branches.

What the tree did have in spades was webworms. In late summer, the tree was covered in webs. The initial little dots inside would grow and begin to wiggle around in their webby womb until mature, then burst through the web and also fall on me as I played below.

I considered myself fortunate when Dad would notice the hatching mess and bring out his webworm-killing tool: a propane torch duct taped to the end of an aluminum pole. He would ignite the torch with his cigar lighter and raise it into the tree branches to burn out all the webs with the occupants inside. The smell was the unmistakable odor of mass death. Some caterpillars leapt to escape the flame only to be squashed under Dad's greasy workboot. I noticed the caterpillars' guts were bright neon green.

No grass grew in the shade of the apple tree. In the summer the dark brown dirt was so powder fine and dry that I could draw images in the dust. I had a fascination with road maps, and with three fingers I drew matchbox car-scaled roads. Thus began my early entry into community and city planning. I would create elaborate road systems daily, spending hours on layouts, with just enough time in the late afternoon to run some cars around the towns and highways I designed.

I remember playing there as early as age five. I could hear my mom through the screen door while she cared for Sandra and Debbie, two- and three-years younger than me. I never wandered away from that tree. It was not until my early thirties that I learned why. Gram told me that once baby Debbie arrived, my parents felt that tending three small children inside all day was too much, so I was set in the grass beneath the apple tree in the shade, with a rope tied to the tree and the other end tied to me. In the years preceding my memory, I may have been the reason the grass died under the tree, just as a dog would do if tied in a limited spot for too long.

This revelation shocked me, but explained how I became so willing to stay in one spot day after day. Like a new puppy, Gram described how I was consistently trained until the rope was no longer needed.

I carried this heavy knowledge of being tied to the tree around with me throughout my thirties until, while working with a therapist, the story spilled out, and with it the repressed trauma of being isolated outside, away from my family just inside the house. Releasing that trauma was a brutal physical experience, but ultimately brought me peace on the issue.

"Lunchtime, Butchy-doo!" Gram called down from the edge of her lawn above "Dover Cliff," the northernmost edge of Long Sands, in York Beach, Maine. I was down on the beach playing with my sand toys. Looking up, I saw her wave and would wave back. Knowing I heard her, she turned and walked back to the cottage beyond, out of my view. I packed the sand toys into my pail and walked up the beach towards the large, granite stairway which led up to the sidewalk along the shore highway. Following the sidewalk north several hundred yards past the motel on the corner, I reached the slate flagstone walkway my grandfather laid so long before that the thickening sod threatened to cover the stones completely. I made my way across my grandparents' yard, sticking to the stone path and working to knock as much beach sand off my feet as I could without stopping. Gram would meet me on the back porch with a warm washcloth, scrubbing away most of the beach that still clung to my skin and trunks before admitting me inside for lunch.

I had been down on the beach by myself for around three hours, digging in the sand and exploring the tidal pools that filled at high tide. I was fascinated by the crabs and starfish that came in with the tide and stayed the night. While I played, Gram had prepared and

Long Sands, York Beach, Maine, ca. 1960. The white cottage to the right of the blue umbrella was Laurie Lee's grandparents' house. Courtesy York (Maine) History Group.

served breakfast to her house guests. After sending them on their way, she had made up the rooms again for her next guests, washing, drying, and pressing the linens. Gram repeated these tasks every day from Memorial Day through Labor Day for more than twenty years.

Back when World War II broke out, Gram and my grandfather, who was trained as a mechanical engineer and machinist, moved with their only child—my then three-year-old mother—to this small home in southern Maine by the oceanside, near the naval yard in Portsmouth, New Hampshire, where he worked building submarines through the war. After the war, the family returned to Massachusetts but kept the beach cottage in Maine. Every summer, Gram opened the main floor of the house to bed-and-breakfast guests, while Grandpa stayed in Massachusetts during the week to work.

Growing up, Mom spent all her summers in Maine. When I became old enough, I took Mom's place as Gram's companion at the guest house. I'm sure I was never any help to her as a child, but the long and peaceful summer days were a cherished alternative to my summers spent under the tree at my parents' house. My happiest childhood memories took place at the beach.

After enjoying a sandwich and a treat at the old maple breakfast table where Gram's guests had just eaten, I would tidy up, find my pail on the back porch, then trot back to the beach to spend a few more hours completely unattended. The independence I enjoyed at the beach starkly contrasted with the subjugation of being tied to our tree back at my parents' house. I loved the freedom and did not take undue advantage of it.

Gram didn't have to call me from the cliff in the late afternoon. When the sea turn came, bringing with it a cold breeze off the ocean water and dropping the air temperature considerably, I knew it was time to go home for the day. I'd climb into the tub to wash the sand off, then put on dry clothes, including a sweatshirt or hand knit sweater against the chilly, Maine evenings.

From a twenty-first-century perspective, it is unbelievable that a small child could be sent off to the ocean to play unsupervised day after day. Apart from being taught to avoid strangers, my training included severe warnings from Dad to never go near the water. He frightened me to death by telling me what the water would do to me if I ever went near it. And I never did—no rope required.

Once, when I was perhaps six, mom and my sisters arrived unexpectedly at the cottage, brought there by my grandfather, who came up every weekend to cut the grass and tend the gardens. Though I cannot remember many details, apparently Dad's angry tirades may have caused Mom and my sisters to leave our house in Massachusetts and escape to Maine, too.

Perhaps things weren't good at our house that weekend. Mom and my sisters took an unoccupied guest room on the main floor while I continued to sleep in the north attic bedroom, which had been Mom's room growing up.

I awoke one morning to find myself in the cot on the edge of the attic room under the eaves. I looked back at my big double bed where I had fallen asleep and felt shocked to see Dad asleep in it instead. He wasn't supposed to be there. His presence in my bed stripped away my sense of peace and protection. This place I trusted was safe, and his presence somehow shattered it. I felt beyond frightened; I was genuinely terrified of him.

I don't remember why I felt that way about my dad. I don't know why I felt like I needed to leave our house in order to feel safe at Gram's cottage. I don't know what I witnessed or experienced that destroyed my sense of safety around Dad. Whatever it was has been repressed and lost. But that feeling remained painfully real.

I crept out of the attic bedroom that morning without waking Dad. Downstairs, I learned that he had arrived late the previous night, determined to take us back to Westminster. Although he was an auto mechanic, our family did not own a car then. He had borrowed the only vehicle he could get the previous night when he impulsively decided to retrieve his family.

It was a nice car, though, an all-black 1957 Thunderbird coupe. The obvious problem it posed was how a family of five would travel 100 miles over two-lane roads in a two-seater. Dad's solution was as practical as it was cruel. Behind the driver's bucket seat was a small void where one could store a flashlight or a road flare. "Get in!" Dad told me as he opened the car door and folded the red leather seat back forward. That was all I needed to hear. I tucked myself into the tiny space in the fetal position, my arms pulling my legs to my chest. Dad threw the seat back to its original position, making the compartment I had crammed myself into very dark. I heard Mom hustle Sandra and Debbie into the car, and onto her lap. I don't believe I made a sound during the two-hour trip, nor could I make a move. I understood I was required to do this by someone whose will far exceeded mine.

Like being tied to our apple tree, that car ride was yet another metaphor for being constrained in unsuitable spaces during my childhood years. My first sleeping space was at the top of the stairway above the old house's living room. The area had no doors but led to my sisters' dormered bedroom on the left and my parents' on the right. My "room" was essentially the upstairs hallway.

As I lay in bed each night, I could hear the TV and everything else going on downstairs. Since Dad rarely returned from work at the garage until after we were in bed, I listened from my bed as he arrived home. I could tell when he was exhausted or had a bad day. I heard my parents' conversations, particularly when arguments escalated, which happened often.

Mom once angrily challenged why Dad ever had kids if he didn't want anything to do with them. A heated argument followed. Another time, I heard Dad emphatically describe how he was determined to keep Mom and us kids in a bubble and protect us from all outside influences. My young mind was troubled by the idea of being so controlled to have to live in a bubble.

I wanted to find ways to help things be more peaceful in our house. I thought a lot about how I could help everyone be happy and get along. I took responsibility at a young age to keep the peace and never do anything to rock the boat. I felt a constant sense of vigilance for anything that might set off an explosive response from either of my parents.

But Dad could not keep us in a bubble. Nor could I keep my desire for a happy home from blowing up.

Once, while rummaging through an old box in the storage room where Mom's dresses were, I found a model railroad set which looked relatively new. Thrilled, I pulled it out and began setting it up. To my joy, the transformer worked—though the engine ran a bit jerkily. I couldn't understand why it was in a storage box. Later, I went downstairs and told Mom about my discovery. Her face immediately changed. "You are not to play with that," she said, "you've been told before. Now put it away before your father sees it."

I could tell Mom was serious, and she likely saw that I was hurt. I couldn't remember ever being told not to play with the train; I couldn't even recall ever seeing it. Slowly, I picked up and examined each piece before I returned them to the box, leaving the engine for last.

When I picked up the engine, I noticed it was much heavier than the other cars because the electric motor that moved the whole train was inside. Turning it over, I saw that it had been damaged and imperfectly repaired, causing the engine to jerk as it ran. It was then that the lost memory returned. I had been with Dad playing with the train set when I was quite small. He was very excited about it. Somehow, I was guilty of breaking the engine, and he became outraged. Although Dad attempted to repair it, it didn't run just right, and he could not make it right. Out of frustration, Dad put it all away in the box, and I was ordered never to touch it again.

A few years later, after working in almost every garage in the area and burning bridges with everyone he worked with, Dad decided to open his own shop at our house. I saw no advantages to our family in that situation, with Dad always nearby, distracted by everything we were doing and any problems around the house. Dad was volatile and triggered to the point of rage by typical household problems that other folks could simply brush off or work through.

Everything came to a head in 1975, the year I turned fourteen. Dad was spending his days trying to fix the old house's roof before winter set in, then working long hours into the night on his customers' cars. He was barely keeping it together until our septic system backed up just before Thanksgiving. From the window above my desk, I watched Dad futilely digging at the lid of the septic tank so it could be pumped. Then I heard him come inside, coughing and violently upset. We knew to stay clear when he got this way. He went into the bathroom, vomiting. Soon, Mom called the fire department rescue truck to our house, believing her thirty-six-year-old husband was having a heart attack.

Everything changed that day for our family, and not for the better. I mark it as the last day of my childhood. The firefighters took Dad to the nearby hospital in the rescue truck. When Mom talked to us the next day, she told us Dad had a heart attack and needed to stay there for a while. The coincidence was freaky since his father died of a heart attack on Thanksgiving weekend twenty-three years earlier.

Several days later, Mom told us Dad had a second, even bigger episode in the hospital and that we all needed to see him before he was moved to Massachusetts General in Boston. Dad was awake but heavily sedated when we went in to see him. He seemed glad to see me and called me to him. When I came closer, he propped himself up on one elbow, drew close to my face, then started ranting incoherently about how I needed to lock the garage and not let anyone inside. Everything in there was mine now, Dad told me, but the guys around town would try to take it. He warned me to do everything I could to prevent that from happening. Frightened by his speech, I pulled away as soon as I could. He didn't speak to Sandra or

Debbie. Mom whispered a few things to him, and we left. It would be months before I saw him again.

With Dad away, the tension in the house dissipated, but other pressures increased. Mom had been working at the elementary school as a lunchroom and recess aide. Now, she took a second job working after school and into the evenings as a bookkeeper, ironically for one of the other mechanic shops Dad had warned me against. With Mom gone so much, I took over much of the cooking, and Sandra became responsible for keeping the house clean.

There was minimal conversation in the house. We just did what we needed to do. Most days after schoolwork and preparing the family meal was done, I retreated into my room and lay on my bed, staring at the ceiling with just a nightlight on and listening to music. I became withdrawn and depressed. That winter was also when I started dealing with the reality of the onset of male puberty. I felt ugly and sad, and I couldn't control my temper. Recognizing that my body was betraying me, I saw I could no longer fight against all the forces that aligned to convince me I had to be a boy.

The following summer, Dad finally returned home from Boston, gaunt and looking like he had aged ten years. He didn't make eye contact and barely spoke beyond grunts. Day after day, he sat slumped over in his chair, hardly moving. Over the previous years, our house was filled with stress. Then briefly, it was quiet. Now we faced a heightened level of anxiety to not do anything to disturb Dad. We fell deeper into the axiom of dysfunctional families: "The whole household will desperately cater to keep the most toxic family member happy at the expense of everyone else." The only positive thing that seemed to come of his prolonged hospital sojourn was that he was through with smoking cigars for good.

Things only worsened as Dad regained enough strength to talk and get around. He was even more prone to angry outbursts and unreasonable demands. He slept most nights in his chair, having fallen asleep there, only to head to bed when Mom got up in the morning for work. At the time I never considered the places I could have moved to be away from the daily dysfunction. Though I wanted more and more to leave the house, I stayed because I felt I needed to support Mom. But I hibernated in my room, turning inward to the seclusion of my thoughts and imagination.

Learning to do what I was told "or else" left its imprint upon me. I grew into a strictly obedient adult who followed all the rules precisely and rarely questioned authority.

Looking back, I now wonder whether Dad actually had a heart attack in November 1975, or whether it was a panic attack or a nervous breakdown. Though I took the explanation of two heart attacks at face value for decades, I now realize it is far more likely that Dad was admitted to the hospital with symptoms of panic or emotional collapse. Once confined to the hospital, I wonder if a second and worse emotional outburst occurred, perhaps as he attempted to leave. That was the day we saw him in the hospital, heavily sedated and talking paranoid gibberish. Then he disappeared to Massachusetts General for months, only to return looking utterly wasted, a shadow of his former self.

Mom said he had reacted severely to Valium. Perhaps he did. Or maybe he refused to take his medications any longer and his doctors gave up trying to get him to conform, sending him back to the house, where life became a living hell for all of us. Our experiences over the next few years were not those of living with a recovering heart attack victim, but with a parent suffering from untreated and severe mental illness.

5

My Gettysburg Address

I didn't play team sports growing up. The idea of competing athletically against boys did not appeal to me. The feeling was mutual. When pick-up teams formed during PE class, I was always the last one chosen. Often, the team who had the final choice offered me to the other team to avoid having to include me. I was awkward and uncoordinated. Guys complained that I ran "like a girl," threw "like a girl," and was timid rather than aggressive.

Dad and Mom were athletic growing up, and I suppose they assumed all their children would be, too. One evening, Dad called me to his shop. "Wanna play some catch?" he asked, already wearing his baseball mitt.

This had never happened before. I ran back to the house for my glove, then met Dad on the newly-built ballfield next to his shop. He crouched down like a catcher behind home plate and had me stand back a distance to pitch to him. He called out where my pitch should land, mixing it up each time. After several throws, he stood and, saying nothing, walked off the field and back into his shop. Nothing was ever talked about, and he never asked me to do it again. I wandered back to my room, figuring I had failed to meet his expectations as a son once more.

At one point, Mom agreed to coach Sandra and Debbie's after-school softball team. To everyone's surprise, Dad got interested in what the girls were doing and proposed to close the shop during practices and games to act as an assistant coach. Mom agreed, happy that Dad was finally doing something that included my sisters. Dad's obsessive tendencies soon kicked in. He began tracking every metric associated with the performance of each young girl on the team, directing batting orders and defensive positioning like a major league manager. All Mom had to do was manage Dad. They got the most out of those girls, somehow never making any of them cry nor making enemies of their parents.

Being the only family member not involved, I watched every minute of the entire affair from just outside the fence behind the dugout. I went because I enjoyed watching my sisters and their friends compete while longing to be their teammate. The more I watched, the more I wanted to be included. I didn't care if Dad's metrics would have me batting last or playing in deep right field where no girl would ever hit the ball. I just wanted to be on a team like theirs.

One photo captured that entire summer. Mom wanted a picture of the girls in their team jerseys, so she lined them up, holding their gloves. Then she told me to get my glove and hop in the picture, too. I protested, but Mom persisted, perhaps noticing that I felt left out and wanting to include me, at least in this way. The resulting Polaroid didn't lie. Sandra and Debbie are grinning from ear to ear, looking cute and sporty. I am on the right, leaning a bit like an old fence post with an expression between grief and anger.

With my lack of ability in sports, Mom picked Scouting as an alternative and signed me up to be a Cub Scout, which Dad protested, he not having interest in anything like scouting. I took to it immediately. Our pack did crafts and plays and the leaders were women, not competitive-type dad coaches.

By fifth grade, the boys who attended Webelos on Saturdays also hung together during school recess. One of the guys, Hal, was the born leader amongst us, commanding the attention of all the others. He was smaller than me, and I found him very cute. Hal had wavy blonde hair, blue eyes, and an infectious smile. He was the lead in all the school plays and participated in a community dramatic club, whose performances I attended as often as I could. Hal had the charisma that I lacked. I contributed to our gang by being clever and imaginative. Before long, I worked my way into being Hal's "second-in-command"—the Robin to his Batman. I liked the role; it put me close to him and allowed my ideas for play and exploits to find voice.

The dynamic continued after we moved on to Boy Scouts. Hal was the patrol leader and I was his assistant—subservient and supportive, but full of ideas. Until one night after a scout meeting, when our new scoutmaster took me aside and changed my trajectory forever. He asked me why *I* wasn't the patrol leader. I told him Hal had always been the leader. He didn't buy it. After watching us for a few weeks, he informed me I was leading and was already calling all the shots. He encouraged me to step up and offer to be a candidate for patrol leader at the next opportunity.

I felt hesitant and told him so. I did not feel it was my role or place. But thanks to his coaxing, I said I'd think about it and, the following week, I sheepishly agreed to do it. I was elected, and for the next five years I led in every facet of our scouting experience, taking our troop to places and levels never before accomplished in our town's memory. We participated in regional and national events, produced several Eagle Scouts and grew participation to include dozens of scouts. I will always be grateful for a thoughtful scout leader who recognized my unseen abilities and encouraged me out of hiding and into roles where I could flourish. After that, I wound up leading whatever I joined.

Then there was one other occasion when I competed with my friend Hal and won. "Four score and seven years ago, our fathers brought forth upon this continent a new nation, conceived in liberty and dedicated to the proposition that all men are created equal." Slender and tall like the man I was quoting, I stood erect at the podium and thundered out those famous words as though I were Lincoln himself. Instead, it was five-score and ten years after Lincoln's Gettysburg Address, and I was speaking on my Westminster Elementary School's stage. I figured it would be more impressive if delivered with some force. Having never used a microphone, I underestimated just how forceful my voice would sound! My audience of sixth graders and their teachers recoiled in their folding chairs at my powerful oration.

I followed perhaps a dozen boys who, like me, had fully memorized the Gettysburg Address. We were competing for the honor of reciting the address from the bandstand on the Westminster Town Commons at the closing ceremony of the upcoming Memorial Day festivities. Girls, on the other hand, competed to recite the World War I poem, "In Flanders Fields," I suppose because it starts by mentioning poppies. I imagined myself as the girl who recited that poem, but I knew my only chance at the pulpit was to deliver the boy's speech, Lincoln's address. Most of the boys ahead of me rushed through the words in soft voices while studying the tops of their shoes. My best friend Hal, with his vast stage experience, was expected to win the role, as he had in every school performance since his family moved to town.

For years I had watched the Memorial Day parade from in front of our house, then followed the parade route up to the old town commons—a triangular field at the top of Academy Hill ringed by some of the town's most prestigious white clapboard colonial homes. There, the town gathered and listened to the closing ceremony.

When the parade passed a couple of years before, I saw my third-grade teacher, Ms. Waterman, riding on the tonneau cover of a brand-new, forest green, 1968 Mustang convertible, with a large Gold Star on the door. When I asked Mom why, she explained that her son Michael was killed while serving in Vietnam. I felt shocked and sad for her and wondered why she had not told us about her loss in class. The purpose of the Memorial Day parade and ceremonies sank deep into my heart. The following year, and each subsequent year, I marched in the parade in my scout uniform. Being the tallest in my troop, I got to carry the American Flag, flanked by others carrying the flag of the Commonwealth of Massachusetts and our red and white troop flag.

Each year, I had seen the sixth graders, one boy and one girl, deliver their memorized speeches from the bandstand. Once I decided I wanted to be one of those sixth graders, I realized I would have to edge out Hal for the chance to represent our school. I went all in when the assignment came to learn about and memorize the Gettysburg Address. I recorded myself saying it using our portable cassette recorder and played it back hundreds of times, perfecting my delivery. I knew this was my chance to excel, and I wanted to win it as I had never competed for anything before.

It worked. My surprised and overwhelmed teachers, who knew me as quiet and soft-spoken, chose me to give the Memorial Day Gettysburg Address to our town. It was going to be a day to be remembered.

The morning dawned with heavy rains, predicted to last the entire day. I was stunned. I could not remember it ever raining on Parade Day. I assumed it wasn't allowed. After a series of phone calls, we learned the parade would take place anyway. I dressed in my full scout uniform, donned my orange nylon rain poncho, and walked from our house to the top of Main Street, where the parade participants lined up. I received the leather holder and American flag from our Scoutmaster and took my place at front and center of our troop. I was already soaked when I passed by my family at our customary spot in front of our house.

The parade suddenly disbanded as it reached the halfway point, by the drug store where my kindergarten teacher once lived. Some people were leaving, but many were headed into the Unitarian Church. That church always looked boarded up and abandoned to me, not open and welcoming like the others on Main Street. Someone spotted me and whisked me towards the church and inside, where I was surprised to see the abandoned church had a lovely, warm interior, filled with townsfolk. My sixth-grade teacher saw me, and his anxiety was replaced by relief as he escorted me to the rostrum to sit next to the girl who had been selected to give "In Flanders Fields." Somewhere along the way, I handed off the flag and holster. My poncho had come off, but my khaki green scout uniform was a darker green than usual, soaked to the skin. My teacher told me they feared I wouldn't attend due to the weather. I never told them I had walked in the parade.

After a beautiful rendition of "In Flanders Fields," I stood, dripping on the podium, and fell into a trance, unaware of my surroundings or the words that flowed from my mouth out of reflex. I'm told I recited it perfectly. I don't know, it had been such a bizarre rush to get there and it was so disorienting not being on the Town Commons that I wasn't even aware of what I was saying. It was my first time addressing a crowd from a church podium, but it would definitely not be the last. Besides winning out for once over Hal in a public presentation, the chance to give the Gettysburg Address to the crowd of the town celebration was perhaps the first time I set a long-range goal for myself and did all I could to achieve it. I was only beginning to find that tenacity within myself, and didn't stop until I achieved my determined goal. That tenacity would become a driving force throughout my life.

At age twelve I began attending the weeklong summer scout camps held in the central New England pine forest. I enjoyed the independence of being away from the house. I shared a platform tent the first year with a new scout named Mike, who was a year behind me in school. We did everything together all week.

The scouts were allowed to light a candle and keep it in a large tin can for light in our canvas tents. One night, Mike and I stayed up so late talking that our candle completely melted, leaving only hot wax that began crackling in the bottom of the can. Thinking it would flare up, I grabbed a canteen of water and poured it into the can of molten wax . A tower of flame shot straight up like a rocket's engine. The sudden flash and roar brought everyone running to our tent, where we were stunned but otherwise okay. Candles inside tents were outlawed campwide by breakfast the following morning.

Mike and I continued to be the best of friends following camp. We shared many interests: drawing and designing things, a love of old music, skating and hockey in the winter, and exploring in the summer.

In my ninth-grade English class, we were assigned to write a short story. The first step was to prepare and submit an outline of our story. I chose to write one based on the experiences Mike and I had while exploring the woods behind our houses, imagining some mystery might be uncovered and solved, like the Hardy Boys and Nancy Drew books I read.

I was excited about my story outline, perhaps more than I had been about any English assignment since I fulfilled a writing assignment in seventh grade. My English teacher at the time was a dead ringer for teacher Gabe Kaplan in the popular TV show "Welcome Back, Kotter." I drew my teacher in a comic strip I titled, "Super English Teacher," who solved his community's dilemmas by flying around, correcting everyone's grammar. It was a huge hit!

But my ninth-grade story outline met with disaster. The teacher read aloud several outlines without revealing the authors' names in order to critique them as a means of instruction. Finally, she read mine. Instead of offering constructive criticism, my teacher's words felt like a taunt. It felt like she was "killing me softly" as she read my words about two boys who make a surprising discovery as they explore the woods together. She mockingly implied that the outline told the story of two gay boys going into the woods to perform lewd acts. She even added a few comments to flesh out the idea, making the class erupt in laughter. I imagine some thought it was a joke, not an actual student outline. But I knew better, and was mortified. I discarded my story idea and instead submitted a meaningless one I cared nothing about, for which I received a poor mark.

I wondered if I had exposed myself with the outline. I was attracted to Mike, although I never told him that he was my secret crush, my first that was also accompanied with feelings of sexual attraction. If I proceeded with the original story, I might have found a voice for my sentiments, but it was not to be. The outline debacle that day in class made clear to me that such attractions were socially unacceptable and must never be revealed. Over the next several years, I vacillated between exploring and hating my feelings and my expressions of appearance.

I always liked wearing hats. When I was little, Dad had a bright red felt hat with a broad brim turned up on one side and clipped in place with a large gold safety pin. He used to wear it as he wandered around the pit crews at drag races, checking out and tuning friends' race cars. It made him easy to find in a crowd and kept his crew cut head from getting sunburned. I often borrowed that hat and wore it around the house. One night, as we watched TV as a family, I was wearing the felt hat and zoned out watching the show.

Suddenly, Dad grabbed the hat and flogged me with it repeatedly. The safety pin was on the side toward my forehead and I felt it hit me with every blow. He was shouting something about how I might get away with treating my mother like that, but *he* wouldn't put up with it. Apparently, he had asked me several times to hand him the TV Guide, and I hadn't heard him. My sisters cowered into Mom while she pled with him to stop. I am sure he struck me before, but this is the only time I remember being hit. I never wore the felt hat again.

Instead, in time I found a hat of my own. I spotted it in a bin at a department store and fell in love with it as I scooped it up and tried it on. I had to have it, and Mom relented. It was a unisex, brimless bucket hat with a beige and brown print that looked like some of my school shirts. It had patterned stripes and circles. I wore it everywhere, outside of school, until it faded and frayed beyond usefulness.

I replaced it when I was about thirteen with an identically shaped but red, white, and blue paisley print, which gave me the advantage of being visible in a crowd, especially now that I stood nearly six feet tall. I continued wearing the bucket hat throughout my teens—on bike rides, camping trips, and around the house. I felt safe with the cap on. It gave me the sensation of longer hair than I was allowed to have or effectively hid my hair when I had grown it out longer than acceptable. Although I did not understand how unisex it was—or even what unisex meant—the hats seemed to be one of the few outward expressions of gender presentation that suited me. It became my style statement, and I was well-known for it around town and at all scouting events. I even got away with it when in my scout uniform wearing the bucket hat instead of the standard, red, BSA beret. It was my way of declaring my individuality that those around me seemed willing to accept.

I felt I needed to hide myself in my school PE classes, which were always a nightmare for me. Besides not being athletic, young men's locker rooms were terrifying to me. Most of my classmates would strip down after gym class, parading their naked selves and running through the gang showers to clean off. I always selected a locker in a corner, forgoing the showers and changing back into my school clothes as quickly as possible. I suppose I had a reputation for being unhygienic, but the alternative was beyond my emotional capacity to bear.

My athletic performances in gym class were equally embarrassing, with a few memorable exceptions. I loved hockey. I played street hockey with my sisters and ice hockey with my scouting friends on frozen ponds. I surprised all the tough guys in gym class when I took my favorite position as goalie when we played indoor gym hockey. Initially, the thought of turning me into a target for hardball slap shots seemed entertaining to the others, but to their shock, their shots weren't pelting me at all. I was deflecting them with my

Wearing my first "bucket hat," age ten, at the cottage in York Beach, 1971. Courtesy Laurie Lee Hall.

hockey stick. Then their aggression turned to just trying to score a goal on me, which they found impossible. My super-power was my artist's eye-hand coordination. Their disbelief turned to audible muttering when they could not get their way.

I had a secret love of softball. I was a lousy fielder, but I could hit. Once, in PE after getting several hits, I heard members of the varsity baseball team lament, "he would be a good ballplayer if he weren't so uncoordinated." One positive situation stands out beyond the rest: wrestling. If I'd had time in advance to think about it, I might have become terrified at the prospect. But after showing us a few basic moves, the gym teacher, whom I knew harbored a bad attitude towards me, immediately paired me to be the first to wrestle. My opponent was a rough, muscular young man named Ronnie, who worked at the local lumber mill. He was the meanest of the guys in our class and hung with the same bully who had smashed my head into the water fountain eight years earlier. Ronnie verbally taunted me more times than I could remember.

His bravado erupted when he received the sanctioned chance to fight me in front of the whole class. This would be the beating of the century, the opportunity to smear, the effeminate "fa**ot," as he had many times called me, on the mat for all to see. As the match began, Ronnie's strength initially struck me. But quickly I thought, "I know way more about geometry than this loser; let's go with what I know." I triangulated my body as best I could so I couldn't be toppled. When that resisted his strength, I went to work on his chaotic, flailing efforts. To the surprise of all, I flipped him down to the mat and did my best to smother and pin him. At that point, it got messy, and the teacher broke it up.

Ronnie's buddies chided him, "Dude, what happened?"

"His fingernails are too long!" Ronnie stammered out his breathless excuse. Immediately, one of the Ronnie's friends crossed the mat and took my hand, examined the nails, held my hand aloft, and exclaimed, "He's right." Turning back to me, he said, "You should cut your nails." I knew better. My nails weren't that long. I had beaten the bully for everyone to see, but it didn't gain me much respect. I was now the queer with the tiny hands and long fingernails, though I don't recall ever getting drawn into a fight after that.

I qualified for my Eagle Scout Award, and a special Court of Honor was held on my behalf, attended by extended family and friends of my parents. With all the accolades and attention focused on me, I forgot myself in the excitement. My anxieties and insecurity were absent for an evening, replaced by the positive recognition of self-accomplishment. As things were winding down afterward, I overheard my scoutmaster remark to my parents that he had never seen me smile as I did on this night. His impression wasn't a surprise to me. Although I had many fun experiences in scouting, I knew he was speaking the truth. I wasn't often an outwardly happy soul. I took his observation about me to heart and never forgot it.

I liked almost nothing about my history teacher, an Assemblies of God minister on the weekends. He was stern and cold. He was among those who, no matter what I did, believed I was not living up to my potential, as revealed by my IQ test score. The one bright spot all year was following a unit on medieval feudalism. I managed to convince him that, instead of a paper on the subject, I would develop a classroom-sized mural of a medieval feudal farm, complete with a castle, villages, farmers' huts, and all manner of activities depicted. It was a large-scale project, so I asked him if several of my friends could work under my direction. This got them out of writing papers—a real win for me! He agreed and secured us a roll of forty-eight-inch-wide newsprint paper, which we stapled to the bulletin boards around two sides of the room, covering about twenty-four feet in length.

Five or six of us gave up our study hall time for a couple of weeks beyond history class time to work on the mural. I was responsible for the overall placement of everything in the scene, along with drawing the key buildings. The other kids colored fields of different crops, drew dirt roads and fences, and added all the people and animals to the vast panorama. When finished, our mural was the talk of the school, and classes from all the grades arrived on field trips to our classroom to see it. On the last day of school, I couldn't bear to see it destroyed, so we carefully took it down and rolled it up, and I carried it home. It hung, overwhelming the walls of my tiny hallway bedroom, for a couple of years. This project was just one of the ways I developed joy and confidence in my leadership and artistic abilities.

"Look what he's doing!" my friend blurted out in the middle of English class instruction one day. The teacher and the whole class stopped to look at the paper on my desk. I was drawing the title of the school newspaper we planned to publish as a class assignment. What made it special was the letters were in Old English script, just as one would see in a newspaper like the *New York Times*, which I could draw from memory. I practiced the font many times until I perfected it. I cannot say I started doing it in the middle of class to gain attention, but once the focus was on me, I kept going, enjoying the praise it brought.

I could visualize things so clearly in my mind that I could replicate them on paper. On one snowy Thanksgiving Day, my Uncle Bill, a professional artist, asked if I could draw Mickey Mouse from memory and handed me a pencil and a sheet of paper. I looked at the blank paper and thought about how Mickey typically stood with his tummy tilted forward and gloved hands on his hips. Then, starting at the bottom of his shoes, I drew Mickey from bottom to top as though it was coming out of a modern-day printer, ending with the iconic ears. Bill was dumbfounded and had my whole family listen as he explained why no one ever drew the famous mouse that way. Artists always started with the ears and the shape of the head. He couldn't comprehend why I started at the feet and drew it so well. I told him it didn't matter. I could have started with the gloves, his shorts, nose, or anywhere I knew how the end product would look.

Even as my self-esteem faltered during my teen years, I knew I had two gifts that adults and my peers valued in me: my leadership abilities and my artistic talent. To offset the negative things I felt about myself as a pubescent boy who knew she was a girl, I poured myself into my art to gain the acceptance and praise of others. Nothing made me feel greater worth.

6

Not Wanting To Be Seen

When I turned eleven in the summer of 1972, Dad started his own garage. He also embarked on an ambitious, single-handed rebuild of our old house, which years before had been converted to include a second apartment in the wing off the back. My parents leased the apartment to another couple—friends of theirs from high school—until the project began. I helped Dad demolish the rear wing, which fascinated me as I grew to understand how houses, particularly historic houses, were built. A primary goal of the "house project" was to get our family all living on the main floor and out of our attic bedrooms. The old roof structure had been cannibalized too many times and was leaking. Dad said the whole attic needed to be removed and rebuilt someday, and his plan was to use trusses, which meant the attic rooms would be no more.

By the end of summer, we all moved downstairs. My parents took over the former apartment bedroom, and my sisters' new bedroom was the apartment's previous living room. We got rid of the back wing's old kitchen, bathroom, and storage porch. That left only one space on the main floor for me. Dad knocked out the wall between the stairway to the attic and the pantry of the old apartment. The result became my "bedroom," a misshapen connection of the leftover pantry and stair hall, only a bit bigger than Harry Potter's fictional "cupboard under the stairs." Every inch of the floor, not under my single bed, dresser, and desk, was a public right-of-way between our living room, my sisters' room, and the attic. Privacy was non-existent in the pantry which now substituted as my bedroom.

If Sandra or Debbie had to get up at night and pass into the main house for any reason, including to use the bathroom, they had to open the faux-wood accordion door and pass right by my bed. Yet, I have no memories of ever being interrupted by them at night. Living in that space must have made me a sound sleeper. I got a small transistor AM radio with an earphone jack that Christmas. The expectation in our house was that when you went to bed, you went to sleep. But I couldn't resist putting on my earphones and surfing the dial for my favorite fifties "oldies" music. Sequestered beneath my covers, I might not be caught, should anyone enter from either door. I discovered that on crisp winter nights, especially on weekends, I could find music programs from as far away as New York City or Chicago! Several months of listening to the radio helped me feel that even the pantry could be private at night, perhaps even safe.

Back when my parents bought the old house, they also obtained a matching new clothes washer and dryer set. Not long afterward, Mom began using the clothesline in the backyard to dry most clothing and all the linens. I asked her once, as she handed me a big stack of laundry to hang in the back on a very cold day, why she never used the clothes dryer. The official answer was that she liked how fresh the line-dried laundry was, but she eventually confided in me via a whisper that the dryer had stopped working years ago. She didn't dare upset Dad by telling him since he would tear it apart trying to fix it, accompanied by unlimited cursing. When they finally moved from that house, the dryer sat unused for at least eighteen years.

Between the laundry room and our garage was another room we called the "backroom." Ironically, it was big enough to be a bedroom and a private one at that, but instead, it was Dad's playroom. He built an elaborate 1:32 scale, slot-car track in the room and played slot cars with his buddies. Later, the slot car track disappeared, and its base became Dad's big workbench. For the room's décor, every inch of every wall was papered with Playboy magazine centerfolds, in what must have taken years to collect.

As children, we were prevented from seeing the nude pictures on the walls. Even opening the door to the backroom was grounds for discipline. Of course, Sandra felt obligated to go in there when she could get away with it. I even remember seeing the slot car track a few times, but only rarely. When the track was removed, the centerfolds remained.

When I was old enough to take out the trash, I needed to walk through that room or carry the rubbish outside and back into the garage, which I often did in good weather to avoid the backroom altogether. I was embarrassed by it. Most of Dad's buddies were single, but Dad was married, and I felt it wronged Mom to "decorate" his room like that. Maybe Gram helped me have that high moral opinion. But I didn't like it. I didn't like what it meant about how Dad felt about girls and women.

By the time I was in junior high, word got around about the backroom at my house, and guys started coming around trying to be my friend so they could go in there and see it. Mom saw that happening and put her foot down, so Dad was finally required to take down all the centerfolds late one night and put them into the rubbish barrel. All that remained of the backroom walls was old, olive-drab paint I had never seen before, riddled with staple holes.

Dad wasn't the only one who had magazines of adult interest. "Mom's magazines have pictures of women who made their boobs bigger," Sandra shouted one day, coming out the front door and running up to me and Debbie, out of breath. "Come on!"

Debbie and I were playing in the shell of a red Volkswagen Beetle, which had surrendered its undercarriage and drivetrain to a dune buggy dad built for a customer. The body, sitting in the weeds of the backyard beyond the garage, became our playhouse. Just ahead of it was the larger-than-life fiberglass Esso Tiger mascot that had stood on the roof of Dad's short-lived gas station downtown.

Sandra led us into the living room and up to Mom's stack of magazines on the maple coffee table: Redbook, Cosmopolitan, Good Housekeeping, and more. Sandra flipped to the ads in the back of one and showed us an advertisement with two photos of the same young lady in a tight tee shirt. The photo on the right was much bustier than the one on the left. "See!" she exclaimed.

Though I had just entered sixth grade, I remained somewhat naive.

However, nine-year-old Sandra, a fourth grader, was clued in beyond her years.

"Well, over the summer, Mary Catherine's boobs have grown a lot," I said, hoping to compete with her.

"How do *you* know? Did she *show* them to you?" came her immediate return volley.

I had no reply, as usual. Sandra knew that even if that had happened (it hadn't), I would be too modest to say so. I wondered what would cause a girl to show her naked boobs to a classmate, and where would that occur at school? My only point was that the change in Mary Catherine since the fifth grade was as evident as the two photos in the ad. Seeing that ad, and the many more I found later as I began scouring Mom's magazines for similar ads, pictures, and stories, encouraged me. I began to connect the dots that young people's bodies change, and that some people could buy or do things to change their bodies too, like give themselves boobs where they weren't before. More than anything, the magazine pages reassured me that my body might be able to change to become the young woman I wanted to grow up to be.

By then the days of dress-up play were behind us, and playing with Barbies was becoming less frequent. I still liked fantasy play, retreating into my own space or on endless bike rides around the dead-end road, telling myself elaborate stories of what I would be like growing up. Part of me believed it would be possible to become the young woman I saw my female classmates becoming.

I watched for Mom's magazines when she threw them out after she finished with them. I became very cooperative at taking out the "rubbish," as we called it. When I emptied the household trash into the barrel destined for the town dump, I tore out certain pages of photos and ads and stashed them in my pockets. I kept them between my mattress and box spring on the side of the bed against the wall, where they were less likely to be found.

With the clothes dryer defunct, most smaller items were dried on a folding rack in the bathtub, behind the shower curtain. The frame was moved onto the bathroom floor when it was time for a bath or shower. The bathroom was the most private place in our house. There, I became interested in articles of Mom's clothing hanging on the rack to dry. I wanted a way to continue to feel the validation of self I found in playing dress-up with my sisters, though now at thirteen, I knew that was no longer socially acceptable for me. Occasionally, I would "borrow" Mom's clothing items from the bathroom rack and hide them with the magazine pages between my mattress and box spring. Many nights in my pantry bedroom included dressing in Mom's clothes, under my bed covers. It began simply at first, growing more elaborate as my experience increased. I used rolled-up socks or yarn balls as bra inserts. Sometimes, I would fall asleep dressed in Mom's clothing, awakening in the night terrified I would sleep until morning and be discovered.

At first I made sure that something I took in the evening was always returned to the bathroom rack when I awoke in the morning. After forgetting to do this return trip a few times and getting away with it, I became emboldened at the ease of repeat-wearing the same item the next night without having to retake it. In time, after not being found out, I began to keep my stash of clothing items for several days. That worked until Mom changed my bed sheets and I discovered that her stashed things were gone. I panicked about what I would say when she would surely asked me what was going on. I felt guilt-ridden for days and, penitent, I abstained from dressing in her clothing. But Mom never asked. Before long, my guilt was overruled by an increasing willingness to take risks again to fill the hole in my unrealized female identity, which drove me to return to stashing and dressing. The cycle repeated itself several times through my teen years. Items stashed and used were found, removed, washed, hung to dry, and stashed again.

I had no idea until I was older that most adults would quickly realize some of their laundry went missing. Still, to this day, I cannot explain why Mom kept taking her things back but never confronted me at all.

I missed openly acting as a girl, like when my sisters and I had played. Dressing under the covers at night in the pantry allowed me to feel a connection to being the girl I was, though not allowed to be publicly during the waking hours. It wasn't that I particularly liked the clothes or the feel of them per se; it was the confirmation that this is how I should be able to look. I should have developing breasts to fill out a bra and not need balls of yarn. I should grow up and be the young woman I knew me to be. But at least I had a few hours in the dark of that little room at night.

There were more than a few drawbacks to secretly presenting as female in the pantry at night. I was in the dark. Turning on a light would have been a dead giveaway that I was awake since the doors to the pantry didn't close tightly. In time, I worked up enough courage after dressing to slide out from under the covers and walk around the room. I reasoned that if I heard someone else awake, I could dive back under the sheets before someone came in. I tried, mostly in vain, to see myself in the mirror above my dresser. Only brightly moonlit nights gave me any chance of seeing my reflection.

Given its past purpose, my pantry bedroom also had no heat. All the other rooms in the house had a large cast iron radiator that filled with steam from the fuel oil burner in the basement. Once filled, they would hiss and whistle, then clank as the condensing water returned down the pipe to the boiler. But not my room. Winter nights in the pantry were so frigid that thick ice formed, not only on the window glass but on the wooden frame as well as the wooden window sill almost to the surface of my desk. Many nights, it just didn't make sense to leave the blankets until morning.

The onset of puberty brought miserable emotional feelings, including frequent self-loathing. I did not like who I was becoming at all. I became more self-conscious each year about how others were perceiving me. Did I act too girly? Could anybody see how I felt about myself? Was I hiding my attractions well enough? As a child, I had wanted to be seen for who I was. But as a teen, trying to hide who I was became my full-time obsession, filling me with anxiety and panic. I wanted to wear my hair longer, but fear that it would give me away caused me to periodically give in to Mom and let her cut it, only to hate how I looked. No matter where or what I was doing, feeling uncomfortable in my skin became my constant experience.

The teenage years can be hellish for everyone at different stages. But most youth don't have to wake up each day trying to decide if they are male or female. Back then, I had no idea whether anyone else experienced gender conflict like I did. I also didn't know anyone I could safely talk to about my feelings. My gender conflict and discomfort felt like being on an airport runway standing next to a non-stop, roaring jet engine. The sound felt so loud, the air movement so disarming, the vibration so bone-jarring that it was impossible to think clearly. The experience felt so threatening that I could barely look around and see, let alone appreciate the beauty around me. I could only endure the constant drain of the engine's effects on me while doing my best to function.

Dressing as a girl at night brought me interludes of inner calm, as if the jet engine was being throttled down. I wasn't able to find relief in any other way. However, reducing the pain of gender conflict in this way came at the cost of increased anxiety over being found out. Nonetheless, the self-medicating effect of dressing compelled me to keep doing it.

There were other side effects. I dealt with not getting enough sleep on the nights I secretly dressed. I felt the shame of being so messed up that I couldn't be satisfied with who I was told I was. I felt guilt for doing something every night that appeared so incredibly unnatural. Some nights, I would collapse on the floor next to my bed, partially dressed, wishing someone would come into the pantry and catch me so whatever was supposed to happen next would just get started. I would sit there sobbing silently, wondering what evil, destructive force controlled me to the point that I could not change how I felt. But the need was so strong that I kept up the cycle of dressing, struggling, and fighting within myself for years to come.

7

Coming Out of the Pantry

In addition to drawing cartoons and pretty much everything else, I liked doing crafts of all kinds, whether it was the mail-order latch hook rug I made as a kid or the sand painting projects Mom first introduced to me and my sisters. We filled acrylic double-wall bowls with colored sand, layer by layer to create decorative flower pots or terrariums. I kept making them until I had made one for everyone I knew. Then I built the ultimate one, a cactus-filled terrarium from a huge sand-painted globe that resembled the planet Jupiter, which hung by hand-tied macrame from the ceiling of my little room over the foot of my bed. My friend Mike helped me hang it because it was far too big and heavy to do by myself.

When Mike and I were teens, we drew all kinds of cars, jalopies, old classics, and hotrods. I imagined we might grow up to illustrate one of the classic car magazines we received monthly in the mail. Once our design juices really kicked in, we began developing original ideas.

Mike leaned toward sports cars, whereas I became interested in how automotive design needed to adapt, given the energy crisis the world was then experiencing. I considered how to get the most efficient interiors from the smallest, sleekest cars. I was convinced fossil fuel engines were on their way out, and the future lay in alternate power sources. A school chemistry experiment using a reaction between hydrogen and oxygen that caused a small pop with only a trace of water as its byproduct captured my imagination. I was sure an engine could be produced based upon the principle, which ran on abundantly available hydrogen gas combined with oxygen from the atmosphere. Instead of harmful exhaust pollutants, clean water would come out of the exhaust pipe! After high school, Mike left for Detroit to study automotive design and later worked for General Motors and Ford, designing Camaros and Mustangs.

I went another way, setting my educational sights on architectural design. By the time I reached high school, my artwork became my constant concentration and desire for my future vocation. Artwork was the thing I strove to be known for.

I was the "art nerd," the kid who took multiple art classes during the school day, then hung out in the art room, usually alone, for two hours after school, working on ambitious projects. I preferred being in the studio to being in the house those days.

Every afternoon, I took the late school bus home. I often got off the bus at the center of town by the drug store. Instead of walking home, I went straight to my job at the pizza parlor, where I also ate supper. Closing up after 9:00 P.M., I would finally go home and go to bed. Because this late bus left after the school's athletic practices ended, I tried to be on that bus first, before the few dozen sweaty, charged-up young men of the JV and varsity teams arrived. These were not average players either. Our school's teams won the small school division state championships in football and basketball in my junior and senior years. These were the best athletes around, and they knew it. The bus jolted back and forth as they boarded, bounded down the aisle, and piled into their seats. I felt intimidated by them as I sat staring out the window to my side, rarely making eye contact and never speaking. I was not one of them.

The "jocks" never bothered me on the bus, perhaps because I went unnoticed. During the same two years they were capturing multiple state titles, I produced artwork that won regional and statewide competitions, representing our school. While the boys' teams garnered well-deserved and abundant praise at school assemblies and in the local media, I'm sure few people noticed the illuminated display cases outside the art rooms where my peers' and my drawings and paintings hung with their own ribbons and medals. I didn't care

Voted "Most Artistic," Laurie Lee stands next to her painting, *Steeples,* for this photo in the Oakmont Regional High School yearbook, 1979.

too much about the accolades of the school's elite. The people who mattered and whose opinions I respected, saw, and appreciated my work included my art instructor, Nancy Gallo, the mechanical drafting teachers, and my guidance counselor. I approached high school like a track athlete might run the 400m hurdles by this point. I had my head down and sprinted, clearing each class and semester like hurdles. I had near-perfect attendance throughout high school because what was the point of staying in the house? My grades were also near perfect, only getting an occasional B in English because I couldn't always figure out how to replace an essay assignment with a drawing.

I was independent and creative. I chose those classes I felt would best propel me toward attending architectural school. For example, the college track for the first year included biology. By faking an illness for an entire week in eighth grade, I avoided dissecting frogs, wanting nothing to do with it. An architect should study geology, not biology, so I chose ninth-grade Earth Science, not realizing it was the introductory science class reserved for the weaker students. I loved the course and found a lot of applications for the knowledge presented. Plus, I was reunited with friends from elementary school who were not in any of my junior high classes that had been segregated according to "academic potential."

After I made my case for my course selections while still in the eighth grade, I was placed with the junior guidance counselor, Eugene Sullivan, instead of with the head of the guidance department, who took all the legitimate college-bound students unto himself. Mr. Sullivan understood my plan, supported my path, and told me to look hard at Rensselaer Polytechnic Institute (RPI) in Upstate New York. I took every available math class, and every available art and drafting class, ultimately doing independent projects during my senior year. I finished high school with a 3.9+ GPA, second only to Mary Catherine Pinkerton, but because of a discriminatory quirk, I was not ranked in the top ten percent of my class.

When reviewing my college application, the Rensselaer admissions people raised the question, how could someone finishing second overall in GPA not be in the top ten percent of their graduating class? My answer was simple: An A in senior year Art IV, for example, was equal in grade points to a D in senior English. Whatever honor I brought to the school's art program around the state didn't matter.

One of my high school classmates recently described me as having been "very quiet and sweet, but contained." The perfect storm of my ongoing puberty, increasing depression, and turning socially inward to conceal my gender identity all played into my deep diving into my art. In the years that Dad was hospitalized and after he came home, I escaped from reality by lying on my bed, doors shut, headphones on, drawing pencil or pastel still lifes on my large drawing board propped up against my bent legs. Staying late at school, I focused on painting large canvases, usually of building exteriors in tight, collage-like compositions. Ms. Gallo told me my style reminded her of the twentieth-century American realist Edward Hopper.

Focused on my art, I could emotionally disconnect from the

painful aspects of my dysfunctional family life and the social pressures and abuses I felt at school. The harder I worked on my projects, the more well-received my creations became. Art accomplishments became the vehicle that brought me acclaim and acceptance, which in turn caused me to apply myself all the more. Encouraged by Ms. Gallo, I offered my works as submissions to statewide scholastic art shows in Boston, where I won several awards and competed in national scholastic shows. Nearer to Oakmont, I won several local shows and public competitions during high school. I was amassing a solid portfolio of completed works and a resume of accomplishments, with my eye solely on obtaining architectural training.

My social identity as the art nerd served me well throughout high school, bringing me a form of validation and acting as a foil to conceal my sexual attraction and gender identity. Rejoicing in my artistic successes publicly offset the self-loathing I felt in private.

"How do you expect to sign a commitment to attend a school that costs more than I make in a year!" Dad bellowed from his recliner chair in the living room corner where he sat all day. I had just told my parents I was accepted via early admission to the School of Architecture at Rensselaer. Ecstatic over the news, I was utterly unprepared for his question. My focus for so long had been to find the architectural program that would be the ideal fit for me and to get accepted, and I had not given much consideration to the high cost of college. My parents were fully aware of my efforts to apply to Rensselaer. Still, like me, they were caught off-guard by the need to commit before the Institute would disclose their level of financial support for my education.

This was a milepost moment, in which everything that would follow in my life hinged on what happened next, and I sensed it. "It will work out. I will take care of it myself. I do not expect you to pay for it," was my reply, not knowing what that would require. Neither of my parents went to college, and Dad had not even finished high school. As their oldest child, I was crossing this bridge for the first time in our family, taking a step through a door and out into the dark.

I also knew that moving away to attend university instead of commuting to a local college from Westminster went in direct opposition to my dad's long-held desire to contain our family in a bubble under his control. Long before his illness, Dad had planned that I would become his partner in his auto repair shop, eventually taking it over. He never asked me how I felt about it; he simply assumed that was what I wanted. On the other hand, Mom would often secretly impress upon me, "Don't you dare stay here and become a mechanic like him!" Although I appreciated her encouragement and secret support, I didn't need her words to know for myself that nothing could keep me in Westminster, fixing cars for a living.

Just before graduation, our high school class and many teachers held a "Senior Show" designed to showcase the talents and accomplishments of members of the senior class. The head of the guidance department, Mr. McKay, conducted it. My classmates gave several musical presentations, including an outstanding, acoustic guitar solo of all seven verses of "American Pie," accompanied by a boy I had never heard sing before that night.

Tributes were paid to the state-champion football team and to the basketball team. Mention was made of the various musicals presented throughout the year. Finally, Mr. McKay read the names of his top students and the universities they were bound for in the fall, concluding our two class salutatorians—both accepted at the US Air Force Academy—and our class valedictorian, Mary Catherine Pinkerton, who was headed to Harvard Radcliffe to study law. Proud parents and family applauded with enthusiasm. The whole affair was awe-inspiring.

Mr. McKay was just about to conclude the celebration when the unthinkable occurred. Nancy Gallo, my mentor and the head of the art department, rushed to the podium, taking the microphone from his hands. Ms. Gallo barely contained her emotions as she described the many art shows our high school competed in across the state over the past year, congratulating all the senior girls who had participated.

Then she turned to me and asked me to stand. I stood up for the first time that night to be recognized, feeling awkward. Ms. Gallo then described every show I competed in and won, bringing notoriety to our school and its art program. She explained that she hoped I would go on to study fine art or commercial art, but that I had always had my heart set on becoming an architect. So, she was pleased to announce that I had been accepted to one of the most respected architectural schools in the country, Rensselaer Polytechnic. Based on the strength of my high school portfolio, I had received a full scholarship to the five-year program, the most significant financial award to any member of our senior class. I was embarrassed and shocked. To me, it seemed that McKay's program intentionally planned to ignore me, but she would have none of it. As a result of her timing, the final focus of the night was entirely mine as I went from being ignored to distinguished.

This felt like a fitting conclusion to my high school journey, with me always running against the grain of a system that discounted my value despite my potential. Ultimately, I triumphed over the school administration's discriminatory actions, and this triumph was underscored.

Until the end of high school, I had kept up the cycle of secretly dressing in female clothing. One night in the summer after graduation, I decided to take it a step further: I would dress all the way and leave the pantry. The idea electrified me so much that I felt completely driven to proceed despite the risk. Mom and the girls were asleep in their rooms. Dad was sleeping in the living room, snoring loudly in his chair, preventing me from leaving the pantry through that door. My only choice was to go out through the window. I dressed in Mom's top and shorts, as best as possible, then cleared off the top of my desk and raised the window screen. I climbed onto my desktop and headed feet first out the window. The aluminum frame of the storm window bit into my thighs as I inched my way out. As my feet dangled out the window, my toes searched for the pile of boards and ladders stacked up outside my window from the never-ending house project. It occurred to me that the pile might not be stable and could fall with a crash if I landed on it wrong. And there I would be found, halfway out the window, a six-foot-tall, young adult male dressed as a girl, ready to be hauled off to a padded cell somewhere. But I kept going.

My foot gradually found the pile and I continued to slither out the window, placing more weight on the pile of old boards. I crab-walked across the wood and equipment until I reached the ground and could sort myself out. I was sure I looked like a complete mess. Fortunately, it was dark on the backside of the house. I stood up straight and took my first deep breath outside, presenting as my true self. It felt good.

Oakmont senior David Hall and his award-winning drawing. Telegram Photo

Oakmont Student's 'Hobby' Wins Him Full Scholarship

From a newspaper clipping about Laurie Lee's receiving a full scholarship at Rensselaer Polytechnic's School of Architecture, *Worcester Telegram & Gazette,* 1978.

But I had no idea what to do next. Where could I go looking like this? I needed to try. I carefully walked across the back of the house, ducking the kitchen window in case anyone heard me. I headed out behind Dad's garage. On the east side of the shop, the ballfield was bright from the floodlights of the nearby parking lot streaming across it. Pushing slightly past the corner of the shop into the light, I saw myself, illuminated for the first time in years, dressed as a girl. I smiled and looked down at the soft fabric laying over my pretended breasts and further down to my long, bare legs.

So much of me wanted to make a run for it across the field, head past my neighbor Skippy's old house, and walk through the town's deserted streets. That was why I came this far out of the pantry, perhaps even to be seen. But then I looked to my left. The house behind ours was owned by none other than the young mechanic who had made fun of my Bermuda shorts before. What would he say if he looked out his window and saw me now?

I thought about my empty bed back in the pantry. There was no return if I proceeded to walk downtown. I couldn't do it. I retraced my steps carefully, back to the wood pile, back through the open window, and across my desktop, landing in a heap on the pantry carpet.

My expedition outside was over. I hadn't been caught. But I hadn't dared to push myself all the way out either. I had too much fear of what wasn't known or knowable. I could see no pathway forward for someone like me. I fell into a deep depression for several days, crushed by my inability to realize more than just a few minutes outside, free to be me.

As that summer of 1979 drew to a close, I prepared to leave my parents' house to begin training as an architect. I understood I was at a crossroads, the first crossroads I ever experienced. There was so much about my childhood and teen years that I wanted to put far behind me. The pain and anxiety of dysfunctional family life. The abuses and apprehension at school. Not being seen or understood as a child and then being unwilling to be seen or understood as a teen.

Leaving the old house and the pantry, gone from Westminster altogether, seemed like the opportunity to start with a clean slate and create a new life. If I knew then what I know now, that new, independent life would likely have been to live as my true self, as Laurie Lee. But in 1979 I couldn't begin to imagine how it could be possible. All I could conclude was that there was no pathway forward to living authentically. I believed that the only way to escape my past was to give up my "fantasy" of being a girl. I needed to look forward, live the life of the guy everyone said I was, and end the conflict. I turned and faced the figurative jet engine beside me and shouted, "I can't hear you. I'm not listening anymore!"

I decided to never allow myself to think about being a girl again. I would never dress up. It was over. I was done. I took the things still stashed between my mattress and box spring to the parking lot next door and shredded them, throwing the scraps of the dreams of my teen years into the rubbish barrel. I turned my back and walked away. I forever buried my gender identity that day.

Or so I thought.

8

Following My Chosen Paths

Even though I had never met an architect, I somehow knew I would become one since I was fourteen. I have always felt grateful that I discovered I wasn't limited to just dreaming about it, but could set my foot on the path to fulfill that dream. Yet I can't pinpoint the influence that placed me on that path. The unrelenting focus that carried me through high school was solely to get into architectural school. Once I committed to Rensselaer's early decision letter, the Institute awarded me a significant scholarship which, along with my earnings and careful planning, meant I could pay my way to college as I told my parents I would.

In late June 1979, I drove to Troy, New York, to attend freshman orientation at Rensselaer. I had visited there almost two years earlier for a pre-admission interview. This trip felt surreal to me—being only my fourth time outside New England and the first time I had traveled alone. In contrast to the pre-admission interview when there were architectural students everywhere, looking like bands of Woodstock hippies, this time the only people in the school of architecture's Greene Building were the few professors assigned to provide the orientation to about one-third of my new classmates. It was a "pinch me, am I really here?" experience. I could not wait to begin in September.

After listening to several presentations, I went on a walk with one of my new colleagues, Jane. She was pretty, blonde, and wearing oval, wire-rimmed glasses. She wanted to get to know me better, so we stopped in front of the engineering building and sat on a low concrete wall to talk. Jane told me all about herself, her family, high school accolades, and activities. She then asked about me. The sparse facts I shared about spending my teen years doing artwork and making pizzas didn't satisfy her. What else did I do? "Did you live under a rock?" she queried. It was as though I didn't know who I was or how to describe myself to someone else. Very few people had ever been interested. For the first time, it occurred to me that I may have led a monotonous life. As I struggled to share something more interesting about myself, images about who I really was inside passed through my mind—the teenaged girl in the dimly lit mirror in the pantry, the identity that constantly occupied my thoughts but only found expression in secret and late at night.

I felt intoxicated by the new-found freedom I was experiencing. Freedom that allowed me to be who and whatever I wanted. Was it enough freedom to openly explore my female identity and start a new life at school in spite of my recent, inner commitment not to? No, I decided, and told Jane nothing of substance about me. I took one more step in my conviction to leave my identity buried in a silent past.

On Mom's fortieth birthday, I returned to Rensselaer again, this time to stay. My parents dropped me and my suitcases off at my dorm. I stood on the parking lot sidewalk in front of Bray Hall, one of five identical L-shaped, three-story male dormitories, and hugged her goodbye. She was crying as she would every time I hugged her goodbye going forward. This first time, though, was the hardest.

After watching the big red Country Squire pull off onto the street, I turned to head into the dormitory, my first new address since I was two years old. My heart was bursting at the taste of freedom. I got away from the house in Westminster!

I was tidying up my side of the dorm room, my clothes put away, and my bed made with my flowered, quilted bedspread when the door thrust open. My heart sank as my new roommate burst in. Rich was magnificent in size and larger than life. Athletic and muscular, Rich was indeed testosterone's finest creation.

Up to that moment, I had not given any thought to the fact that, for the first time in my life, I was about to start living with a man who wasn't Dad. Here was the person I would share this small, concrete cell of a room with for the next nine months. I had crushed on some boys in the past, but they were tender, creative, male versions of me. I felt like I had been assigned to the gorilla cage. Rich's first words were aggressive, loud, and so in my face that I recoiled onto my bed.

"Hey, roomie, whatchu doin'!" he thundered, eyeing me with contempt. "You're not a dickfor, are ya?"

"What's a dickfor?" I asked sheepishly.

"Aw huh! Ya don't know what a dick is for!" he shouted even louder, making a repeated obscene gesture involving his right arm and his ample groin. I was doomed to hear that inane joke dozens of times in that room before the following spring.

In spite of my excitement to move out on my own, by nightfall I was yearning for what little privacy I had enjoyed in my pantry bedroom. At least in there I could change my clothes without being seen. I set about as discreetly as possible to change into my pajamas in my corner of the room as Rich and his new friends went back and forth between the room and the hallway, never closing the door. When Rich finally decided to get ready for bed, he threw off his tee shirt onto the floor, scratched his groin several times, thumped onto his partially-made mattress, and grunted, "G'night, roomie!"

The Bray Hall common restrooms were located at the corner intersection of the two legs of the L-shape. The urinals did not have privacy screens but were lined up along the far wall under the glass tile windows. I never used a urinal and so I avoided that side of the room. A few toilets were within stalls. I will never understand why men need three times as many urinals as toilets. To my horror, beyond the toilets was a gang shower—one large room with shower heads on every wall without a curtain in sight.

Even though I had consciously buried my female gender identity a few weeks earlier, I had not realized that accompanying my identity was a heightened level of modesty. It frightened me to think I had to live like this. To avoid Rich and our perpetually open room door, I started dressing in one of the toilet stalls. I only used the gang shower in the middle of the night or very early in the morning when no one else was there. I did not want to see any of those guys naked, and I didn't want them to see me undressed, either. My inner self wouldn't permit it.

There were 100 men on this dormitory floor, three-quarters of them from New Jersey. I found their behavior appalling and their language worse. The dorm shook with unending raucous chaos, all set to the constant thundering of Bruce Springsteen and the E Street Band. They made fun of my heavy New England accent and pretended never to understand anything I said the first time I spoke. The only other "downeaster" on the floor was a slight, timid boy they called "Soap," from Bangor, Maine. I liked Soap, but we never hit it off as friends.

Classes began just after Labor Day. I was glad I had already made a friend in Jane. She introduced me to Glenda, another architectural student who also lived in the only first-year female dormitory building, Warren Hall. We also made friends with Pete, a slender, nerdy fellow who was into model railroads. To begin the semester, we were given class group assignments. One was to draw the building facades and landforms of a one-block-wide section of the city of Troy, from the Hudson River up to and across the campus, a distance of about a mile. Jane, Glenda, Pete and I formed a team and set out with our charcoal sticks and sketch pads to get to know each other and the city we now called home.

Our group of four frequently studied together in one of the girls' dorm rooms. Their rooms were more civilized than the male rooms, with a wardrobe dividing the sleeping areas into two and an ensuite bathroom for each room. A few weeks into the first semester, Glenda's roommate moved out, apparently into her boyfriend's room in the old quadrangle dormitory in the center of campus. This left one-half of Glenda's room open to create a study area using the bed as a sofa. With end tables and thrift-store lamps, it became our gathering place.

When focus on assignments waned late at night, we talked about other things like music, philosophy, or religion—especially religion. Glenda was a Mormon and usually led conversations about each of our beliefs. Jane was Methodist, and Pete was Catholic. All three were practicing members of their faiths, possessing firmly held convictions. I had no strong beliefs, having not attended church since being put out of the childrens' choir at age ten.

One evening, the other three discussed the nature of God while I listened. As Glenda described the Mormon or "Latter-day Saint" belief in a loving, tangible God, and of God the Father and his Son Jesus Christ as individual, embodied beings, I thought that made good sense. I resonated with hope when she described the LDS belief in eternal families. I had unfettered optimism that my future family could be like the kind of families she described. Soon, Glenda and I began more direct, individual discussions related to the basic story and doctrines of Mormonism. It all felt increasingly sweet to me.

At Halloween that fall, our first-year class of architects planned a party. Like usual, I had no intention of attending, but when Jane and Glenda discovered I wasn't going, they hatched an idea. They would help dress me in their best clothes and do my hair and makeup, and I could disguise myself as one of their friends. They knew nothing of my history, nor my determination to never dress as a girl again. Yet I could not resist their enthusiasm for this prank. Once they had themselves and me ready for the party, we walked several blocks to the apartment where it was being held. To be out in public with friends, presenting as female was my dream come true. It was all I sought when I briefly escaped the pantry wearing women's clothing a few months earlier, and I found it intoxicating.

When we arrived at the party, Jane and Glenda were welcomed by our classmates while I was introduced as their friend who attended school elsewhere. The whole evening went that way. After a bit of liquor, some of the guys I went to class with every day began to hit on me. We stayed together, the three of us, for mutual protection. My head spun all night with the sensation of being out and social as a girl and finding acceptance.

When I came into the studio the next day, someone pointed to some words spray-painted on the center wall of the room, some twenty feet up. "Dave Hall is GAY," the words said. Someone had figured out my disguise, and soon everyone knew. Each of the professors took note of the graffiti, but to my humiliation, it remained there for all to read until it was finally painted over during the winter break.

In the design studio late one night towards the end of November, Pete, Jane, and Glenda found me slumped over my drawing board, my face smudging the graphite of an unfinished, site plan drawing.

Freshman class of architects at Rensselaer, September 1979. Laurie Lee (seated at center), surrounded by friends Glenda (to her right), Jane (seated in front of Glenda), and Pete (to Jane's right). Courtesy Class of 1983 thirtieth reunion committee.

I was burning with fever and incoherent. My friends got me to my feet and, supporting my weight, walked me to the campus infirmary.

The central ward of the Rensselaer's infirmary was full of university students who had succumbed to infectious illnesses as the Upstate New York winter set in. By morning I was diagnosed with mononucleosis and moved to a private room, deemed too compromised to remain exposed to the others.

Accustomed to excelling academically compared to my peers while growing up, like many first-year university students I discovered myself to be academically average at best in the mathematics and science courses that formed the educational core at RPI. My small-town regional high school had only just experimented with teaching an introduction to calculus during my senior year. I was unprepared to compete against highly qualified engineering prospects and future scientists who had been groomed for the university experience at prestigious prep schools.

On top of that, I had almost no experience traveling outside New England, and hence lacked exposure to much of anything capable of challenging my own biases or causing me to develop and defend my ideas. All I initially had going for me at Rensselaer's school of architecture was my ability to draw with the very best. Conveying my imagination visually and graphically was the one talent I had developed as a youth. As a result, the architectural design studio had become my principal focus, where I devoted all my energy until I was utterly spent.

I slept most of the time during my first several days in quarantine. A welcome respite to my mind and body after being overwhelmed by the rigors of my first semester in the school of architecture. After several days, I became lucid enough to finish the few assignments necessary to complete or nearly complete my coursework as the semester drew to a close. I had taken seven, three-credit courses, but only one of them—economics—had a final exam that was not excused by my illness.

I had not enjoyed freshman economics. Our economics instructor was a visiting professor from Iran. His thick accent was unfamiliar, and I had difficulty following him. During the semester, we learned his father's family was close to the Shah of Iran, who had been the head of his country's government. He was absent on the day of the final exam, the proctor was a graduate student from the school of management. The whispering around the room made me understand some significant events had occurred in Iran, and our professor had left RPI abruptly.

As I took the exam, my head was far too muddled from the mono to remember hardly anything I heard in the class. Somehow I managed to pass the exam, but I remember nothing from the course. I will never forget what I learned that week, though. I ventured out of my quarantine room one evening following supper to the common room, where I slipped into an old oak-trimmed phone booth with a wooden bifold door to call my parents. Through the glass in the phone booth's door I could see the common room's TV. There was grainy news footage of men and women wrapped in cloth blindfolds and being paraded before the cameras to create footage devised to goad the United States government into returning the Shah to Iran to face trial before Iran's new theocratic regime.

Once my call was over, I opened the bifold, and sat in the phone booth transfixed by the reports on the TV screen. The government of the Shah had been overthrown, extremists had taken control, anti-American protests were rampant, and hostages, these blindfolded people, were Americans who worked at the US embassy in Tehran. I began to understand my economics professor's sudden departure and wondered about his family's situation. It was early December 1979, just over four years since the end of the Vietnam War, which had been going on my entire life, frightening me as a child every night during its news coverage. Were we about to return to war?

I remembered, with a sense of dread, walking over to the post office in Westminster the previous summer to fill out my Selective Services draft card—a requirement to qualify for the federal student loans that I needed. Dad had been livid with me for submissively registering for the draft. He successfully avoided military service as a young person and was adamant in his opposition to the draft. Now, I could see the grave possibility of armed conflict occurring in my generation.

Along with my textbooks from my dorm room that my friends had brought me, Glenda included a paperback Book of Mormon she had given me earlier in the semester, making me promise to read it. I hadn't. My quarantine room had no television; the only one was in the common room. Once I completed all my assignments and exam, I still wasn't allowed among the living. All I had left to do was to look into this strange little book.

Its shiny gold cover, with so-called "Reformed Egyptian" characters printed in black on the front, was designed to look like a miniature replica of the ancient, golden plates that Joseph Smith, the LDS Church's founding prophet, professed to have translated and subsequently published as the Book of Mormon. Inside the front cover were Glenda's sweet words of testimony of its truthfulness, written in blue, ballpoint ink.

Reading the book's first five chapters, I felt a clear impression that its characters and their story were real. I still think about that moment often. What was that impression? I cannot mince words; the feelings were simple and direct. This account I was discovering felt real. Their story was sweet to me. I later learned how to explain that I had felt the Holy Spirit while reading. I had this experience lying in a hospital bed, alone in a small treatment room of the RPI Infirmary, still under quarantine.

I have told the story of this first experience with the Book of Mormon hundreds of times. Because of that witness, "I must trust the story of Joseph Smith and the book's origin," I told myself. I needed to learn all about this and then act on it, so I did. Studying architecture was my first chosen path. Embracing Mormonism became my second.

At the end of the first semester and just after I was released from the infirmary, Glenda left for home to spend the holidays with her family. I needed to wait a few days until I could catch a ride back to Westminster. I was coming off of three weeks in quarantine and I didn't want to return to my dorm room with Rich, so Glenda gave me her key. Staying in Glenda's room alone, with no schoolwork, felt strange and lonely. One evening, I was sitting on the floor next to her bed reading when it occurred to me that she probably hadn't taken all her clothes home for break. I pulled open the bottom wardrobe drawer and, sure enough, it was full of sweaters and tops. Her underclothes were in an upper drawer and her closet was full of dresses and skirts. Here I was with unparalleled access to lovely girl's clothing, on an empty campus, in a private room, and I had the only key.

A few months earlier, it would have been my fondest desire to have this opportunity to explore dressing and making myself up as the version of me I wanted to see and be seen as. I could have gone out for the evening and even walked downtown into Troy if I wanted to. The Halloween party proved how incredibly affirming that would feel. But I just couldn't. I sat on the floor staring into the sweater drawer, thinking about all the years I struggled in the pantry to feel right and whole. I thought about the progress I was making being away from the house and amongst people who challenged me to think and grow. I had been tagged as gay for all my class to see because I once dared to venture out as a female. I considered the commitment I made to myself before coming to Rensselaer to never cater to my feminine identity again. I thought a lot about my excitement with this new-found religion I was beginning to embrace, and all I could do was cry. Alone in Glenda's room, I sobbed openly for a long while.

When the tears no longer came, I closed the sweater drawer, exhaustedly got up and put on my coat, locked Glenda's door, and went back to my Bray Hall dorm to sleep. I didn't trust myself in her room alone any longer. I did not want to explore my feelings of being a girl ever again. There was no safe way forward to do that.

Instead I had set out on the path I felt I had to follow to be the man I was supposed to be. I did not know then that I was actually on a path in which I was learning to live in denial, only to see my true self surprise me by reappearing repeatedly throughout my life.

Near the end of my winter break in Westminster, after spending the better part of another month in bed recovering, I finally began feeling stronger. With the enthusiasm of an unconquerable teen, I convinced my parents I was well enough to drive out to the Finger Lakes region of Upstate New York before I went back to school for my second semester. The object of the trip was to meet up with Glenda, whose family lived in that area, to further my investigation of the Church of Jesus Christ of Latter-day Saints by visiting the historic sites where Joseph Smith established it.

Light snow was falling when we left her home the morning after I arrived. As we drove north towards Palmyra, New York, the weather conditions turned harsh, nearly to a whiteout. Taking more time than planned, we arrived at what was said to be the home where Joseph Smith was raised. We were told that the "Sacred Grove" where Joseph received his "First Vision" of God the Father and his Son, Jesus Christ, was across the road from where we parked, through the field and back into the woods.

The snowfall on the ground was deep and untouched. The morning's new snow completely obscured the trail across the field into the woods, and it was still snowing hard. We had come this far, I was determined to see the grove for myself.

In the classic film, "It's a Wonderful Life," George Bailey stands on a bridge during a heavy snowstorm, wishing he had never been born. The film alerts viewers that a change occurs in George's life when the snow instantly stops falling. The moment that Glenda and I stepped out of our parked car, the same thing happened. The snow which had been coming down hard, suddenly paused.

The sun broke through the clouds as we waded into knee-deep

drifts of brightly sparkling snow and made our way to the far corner of the field, then into the woods. Once there, we experienced a surreal silence and peace. Was it the sacred nature of the place and Joseph Smith's professed experience, or was it the extraordinarily beautiful physical surroundings that made this wooded area feel unearthly? Either way, my heart was filled with joy!

We eventually made our way back across the field. As we got into the car and shut the doors, we had the George Bailey experience again. It hadn't snowed a flake the whole time we were out exploring, but back in the car again, the snow began dumping as before. It felt as though nature and God were aware of our visit and all things combined for our blessing.

Next, we stopped at the LDS Visitor's Center at the nearby Hill Cumorah, where missionaries recounted the story of the coming forth of the Book of Mormon in legendary detail. The older missionary couple who staffed the center that day welcomed us like royals. We were their only visitors, and it seemed perhaps for several days. They smiled at us knowingly as we excitedly shared what happened at the Sacred Grove regarding the snowfall. Their enthusiasm was boundless as they responded to all my questions. I was as "golden" an investigator as my shiny gold Book of Mormon.

Upon my return to school at the start of our second semester, I began attending Sunday church meetings. As Glenda and I entered the church foyer for my first time, I was met with an exuberant welcome from a middle-aged woman with short spiky hair, big eyes and an even bigger smile. She cupped my face with both her hands, pulled me close, looked directly at me and exclaimed, "What beautiful eyes!" I liked that unique experience of being welcomed and to have my beauty recognized. After a few weeks, I asked the missionaries if they could find the time to come to RPI to teach me about the church because I hoped to be baptized and become a church member. I was pleased they consented—little did I know then that they were probably more pleased than I!

As I recall, there were nine prescribed missionary lessons or "discussions" in those days. I received three at each sitting, every other day, so that in a week, I heard them all and set a date for the coming Sunday for my baptism. I decided to move quickly while the semester was still young and the workload still manageable. Our friends Jane and Pete joined Glenda and I for church services on the day of my baptism, February 17, 1980. It was nice to be together that day. Looking back, I now realize that our late-night discussions about religion had come to an end.

I had shoulder-length hair when I joined the church, having avoided getting it cut since I graduated high school many months before. Not long after my baptism, I was approached by a "brother" after the weekly church sacrament meeting. He was small and thin, and what little hair he had left was buzzed close to his head. "When I joined the church, I was your age and had long hair too," he said. "The closer I grew to the Holy Ghost, the shorter I cut my hair." I realized he was passively implying that the level of my spirituality would be judged by my appearance. In my fresh and vulnerable state in the church, I took his words to heart. I began to gradually conform.

I began observing the benefits of "living God's commandments" almost immediately. Our design presentations in the studio always began Monday afternoons at 2:00 P.M. Determined to obey the Word of Wisdom (the Mormon law of health, which, among other things, forbids the use of alcohol and drugs) and to maintain Sunday as a Sabbath Day only for worship and service, I structured my weekends so all my design materials were completed by late Saturday night. Glenda did the same. In contrast, our classmates took Fridays off to party and rarely appeared in the studio on Saturday, while we worked with the entire place to ourselves. Most of our colleagues would roll into the studio sometime on Sunday, hungover, then work through all-nighters until presentation time on Monday. Most of them looked terrible by the hour the studio came to order. On the other hand, Glenda and I were rested, showered, and refreshed.

The professors were just as anxious as we were to make the design presentation discussions successful, so they almost always called on me to go first because I could with a reliably clear head explain my approach to the project and design solution. With my introduction as a foundation, good critique and discussion flowed, helping others to successfully present. I was soon recognized as a studio leader by my instructors and peers.

I could not have realized at the time how overarching the church would become in every aspect of my life for the next forty years. If someone had been able to foretell the good, spiritual highs and the bad, harmful lows, I would not have been able to comprehend even a tenth of it.

As an eighteen-year-old investigator of the church, my spiritual understanding led me to say I "knew" it was true. When I was being taught the missionary lessons, one of the young women missionaries (I always thought it was cool I had female missionaries, since I was a young "man") asked me if I had prayed to know the Book of Mormon was true. Though I had not, I knew that she needed me to say, "yes." I felt no need to trouble God with a question I sensed had already been generously answered by the witness of the Holy Spirit. When I was baptized, I knew I had found answers to many of life's questions that felt sweet and that I could trust.

The week following my baptism, the ward elders quorum president, Mitch Thomas, ordained me to the Aaronic Priesthood, typically given to Latter-day Saint boys in preparation for receiving the higher Melchizedek Priesthood authority given to men. I was ordained a "deacon," the office typically held by all twelve and thirteen-year-old boys, which authorized them to pass around the sacramental bread and water to the congregation every Sunday. Even though I was eighteen, at times I passed the sacrament with the younger boys as needed. Within six months, I was ordained to the higher Aaronic Priesthood office of "priest," catching me up to the office appropriate to my age.

I also began serving as the "junior home teaching companion" to Mitch, who was a married doctoral candidate at Rensselaer. In the church's "home teaching" program, priesthood holders are assigned to visit each member of their congregation at least once a month, sharing a spiritual message and helping them with any needs they may have. As Mitch and I drove all over the Upstate New York countryside, he took delight in training me in all aspects of serving as a priesthood holder. I was an eager and attentive student of this man, who seemed to me an excellent example of what I was trying to become. He was so enthusiastic regarding my progress that he even began having me assist him in giving priesthood blessings by laying my hands, along with his, on the head of the person requesting a blessing as he voiced the words—a sacred ordinance administered only by Melchizedek Priesthood holders.

All members of the LDS Church in good standing can receive a patriarchal blessing. One man in each larger congregation or "stake," is called and ordained to be a stake patriarch, authorized to give these blessings to members of that stake. The patriarchal blessing is viewed as a personal revelation from God for the individual receiving it, kind of like a chapter of scripture for that person. It might outline specific blessings and warnings to guide a person throughout their life. Occasionally, the patriarch giving the blessing prophetically reveals something unknown about the recipient that he could not have known at the time of the blessing.

Only three months after my baptism, I became interested in receiving my patriarchal blessing. At the time, I was on summer break from Rensselaer, staying at my parents' house. My bishop in Massachusetts told me he felt it was too soon for a young convert to seek their patriarchal blessing. But I pressed him until he relented and issued me the required recommendation.

I understood that spiritual preparation was important on the day of the blessing, so I decided to fast through the day, abstaining from food or drink in order to draw closer to the Spirit. I knew I needed to inform my parents why I wasn't eating, so I wrote them a note the night before explaining the purposes of the patriarchal blessing and the spiritual nature of fasting. The next day, I could sense the level of their concern growing for what they saw as my Mormon extremism.

On that sultry July day, I was working alone as a draftsman of wood furniture parts in an unair-conditioned, second-floor office of a nineteenth-century furniture company. My boss and colleagues were all up at the main factory working on our project to standardize the furniture assembly process. Conditions were ideal to fast and prepare my mind for the blessing. Several times, I followed the scriptural admonition in Isaiah to "anoint [my] face with water" while fasting. On such a hot day, I enjoyed that physical pleasure in lieu of nourishment.

When the workday concluded, I drove Mom's station wagon up into the wooded hills of Southern New Hampshire, looking for the address of the stake patriarch's house in a town I had never before visited. Patriarch William O. Murdoch graciously welcomed me into his home. I thought his family name was interesting because my mother's family ran a dairy farm named Murdock. He was an older gentleman but not yet graying, clad in the same dark suit, white shirt, and conservative tie that all Latter-day Saint priesthood leaders wore. Out of respect for the occasion, I had added a tie to the sweaty, colored dress shirt and Dockers I wore to the office. He and I had never met before; we chatted just long enough for him to know I was a convert of three months and an architecture student at Rensselaer. I may have shared the configuration of my non-LDS family.

After our brief talk, he invited me to sit in a small chair in front of him, placed his hands on my head, stated his authority as an ordained patriarch, and pronounced a blessing, which he recorded on a tape recorder. Once completed, he congratulated me and I left, never to see him again.

On the way home, the words of the blessing filled my mind. I stopped the car on the roadside and scribbled onto a piece of scrap paper every bit of what I could remember, knowing it would be about six weeks before I would receive a hard copy transcript of it in the mail.

The blessing spoke about my eventually receiving the Melchizedek Priesthood the importance of my education, and the impact of my life's work. It foreshadowed my future wife and family while offering admonitions of faithfulness to church teachings, with a promise of a glorious resurrection someday. The blessing seemed beautiful to me, and I treasured it as a sacred roadmap to direct my life's journey.

At the end of our last home-teaching visit, my home teaching companion Mitch summarized my experience. "This has been quite a year for you," he said, "coming to this prestigious university to study architecture and to find and embrace the restored gospel and receive the Lord's priesthood authority!"

Learning about the church and its teachings gave me the excitement of something new coming into my life, a catalyst for change and personal development, which I welcomed. I felt comradery amongst church members, including being welcomed into the all-male priesthood group. The church offered everything I needed to keep my female identity buried and to succeed as a righteous man, husband, father, servant, and leader. I grew close to the men in the church who took me under their wing and showed me the way. Because of the church, I no longer had to worry about how to find my place in a man's world.

For my sophomore year at RPI, in contrast to Rich and the all-male menagerie in Bray Hall, my choice for second-year housing was a small room in an old brick dormitory, which I shared with my architecture-school friend Pete. I came prepared with a folding screen I covered with decorative oriental prints and placed in the room so that and Pete's and my sides were visually separated. It served the trick of a bit of DIY privacy nicely.

Pete was Catholic, kind, and soft-spoken even when defending his deeply held convictions, like when we would debate the meaning of New Testament scriptures. But there was always a high level of anxiety about him, as if he could never relax.

More than forty years later, I learned that a couple of years after we graduated from RPI, Pete self-accepted as gay and found a support group for Catholic LGBT persons. He now lives reconciled with his sexual orientation and his Catholic faith in a loving relationship with another man. It is sad to me today that during the time we shared a dormitory room, Pete and I, both deliberately and deeply closeted, weren't able to open up to each other about our secret truths. The universe had brought a gay man and a trans woman together on the same campus in the same dorm room at a vulnerable time in our lives. We could have strengthened each other to be our best selves. Instead, we each suffered in silence, only to learn of each other's true nature more than four decades later.

In the spring of our sophomore year, Jane and a couple of other girls approached Pete, Glenda, and me with the idea of renting an entire three-story brownstone in downtown Troy, just below campus. It had five bedrooms, lots of living spaces, and a bathroom on each floor. With five or more of us renting, the cost would be reasonable. I was thrilled when we went to look at the townhouse. It would be my first time living off campus in what felt like a home instead of a dorm cell. I liked each of the girls in the group and considered them my closest friends at school. Three of them planned to move in immediately and remain in Troy, working there for the summer.

Although I planned to work back in Massachusetts, I told them I was all in for the fall, as did Glenda. Unfortunately, Pete was a no-go from the start.

Over the following weekend, I shared my excitement and good fortune with friends from church. I was shocked that my news was met with a solid wall of disapproval. Some of my church friends told me that living in a house with several single girls was "the appearance of evil" and inappropriate for a young man preparing to leave on a two-year Mormon mission. I was heartbroken. I had even prayed about the decision to live there and felt very positive about it. But I bowed under the pressure of church members who were desperately worried about appearances, and the risk to my chastity. I told Jane and the others the next day I could not join them in the house. They were angry at me, and our friendships were never the same again. I tried to focus on the fact that I had "chosen the right," but it haunted me nonetheless.

Looking back, I realize I dove headlong into sharing a house with my female friends because I simply saw myself as one of them. When I wasn't focused on gender—whether hiding it or expressing it—I was just me, naturally a girl.

9

Every Young Man

"Why the hell would you do that?" Dad roared at me. "RPI is where you belong. Don't throw it all away for some church!"

I had just informed my parents that after the current school year—my third of the required five—I planned to take a two-year leave to serve a full-time, proselyting mission. I was standing with my back to the kitchen sink. Dad sat a few feet away at the head of the table as he railed on my proposal. I thought how ironic it was that the place he didn't want me to go four years ago was now the place where he wanted to make me stay.

"I plan to come back and return to school. Guys in the church do it all the time," I stammered as the violence of Dad's response reverberated through me. "I will make it work." I didn't know yet that no one at Rensselaer had ever left for a mission.

"Where will you be doing this thing?" Dad snapped back.

"I'll go wherever the church's president calls me to go."

"What if it's somewhere dangerous? You must be out of your mind."

Mom was sobbing quietly because things didn't go well when Dad got that upset, and I was bawling with pent-up emotion and defiance. Opposing his will was nearly impossible for me. It took all my strength, but I could do it because I knew what was essential for my life while he did not.

After I joined the church, a continuous chorus of church members asked me if I planned to serve a mission as all Latter-day Saint young men are expected to do. I felt comfortable saying I was already deeply committed to my studies and too new in the church to go. But in a meeting with the priesthood men one Sunday morning, our teacher played a cassette tape of a talk by Spencer W. Kimball, who was then the president of the church. I had learned to trust that President Kimball spoke the Lord's mind and will on all significant matters. When I heard him say, "Every worthy young man should prepare for and serve a full-time mission," I knew by a strong impression of the Holy Spirit that this included me. I changed my life direction instantly, and I felt my commitment deep within me.

After the confrontation in the kitchen, I returned to Rensselaer undeterred. As time permitted, I went from one administrative office to another to learn how to leave the Institute to serve for two years and how to return. I was surprised to realize no one in RPI's administration was familiar with Mormon missions, nor had anyone ever asked leave before to serve one. Finally, everyone pointed me to the dean of students. After listening to my story and description of missions and checking my academic performance, he decided to be my mentor in helping me depart as well as return four semesters later. With his help and influence, I was able to leave and serve.

Then, the other shoe dropped for my parents. My call letter from church headquarters came, assigning me to serve in the Argentina, Buenos Aires North Mission. Argentina had recently invaded the Falkland Islands, a British territory off its southern shore. This set off a ten-week undeclared war in which the US sided politically with its ally, the United Kingdom. There was no place on earth more notorious and condemned in the US news at that time than Argentina, and I was willing to follow a church leader's direction to go right into its capital.

Dad went out of his mind. Knowing there was nothing he could say or do to dissuade me, he made our family's summer hell as the war in the South Atlantic continued and I prepared to leave. For the six months between my call letter's arrival and my departure for my mission, Dad did not speak to me and I rarely saw him, even though we were living in the same house.

As I had the year before, I worked that summer for Dad's best friend, Wayne. He was an employee of a communications company in Metro Boston called Megapulse, which contracted Wayne and me out to the scientists at the US Air Force Geophysics Laboratory, located at Hanscom Air Force Base near Concord, Massachusetts. I prepared their graphics for analysis and publication freehand, with pen and paper, in the age just before computer graphics. My work the previous summer paid for my third year of college, while this summer would pay for as much of my mission as possible. When the time came to leave work to start my mission, my lab colleagues surprised me by applying a hard press to get me to forgo my mission and stay working with them. I stood my ground, explaining why I was serving and not returning to school that fall. Wayne later confided in me that Dad had begged him to find a way to get me to remain in Massachusetts and not serve my mission.

The morning I left the house to go, I had to find Mom in the backyard to say goodbye. She told me not to try to find Dad. He was in bed and would not see me. I departed my pantry bedroom at my parents' house for the last time and traveled to Provo, Utah, to begin my mission at the church's Missionary Training Center (MTC).

When I arrived in Provo, I attended the LDS temple there in order to receive my "endowment," as required of all missionaries before embarking on their full-time mission. The temple endowment is instructive in nature. In this sacred rite of passage, individuals make covenants, or promises to God, of personal sacrifice, fealty, and chastity. Members are also instructed to begin wearing holy temple garments—underclothing which covers the body from the chest and shoulders to the knee—to wear throughout their lives as a reminder of these covenants and commitment to God.

As the only church member in my family, I had never seen the temple garment before I began wearing my own in the temple. The top for men was cut like a tee shirt, but the bottoms were knee-length boxers, not unlike baggy Bermuda shorts. I understood that one purpose of the garment was to foster modesty, which was fine by me.

I had not even considered that living conditions in the MTC were going to feel like a throwback to my worst experiences at Bray Hall. The schedule was so tight and the bedrooms so crammed (four to a room) that I could not avoid dressing in front of others. I also had no choice but to use gang showers with a crowd of other young, male missionaries, ironically called "elders."

Even though we had all been to the temple and taught the purpose of the garment, I was appalled at how many elders on my floor

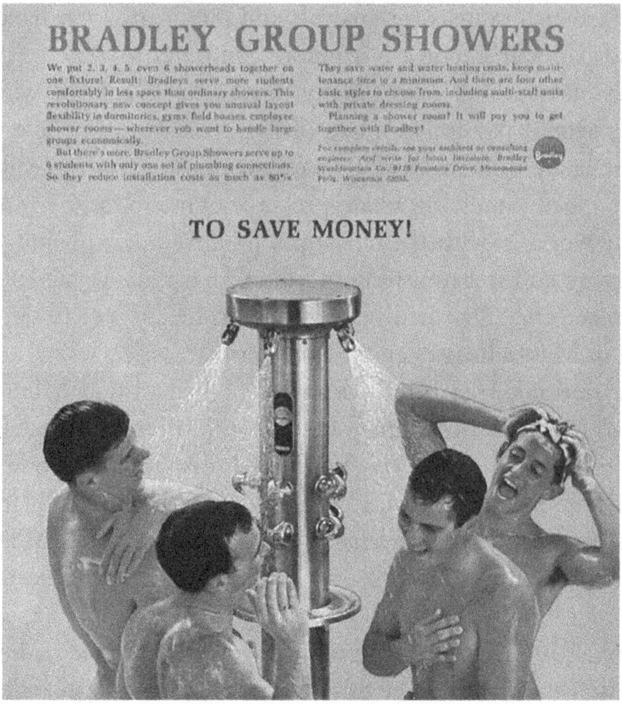

"Gang showers" typical of those found in Bray Hall Dormitory and the Provo Missionary Training Center, Bradley Washfountain Co. ad, 1965.

ran around in the late evening after class with nothing on but their garments. Some wore gym shorts over the bottoms, but the garment legs still extended well below the shorts. It all seemed sacrilegious and immodest to me, dismissive of the sacredness of temple garments as I understood them. I stayed dressed in my white shirt and slacks until bedtime, slipping on my pajamas on my bottom bunk bed just before sliding under the covers.

After the standard two months of studying my mission language and how to be a proselyting missionary, I finally arrived in Buenos Aires, where I met my first missionary companion, Elder Campbell. Even though our apartment bathroom would get hot and incredibly humid, I usually dressed quickly in there, dripping with sweat, rather than in our shared bedroom where at least we had a fan. At night, I undressed in my bottom bunk. Years later, Elder Campbell teased me by recalling that at night, he would feel the bunk rattle, and soon my clothes would slide out from my bed and land on the floor. I never considered how odd my behavior must have seemed. I was just doing what I needed to do in order to feel safe.

After two months with Elder Campbell, he was assigned to serve in another part of the city. I waited alone in our hot, airless apartment for his replacement to arrive. When he did, I was in for a shock. Elder Huston was Campbell's antithesis in every way imaginable. Campbell had been perfectly obedient, driven to work hard, and never uttered a word of English in order to help me learn Spanish. Huston on the other hand was unkempt, shabbily dressed, and spoke to me only in English. He even brought a pet cat with him.

When I challenged him about the cat, Elder Huston informed me that it wasn't a house cat, but a puma cub! He had named it Parley P. Puma, after the early Mormon apostle Parley P. Pratt. Apparently he purchased the cub from a church member in a far-flung community on the edge of our mission, where he last served.

Living with Huston and Parley for the next two months was an adventure. We locked Parley in our bedroom while we were out proselyting during the day because we only rented that room in our landlord's apartment. Each evening when we returned, we found Parley had destroyed something else in our room. I lived out of my suitcase stuffed under our bunk so that Parley could not get to my things.

He grew rapidly and was becoming fierce. Huston enjoyed teasing him, but I kept my distance. What to do with Parley became a daily topic of conversation which I would start, and usually ended in a fight. Finally, Elder Huston hatched a plan: he would take Parley to the home of a member family in our ward, who would care for him until Huston's mission was finished in two months. Transporting an adolescent puma on an Argentine city bus, or "collectivo," was another adventure. Other passengers gave us plenty of space for a change. Parley hadn't been outside in eight weeks, and the city looked appetizing to him. We turned him over to the family, and I gratefully unpacked my things again.

Elder Huston intended to take Parley back home to the States, but when that proved impossible, Parley somehow met with an untimely demise, and Huston took him to a taxidermist whom he met in one of his earlier mission posts. Parley went to California in a suitcase.

Initially as a new missionary, I found learning Spanish particularly difficult. Conventional studying didn't click for me. In time, I discovered that reading aloud Spanish-language church books, including scriptures, significantly improved my diction and embedded my understanding. Then I tried translating things I knew into Spanish.

I kept a photocopy of my patriarchal blessing between my journal and my scriptures, though I read it infrequently. I challenged myself to translate my patriarchal blessing into Spanish. The process and my mission caused me to pay more careful attention to my blessing than ever before. As I did, certain things began to stand out to me.

I was admonished regarding the priesthood and told I would "eventually" receive the Melchizedek (or higher) Priesthood. "Eventually" turned out to mean only eight months in my case, which seemed odd to me. Looking at it from today's perspective, maybe the patriarch was referring to when I might "eventually," or finally, receive it *as a woman!* I also now realize that the second half of my life is not referred to in the blessing at all. Perhaps it was too difficult for my patriarch to describe, like the Old Testament prophet Isaiah attempting to describe a roaring steam engine using terms he was familiar with in 900 BCE.

For me, the most profound paragraph of my patriarchal blessing began with an admonition to continue my education and use my talents to serve people within and without the church. In doing so, I was promised to become "a vessel in the hands of the Lord to spread the Gospel of Jesus Christ to every nation, kindred, tongue, and people." The nature of what that meant weighed down on me so much that I never finished my translation. I stopped on that paragraph.

Thinking about this promise, I saw no possibility of anything in my life ever having a global impact. I saw myself as a humble nobody, a convert to this church who, other than this mission to Argentina, had never left the northeastern US.

My next transfer came unexpectedly, and put me in a bad mood. I loved my previous companion, whom I was training to be a "rock star" missionary, and we had worked hard to build success in my second area. Leaving the excitement of that area as it was cresting only to open a new area from scratch was depressing. Furthermore, it was an area in the city, with far more apartment buildings than detached homes, which made it difficult to reach people to teach. Not that Buenos Aires lacked people; some twenty-six million lived within the city limits, about one-third of the vast country's entire population. There were only twenty-eight missionaries in our zone, which covered the city, essentially making each companionship responsible for reaching some two million people!

The problem was figuring out how to talk with them. The people were cold and untrusting. Admittance into their apartment buildings required a prior invitation. Even church members in our new ward were distant toward the missionaries. My new companion, Elder Bradley, had never served in the city. He believed that if he talked to everyone he saw on the street, on the bus, in the shops, or anywhere, he would find a "golden contact"—a term missionaries use for a person who was ready to hear our message and join our church.

I was less enthusiastic. Seven months in the city showed me that traditional door-to-door contacting or "tracting," was a waste of effort, given that most occupants worked long hours away from home. And cold contacting people on a bus or the street was met with so much resistance to be futile. Yet this elder persisted for weeks. It got to be so bad I just shadowed him for his protection while he completely threw himself into his contacting. I felt terrible not contributing, but worse whenever I tried to help.

Our new mission leader, President Fausett, conducted a mission tour a few weeks after his arrival, sitting privately with each missionary one-on-one. I went into my interview frustrated and almost broken, clinging to the purpose that brought me to Argentina. The Holy Spirit was present in our interview. I know because I said things I never thought of to the president.

"I am the only person in the mission I know of that has served three transfers in a row within the city," I stated flatly. Then I felt inspired to say, "President, there has to be a reason I have been so long in the city, where nothing is working for us as missionaries. I will figure out why I am still here and how to make this work."

I left the interview elevated and slightly astonished at what I just learned and then said aloud. Without the president saying a word, I felt I now had exciting, clear direction. I could pour all my creativity into making missionary work effective in a large urban center, whatever that meant. As I followed Elder Bradley around for the remainder of our six weeks together, rather than complaining, my mental wheels were spinning at full speed. In time, I realized if we had something for people to look at to spark their curiosity, conversations with strangers in public places would be much easier.

We began testing forms of street preaching using pictures from our flip charts we kept in a three-ring binder for whenever we sat down with someone to teach. During my next transfer, I was called to be a zone leader, responsible for the work of all the missionaries in our area or "zone," but still within the city. My "transfer" consisted of changing bunkbeds in the same bedroom, so I could be on the same side of the room as my new companion!

I started making small kiosks out of cardboard with pictures and questions that we could carry to busy street corners. Two of us would stand next to it, talk with curious folks, and share what information we could. We even braved the wild crowd outside an international *futbol* match in December 1983. The Argentine national team fans were hardly in the mood to talk about salvation, but being immersed in a sea of people that way was life-changing for me. I became convinced we must do something big, something extraordinary.

"President, how much money does the mission have from the church each year to fund projects?"

"Two-hundred dollars," came President Fausett's reply to my directness. He looked flustered, but as a new mission president in his first six months of service, he was still learning to navigate.

"If you give us one-hundred fifty dollars, we will build the exposition I envision and do some great things with it." The requested amount was audacious. US dollars went a long way in Buenos Aires in 1984—$150 was enough for two missionaries to live on for a month. But here I was asking President Fausett to commit to our unproven idea three-quarters of his annual budget on New Year's Day. Nevertheless, he consented and gave us a massive stack of Argentine *pesos*, representing our project budget. The truth was I really had no idea what it would cost.

My design for the exposition consisted of four large, two-sided panels. Graphics on the eight faces would depict the principles from the church's six missionary discussions, describe the newly announced temple under construction in Buenos Aires, and show the church's official logo in large font. I also knew where we should set up the exposition, in an ample public space known as Plaza Miserere. The city's principal train station, "Estacion Once," was on the plaza's north side, and another entry to the main subway line to downtown on the south. Thousands of people walked across the plaza between the two stations in the morning and then back again in the evening. Beyond this, my companion and I had nothing else figured out when we approached the president.

We got materials from the church distribution center and building supplies from a lumber yard, and stayed just under our budget. We hauled all this through city traffic back to our apartment tied to the roof of our sedan.

Elder Kenig and I, along with the two elders who lived with us, spent the next several days organizing the images into storyboards, pasting them to the four-foot by eight-foot panels, and protecting it all with large, self-adhesive laminating plastic sheets. The result, along with the two-meter-tall legs set up in our apartment's main room, was a site to behold, filling almost the entire room.

When it was time to set it up in the Plaza Miserere, the other elders asked me, "How will we get this down there?"

"The same way we got the materials here, tied to the car's roof!" I had not thought about the fact that we hadn't done it before; I was running completely on fumes and faith by this point. I believed entirely in the principle of going forth without knowing beforehand what I would be led to do. We would do whatever we needed to make this work. It was too important, and we had come too far to pause or trip over any obstacle.

We successfully transported the display to the plaza and set it up in our determined spot. It appeared majestic as we spread the four panels out in a gentle semi-circle fifty feet across. We came prepared with about 100 slips of pre-printed paper to take names and contact information for anyone interested in a visit to learn more. By that evening, forty-two of the sheets had been filled out. In one day, we received more referrals than I had obtained in over a year in the city!

Elder Kenig and I participated in the initial training of the thirteen companionships who worked a day at the exposition. We discovered on many days the crowds were big enough to justify three and sometimes four companionships on site. Each night, we received batches of new referrals. News spread throughout the mission about this remarkable thing happening in the city and how it benefited every area's list of families to teach.

One evening a few months into the exposition, I stood and watched what was occurring at this beautiful thing that inspiration created. Besides myself, seven other missionaries were operating the panels, one stationed at each instruction face. Around each missionary stood a crowd of twenty to thirty people. We learned to set the panels far enough apart to permit this amount of activity. Seven discussions were taking place at once to as many as 200 people. I watched new missionaries who barely spoke the language upon arrival weeks before, talking a blue streak to their groups, who were glued to their words. The transformative power in the missionaries who served on the exposition was undeniable. The change in the way the public saw us and interacted with us overcame all the barriers I previously witnessed, as well.

On the morning before Elder Kenig and I were to fly home to the US, we were in the mission home with some downtime before our drive to the airport. We talked with the mission clerks, who gave us access to the mission's records. Over the four months since the exposition was launched, it had provided more than 1,200 referrals for the missionaries to teach! An unknown number of families who had met us at Once were being introduced to the church at that time in every zone. We also found the records of several persons we had met there who had now received baptism.

Twenty-five years later, when I would return to Buenos Aires as part of a team renovating the temple that had been under construction when I was a young missionary, I took my colleagues back to Plaza Miserere and Estacion Once. I was saddened to see it had fallen into disrepair and ruin. But I took time to stand on the spot between the train station and the subway entrance to describe the miracle of what we once accomplished at Once.

10

Living With a Woman

Not long before I returned to Massachusetts from my mission in Argentina, my parents sold their old house, the only place I remembered living with them. They relocated to the south shore near Cape Cod, where they built a two-bedroom house and purchased a small convenience store. I planned to stay with them that summer and help out at the store. I hoped this would repair the breach formed two summers earlier, when I determined to serve a mission in spite of their conviction against it.

To my delight, just after arriving I met an architect who lived down the street from the store. He offered me the opportunity to interview with his firm in Boston, where his father was one of the principal architects. After the interview I received an offer for a summer internship, which opened my mind to opportunities and connections for the future. I told Dad about the offer in the back of the store between the soda cooler and his office. Instead of being pleased with this exciting opportunity that came my way, he angrily had it out with me about how I was abandoning him again, after I had committed to helping him.

Defaulting to my desire to repair our relationship, I told Dad I would not take the job in Boston, but would keep my commitment to him. Fortunately, the architect who lived down the street had several moonlighting projects that summer and gave me the chance to draft several house plans to help him.

Debbie was living in Buffalo. Sandra, who was also home from college and working at the store, took the second bedroom of the house, and I had the unfinished, uninsulated attic. I organized one side of the attic with my old bed and dresser as my "bedroom" and the other side with my drawing table and some milk crates with a board across as a table to be my "office." All around me were storage boxes of my parents and sisters' belongings.

I returned from Argentina too late in the year to have access to any of the housing opportunities typically available in the spring at Rensselaer. My former classmates were all graduating, so I knew no one who was coming back for the fall. All of this made me assume I would be scraping the bottom to find a place to stay. But when I visited the school as soon as possible to search for one, I discovered that one of my professors, Dora Crouch, an architectural historian, had a room in her home for rent. She was direct, articulate, and suffered no fools. I sought her out, grateful I treated her kindly before my mission, and she agreed to let me rent.

Dora's house was a two-story Victorian on Troy's east side. Our collective consisted of Dora, a visiting female professor from New Zealand, and a German graduate student whom I rarely saw. I felt vindicated to have the maturity and independence to choose to live in a mixed-gender home with four single people without apology. We came and went as we pleased. I saw Dora more in the Greene Building than at home. We four never had a house dinner together except for one Friday night. Our Kiwi companion treated us to a lovely lamb meal with mint sauce like she would make back home. I never tried lamb before and fell in love with it.

The house possessed an air of order and formality. It was a relaxing, stimulating, and empowering environment in contrast to my prior living experiences. It felt like a privilege to dwell with a group of intellectuals, and I felt enriched when I returned home each night.

I went into the chapel of the Albany, New York, stake center to enjoy sacrament meeting in my home ward for the first time since my mission, choosing a spot in the middle of an open pew towards the front. Suddenly, a whole family arrived at my pew. The oldest daughter, about my age, entered first and slid surprisingly close to me. I caught the bishop's gaze, sitting on the stand right before us, and saw he was trying hard to suppress his laughter. He later told me that he had watched the family arrive in the chapel and move towards the seats in the back when the oldest daughter spotted me sitting alone. She had redirected her family towards the front of the chapel, then pushed past her siblings and parents so she would be first to enter the pew and land next to me.

She introduced herself as Marleen. Her family had moved into the ward while I was in Argentina, and she had recently returned from attending college in the West. Today was her first Sunday in the ward. When church meetings were over, Marleen invited me to her parent's home for Sunday dinner. This routine was repeated every Sunday for the remainder of the year. I felt welcome and grateful for the chance to spend Sabbath afternoons and evenings with a Mormon family.

That Christmas of 1984 was my first time back in the States in three years, after the two I had spent in the middle of the summer in the southern hemisphere. I was yearning for a good old-fashioned, picture-postcard, Hallmark Christmas, and Marleen's family did not disappoint. Their home, known to them and their neighbors as "the old house," was an early nineteenth-century, brick two-story on a bluff overlooking a bend on the Mohawk River. When the Christmas decorations came out, Marleen's family transformed the home into the storybook place of my dreams. I spent several evenings there with the family in the days leading up to winter break.

This was my first Christmas season spent with a family since I was in high school, and those of my childhood weren't at all joyful or magical, even before Dad's health failure and extended hospital stay. It was also my first holiday season spent with a Mormon family. Experiencing the Christmas celebration with the traditions and the spirit of the gospel was beautiful to me. I recognized things about family life with them that I never had in my parent's house. Palatable love, mutual respect, and togetherness felt right while simultaneously unfamiliar. Sensing something you have always missed but never really knew is strange. Everything I wanted to have in my future family was coming into sharp focus.

Unfortunately, my wonderful time living in Dora Crouch's house came to an end after Christmas. Dora accompanied the study abroad semester in Rome beginning in January and rented out her entire house to a family. I was forced to scramble again to find a room on the rental posting boards. This time's spin of the roulette wheel came up a loser. Though I found a cheap, small room with a door, it came with a few drunken upperclassmen I thoroughly disliked. Their parties every weekend with friends, girls, booze, and drugs were the worst living experiences I ever had, which, after living with a puma, is saying a lot.

I shared with Marleen how miserable it was there for me during the roommates' raucous weekend parties. Her parents responded that I was welcome any time to stay in the little studio apartment on the second floor of their home. I began staying there most weekends. I spent Sundays with them, attending church in the morning, enjoying a family evening meal, and returning to Troy for Monday classes. I felt welcome in their family and relished being in their home.

While spending weekends in the studio apartment in their old house, I started thinking how for years, maybe all my life, I had not deliberately chosen the person or people I lived with. Occasionally, it worked out well. More often, it did not, and sometimes, it was ghastly. As I began seriously considering marriage, I realized how important it would be to choose the right, permanent "roommate."

I look back with embarrassment now on the mindset I frequently bought into during my first several years as a church member. The church provided a pattern to follow, enabling me to learn to live as a successful male in a male-dominated world. Since I was certain the world was not designed nor safe for someone like me, assigned male at birth but feeling female, I blocked out my female self, and willingly submitted to the church's way. Predominant LDS thinking of the 1980s filled my accepting mind, and I totally bought into all the teachings of top church leaders, referred to as "the Brethren."

One of the most powerful directives at that time of my life was the charge that young men must marry a young woman early and immediately start their families. The pattern further dictated that the husband get a respectable education and profession while the wife stay at home to raise the couple's children—the church's ideal family order.

Although I had attractions to boys I was friends with in school, by this point in my early twenties, I felt no such attractions. I don't remember consciously choosing an interest for women over men, or feeling overtly sexually attracted to anyone much at all. I based my feelings of intimacy and connection on developing a deep personal relationship with someone.

I remained committed to the pattern I chose for my life. The "priesthood path" I had embarked on had me attend the temple and interrupt my education to serve a full-time mission. I had returned to complete my education and prepare to enter my profession. Now, I knew I also should find the right young woman, marry in the temple, and begin having children. Beginning when I was a young missionary, there was no question in my mind that this was the path I would follow. It was my duty to the church's "Kingdom of God" on earth.

In my last missionary area in Buenos Aires, another young missionary surprised me when she mentioned she was planning to attend architectural school after her mission and was completing her university application to the architectural program. Having gone through that process myself, I provided her some help. In the remaining weeks we served in the same district, I found we were compatible and enjoyed each other's talents and attitudes.

When Shelly returned home to Oregon from Argentina, she was accepted into her program, and we rejoiced over that through letters. Meanwhile, I was also back at school and had been befriended by Marleen and her family. I developed strong feelings for Shelly in my time back in the States. I also enjoyed spending time with Marleen as a friend as we got to know each other well.

I began considering which of the two women would be the most suitable prospect for a wife. Knowing Shelly was being trained in my profession, I was drawn to my former mission colleague and thought about the similar careers and interests we might share. But I also bought into the dogma that women should remain in the home and raise a large family. I knew Shelly wanted to practice her profession and I didn't want to stand in the way of that. I also knew Marleen, a dental assistant at the time, only wanted to work until she married and had children.

I realize now how much power that dogma had over such an important life choice. I feel shame that I allowed that to be the case, mainly because the "ideal family" mantra enforced limitations on girls and women. Trusting that I was "choosing the right," I broke off my long-distance relationship with Shelly and began courting

Marleen. A little over a year later when I stood on the steps of the School of Architecture at Rensselaer, dressed in a black cap and gown and clutching my professional diploma, my pregnant wife, Marleen, stood by my side. I successfully followed the "inspired path" once again. Although I don't regret my decision to marry Marleen, I do regret that my decision was so heavily influenced by those forces in which I immersed myself, which placed independent thinking and following my heart beyond my reach.

After graduation, I began working for a firm for my three-year, pre-licensure internship. Marleen and I had our children in rapid succession. By the time we were twenty-nine, we had two children under four with a third on the way, owned a home, and I had passed my licensing exam to be a registered architect.

Passing the licensing exam culminated a fifteen-year journey that began with my youthful decision to be an architect. The licensing exam was notoriously difficult to pass in those days, consisting of thirty-six hours of testing over four consecutive days. I understood from colleagues in the office that only one in ten candidates ever passed the exam, and as few as one in one hundred passed it all in their first sitting. I was determined to be one of them.

Marleen and I discussed the importance of getting licensed this first time in terms of my career development and for our family economically. We understood how hard it would be to prepare myself while helping with the needs of our small children each night after work. It seemed best for her to visit her parents for several weeks before the exam. Several months pregnant, she bravely flew with two toddlers to her parents' home in the Midwest. I temporarily converted the nursery into an office with my drafting board and all my reference materials so I could study each night.

It was a success. I passed all eight exam sections with an average score in the low nineties. I hadn't just passed but had nearly mastered the professional knowledge. With the exam behind me, I found much more time for family and church service. Soon, our third baby, Liz, was born, and my office returned to a nursery.

I felt tender feelings towards this baby more than with our first two, Isaac and Alissa. She was easier and less stressful than the others, who had challenged our lack of skills as young parents, and she was simply a calmer soul all around. Holding her and cuddling was fulfilling. I imagined being able to breastfeed and bond with her as her mother did. I realized that I had deep feelings of envy for Marleen's role as a mother. For the first time, my female self felt deeply maternal, and I wanted to express that part of my identity.

I had been jealous of the changes Marleen experienced in her body through pregnancy and afterward. How could I have explained that to her? She was going through something she didn't always enjoy, but something I could never experience. Unable to voice my emotions regarding this, far too often, all I seemed able to express was unexplained frustration or anger. The struggle within myself robbed me during those years of opportunities to experience peace and joy.

I frequently felt extreme anxiety in my "male" roles. I worked long hours each week in a taxing profession where I feared the boss walking past my desk and criticizing my work. I was also serving in church leadership callings. The telephone ringing triggered me because of what challenge the call might bring. Money pressures, paying the bills, and maintaining our home and cars all accumulated. Today as a parent of adult children, I see that our challenges then were the common lot of young families, things that nearly all go through, but at the time it was all overwhelming.

In addition to life's challenges in our first home, I still struggled with my undisclosed reality of who I really was. I did not see it as an identity then. I didn't have the knowledge or words to frame it that way. I wouldn't have admitted that I was harboring a secret because I was in denial that I even had a secret. After Liz was born, though, for the first time since before college ten years earlier, I began to infrequently and secretly experiment with wearing Marleen's clothing. After each of these instances, I collapsed with shame, under the weight of guilt that I must somehow have sinned. I swore that I wouldn't do it again, only to break that promise. During these first five years of marriage, it had become increasingly more difficult to resist than it had previously been. Living intimately and closely with a woman for the first time since I was in my parents' house caused a more robust return to wanting to live *as* a woman, and Marleen's clothes were everywhere available, as Mom's had once been. As I walked toward my office building after one of these forays, I looked into the sky and said aloud, "I am the elders quorum president. I cannot be doing this."

11

I Can't Do Male Anymore

At an annual General Relief Society Meeting of the LDS Church, held in the Salt Lake Tabernacle and broadcast around the world on September 23, 1995, church president Gordon B. Hinckley gave a remarkable address that set the course for the modern church. Titled, "Stand Strong against the Wiles of the World," Hinckley's speech centered on "challenging problems," a "world of turmoil, of shifting values," and "betrayal of time-tested standards of behavior," threatening "the moral moorings of our society."[1]

Hinckley lamented that "there are those who would have us believe in the validity of what they choose to call same-sex marriage. Our hearts reach out to those who struggle with feelings of affinity for the same gender. We remember you before the Lord, we sympathize with you, we regard you as our brothers and our sisters. However, we cannot condone immoral practices on your part any more than we can condone immoral practices on the part of others."

Hinckley "felt to warn and forewarn" of "sophistry that is passed off as truth," "deception concerning standards and values," and "allurement and enticement to take on the slow stain of the world." He then issued "a proclamation to the Church and to the world as a declaration and reaffirmation of standards, doctrines, and practices relative to the family which the prophets, seers, and revelators of this church have repeatedly stated throughout its history." He read in its entirety what has come to be known as the "Family Proclamation":

"We, the First Presidency and the Council of the Twelve Apostles of The Church of Jesus Christ of Latter-day Saints, solemnly proclaim that marriage between a man and a woman is ordained of God and that the family is central to the Creator's plan for the eternal destiny of His children.

"All human beings—male and female—are created in the image of God. Each is a beloved spirit son or daughter of heavenly parents, and, as such, each has a divine nature and destiny. Gender is an essential characteristic of individual premortal, mortal, and eternal identity and purpose.

"In the premortal realm, spirit sons and daughters knew and worshiped God as their Eternal Father and accepted His plan by which His children could obtain a physical body and gain earthly experience to progress toward perfection and ultimately realize his or her divine destiny as an heir of eternal life. The divine plan of happiness enables family relationships to be perpetuated beyond the grave. Sacred ordinances and covenants available in holy temples make it possible for individuals to return to the presence of God and for families to be united eternally.

"The first commandment that God gave to Adam and Eve pertained to their potential for parenthood as husband and wife. We declare that God's commandment for His children to multiply and replenish the earth remains in force. We further declare that God has commanded that the sacred powers of procreation are to be employed only between man and woman, lawfully wedded as husband and wife.

"We declare the means by which mortal life is created to be divinely appointed. We affirm the sanctity of life and of its importance in God's eternal plan....

"The family is ordained of God. Marriage between man and woman is essential to His eternal plan. Children are entitled to birth within the bonds of matrimony, and to be reared by a father and a mother who honor marital vows with complete fidelity.... By divine design, fathers are to preside over their families in love and righteousness and are responsible to provide the necessities of life and protection for their families. Mothers are primarily responsible for the nurture of their children. In these sacred responsibilities, fathers and mothers are obligated to help one another as equal partners. Disability, death, or other circumstances may necessitate individual adaptation.... We warn that the disintegration of the family will bring upon individuals, communities, and nations the calamities foretold by ancient and modern prophets. We call upon responsible citizens and officers of government everywhere to promote those measures designed to maintain and strengthen the family as the fundamental unit of society."

When President Hinckley released the Family Proclamation in the fall of 1995,I was working more than sixty hours a week for a successful architectural firm in Albany, New York. I was the managing architect over the design and construction of many of the company's most prominent projects. At church I had been ordained a High Priest and was serving as the High Priest group leader. I was also teaching temple preparation classes to new and reactivated members. Marleen and I also volunteered in the Washington DC temple several times each year. On top of all this, we were raising our four children, ages eight and under, and I was continually working on refurbishing our home and property.

Reading this new Family Proclamation, I was immediately struck by the place in history it would play. President Hinckley had concluded his historic address with a strong admonition: "We commend to all a careful, thoughtful, and prayerful reading of this proclamation. The strength of any nation is rooted within the walls of its homes. We urge our people everywhere to strengthen their families in conformity with these time-honored values."

I took it as my responsibility to study the proclamation deeply and incorporate it into my teaching our ward's High Priests and my family. Like other Latter-day Saints around the world, we hung a framed copy prominently in our home, which we continued to do for more than twenty years. When it was initially issued, I superficially understood that it spoke against same-sex marriage. But I set that aside, choosing, as I had done before with more complex topics, to look at it with obedient eyes, drawing out only the positive truths that I could use to benefit my life and those around me. Only years later would I come to understand the legal background of the church's ongoing fight against same-sex marriages or "marriage equality," which was the basis for the church's decision to officially publish its doctrinal statements about gender and marriage in the Family Proclamation.[2]

As a couple, Marleen and I reviewed each aspect of our parenting against the statements in the proclamation to find ways to improve. I endeavored to preside over my family in love and righteousness and was effective in my responsibility to provide the necessities of life and protection for my family. At no point in my church membership did I feel the clarity of church standards sink more deeply into every part of who I was. I had never felt the need or desire to live perfectly as I did due to this proclamation. I saw that others felt it, too. A wave of cultural retrenchment washed over the active members of our ward and stake. Along with it came heightened means to judge those who might not measure up to the newly proclaimed standards.

I did not realize then that my increased devotion to living these standards was cutting against my underlying and oft-buried identity. Not only did I have a shiny new standard to live by, but I had an inflexible filter by which to judge my soul. The weight of expectations, especially those self-imposed, became increasingly crushing.

I had always thrived on the highest level of performance and was both a workaholic and a perfectionist. At work, I had struggled since I began practicing architecture under a domineering, exacting, and often capricious boss, whose frequent vocal criticism affected me deeply. This led to my growing battle with anxiety around my professional work.

Having grown up trying to keep peace in a dysfunctional family, it became overwhelming when we experienced conflict I found difficult to resolve in the early years of my marriage. All I wanted was a peaceful, happy, ideal family. But I had no therapy, diagnosis, mental health, or medications to rely upon. It was just a feeling that I was struggling to live as I should. I often found relief and "self-medication" by experiencing my female self through flights of imagination or secretly cross-dressing when possible. But those fleeting "fixes" only brought crushing shame that I was imperfect and guilt that I was engaging in "unholy and impure" practices.

By the end of that winter, my health was dangerously deteriorating. I was experiencing crippling panic attacks at home and persistent irritable bowel syndrome at the office. I did not feel right about myself, who I was, or how I was living. I was constantly on guard and hyper-vigilant against either crushing criticism or being detected in my femininity.

"I can't do male anymore!" I cried out on Monday morning, March 11, 1996. I was already late for work, a forty-five-minute drive away. As I attempted to cross our living room, I became overwhelmed with panic and fell awkwardly to my knees against the wall behind a chair. The kids were at school and Marleen had taken our youngest child out to run errands.

Alone in the house, my panic reached a crescendo as I struggled to focus and move forward. Instead, I found myself fixated on ending my life. My weapon of choice was my car. Even when I felt out of control, it seemed to make sense to my harried mind that I could control my end if I were behind the wheel. Besides, I didn't own a gun or have a bottle of pills. Images of concrete highway barricades or the bridge over the Mohawk River chasm I crossed each day flashed through my mind.

If I had been able to stand up, I might have made it to the car. But instead I remained crumpled in a heap on the carpet behind the chair. That's the moment my soul cried out in anguish that I could no longer "do male," that I could no longer function in the male role expected of me. The cry sprang from deep within me, appropriating the term "male" from the Family Proclamation. This marked my first verbalization that I was living contrary to my truth in the fifteen years since I had determined to bury my female identity.

Shouting it aloud, even if I was the only one to hear it, felt empowering. It made me realize that I didn't need to end my life—I just needed to learn how to live in a way that was truer to myself. My problem was not the result of external pressures. I didn't cry out that I could no longer work for that man or in that office. The crisis I faced came from an identity conflict roiling within me, which I didn't know how to resolve. I stayed on my knees, seeking answers, until I found relief as the impression came into my mind that God loved me and that my family loved me. This assurance pushed the suicidal thoughts from my mind. I felt a measure of strength in the reality of the love I felt. By then, I was drained of all my strength.

I went upstairs, removed my clothes, climbed under the covers, and fell into a deep sleep.

For many days following this collapse, I was in a total funk, unable to think clearly or make even the most simple decisions. Marleen brought me food and laid out my clothes for me, but I didn't spend much time outside the bedroom or dressed. I lost all ability to function. After several weeks, Marleen went to my office and explained the situation to my employers as best she could, telling them it didn't look like I would ever be back.

Our bishop arranged for me to meet with a therapist from the LDS Social Services office in New York City. Brother Clifford Campbell was on call to come up to our stake from the city as often as needed. I met with him several times in a classroom at our stake center. My memory of those meetings was that the lights weren't on in the room and that the edges of the room were in shadow. He was an older gentleman in a dark suit and tie, large in stature and possessing the aura of a senior priesthood leader. I had never met with a therapist before and was unsure how to process the questions he asked me.

The shadowy room, his overall appearance, and his direct demeanor set me ill at ease. The interviews felt to me like searching priesthood leader interviews, such as one might have with their bishop to disclose unrepentant past sins. I was accustomed to upbeat priesthood interviews where I could talk about my church service in areas I was doing well. I had no frame of reference to tell this man what I was experiencing. I had already lost my job and wondered how I would ever return to my profession. I was clinging to my family and church like a lifeline. I could not risk losing either or both of those. I had no way to comprehend what telling this priesthood man that "I cannot do male anymore" might do to my future. I didn't even know yet what that meant.

I was unaware that a female identity could legitimately exist inside a male-identified body. It seemed sinful to me to explore an idea that did not have a place in Heavenly Father's "plan of salvation." To me my fantasy of dressing and being female was a category of personal sin that I deceived myself into believing I could suppress and control, but must never share with anyone else, let alone this stranger.

Instead, I only attempted to describe my family and work stress to him and my symptoms. I explained my panic attacks and nasty bouts of irritable bowel syndrome over the past several months. But I could not express my inner secret. Oh how I wish, looking back, that I realized how life-giving it would have been for me to articulate those feelings and express them in confidence to another person! And yet, I do not know whether he, in 1996, would have been prepared to genuinely help me understand my gender dysphoria.

Notes

1. Gordon B. Hinckley, "Stand Strong against the Wiles of the World," *General Conference Report*, September 23, 1995.

2. See Gregory A. Prince, "Gay Rights and the Mormon Church: Intended Actions, Unintended Consequences," *The University of Utah Press, Salt Lake City, UT,* 2019, beginning page 38.

12

My Pioneer Trek

Months after my breakdown, the fog clouding my mind and the strain on my nervous system began to clear. Gradually, I was able to assume my responsibilities for my family. I realized I needed to establish a new direction for me and for our family's future.

Because I hadn't been able to articulate my gender issues to my therapist, that left him and me with only one conclusion: my workplace stress had overwhelmed me to the point that I needed a change in career or place of employment. I knew by then I would never return to my former employer, so I needed to figure out what my next path would be.

I sensed I was at a crossroads again, but didn't overthink it. The increasing clarity that came each day, coupled with no longer having a demanding job to run to, created a season of self-determination. I have frequently looked back on this time and recognized how much courage it took to take the next steps that I did. What saddens me is that although my gender identity and inability to continue living as a male was at the core of my breakdown, addressing what that meant for me did not factor into my plans for our future. Instead, I simply tried to ignore those feelings. This time, I didn't throw them in the trash barrel with a determination to never think about them again. As I healed from my trauma, the issue of gender just seemed to back away into the shadows—there, but not as present. My gender identity was now an underlying part of my adult life that I no longer packed in a sealed box.

I relied on study and prayer to gain confidence in figuring out my new direction. Always in my mind were the words of my patriarchal blessing, directing me to obtain and use my education in service of those within and without the church, consequently spreading the gospel's blessings throughout the world. This notion had previously led me to interview with the church's physical facilities office in Indianapolis. I had subsequently received a job offer to be a meeting-house project manager in Ohio, only to have the position eliminated due to a hiring freeze enacted by church headquarters. If I wanted to work for the church, I decided, I would have to talk to Salt Lake.

Up to that point in my life, I lived under a self-imposed limitation. I was a convert to the church living in the American northeast, a professional, and a local church leader. I felt it my duty to stay rooted in that part of the church where I was planted. Accompanying this creed of mine was my disdain for all things associated with Utah Mormon culture, as I imagined it. Even though I had never lived in Utah, I felt strongly that I never wanted to.

As my conviction grew that I must follow my patriarchal blessing's direction to use my talents in the Lord's service, I had to face my unwillingness to look West. One evening as I pondered what to do, I felt the influence of the Holy Spirit, which, to define it using scriptural terms, "removed the scales from my eyes" and helped "set behind me the incorrect traditions of my fathers." At that moment, I became convinced to expand my employment search to the West and to prepare to move to Utah. I know I am not the first, nor the last, to decide to pack up and move to the Mormon "Zion," but the fruit of that decision bore out that it was the right one for me.

A series of applications and phone calls yielded my first interview at church headquarters in Salt Lake City a month later. Thrilled, I bought an expensive plane ticket from Newark, New Jersey, that would put me in Salt Lake the night before the interview. But on the morning of my flight, I received a disappointing letter from the church's human resources department, thanking me for my interest but telling me I was no longer being considered for the position. Marleen and I agreed that since I had already purchased the ticket, I should go anyway to see what I might accomplish.

I left in my old Ford pickup that afternoon with ample time to get to Newark airport. Knowing the truck had a slow oil leak, I had a case of oil in the bed to be safe. A little into my trip, to my shock,

I spotted the oil gauge dropping, and when it bottomed out, I didn't want to but I knew I had to stop. Four quarts later, the engine was full again. But to my dismay, it kept leaking, until I had used all my oil by the southern end of the New York State Thruway.

The time I lost stopping multiple times to fill my crankcase meant I arrived in the parking lot at Newark just as my flight was supposed to be boarding. The engine was completely dry of oil again. I was frantic, but my focus shifted to getting on that plane. I ran through the pre-9/11 airport with all I had, only reaching the gate once the plane was supposed to have left. It hadn't. I never heard why, but I was able to board. I was drenched in sweat, covered with motor oil, and pinned into a middle seat between two uncomfortable strangers, but I made the flight.

My troubles weren't over. Because we left Newark late, I missed my connecting flight to Salt Lake City. During my layover in Las Vegas, I swapped my ticket for the first flight in the morning but still had several hours to wait overnight at the airport. I tried to sleep on a chair as far from possible from the seductive lights and whirring of the Las Vegas airport's slot machines. I did the math in my head as I dozed. I would have two hours from landing to get a rental car, drive to Marleen's sister's house in West Jordan to clean up, and drive back to the Church Office Building for the 10:00 A.M. appointment—an appointment I had been told was canceled. Plus, I was unfamiliar with these places and had no GPS.

Somehow I arrived at the interview the following day on time as the interview team was finishing up with the person before me. Everyone seemed confused that I had shown up. I pretended that I had not received their letter canceling the interview, so they graciously interviewed me.

Having beaten all my challenges, I felt pretty invincible regarding the job opportunity. All went as it needed to, so clearly, I thought, I was meant to get this position. A week later, I was shocked to receive a second letter from church human resources thanking me for interviewing but explaining that the job had been given to another. I mustered my courage and called the HR man who wrote the letter and was present at my interview. I asked what I lacked or could have done or said to have shown myself to be more valuable to them.

He paused, his integrity welling up inside him. He whispered, "I shouldn't tell you this, but you were the most qualified candidate. You have the wrong address." I thanked him for that critical piece of information that I lacked. I concluded that the church must be unwilling to hire and move candidates from outside Utah.

So I determined to get a "correct address" in Utah and try again. Marleen and I created a plan with no plan B. I changed the address on my applications and resumes to her sister's house and got busy preparing our house for sale and a big move.

It wasn't long before church human resources informed me of an open construction position in its Welfare Services Department. I was flabbergasted and queried, "Why does welfare need an architect?" They had a separate facilities program, I learned, so I arranged an interview in Salt Lake in two weeks.

Then, according to plan, I took Alissa and Liz, our seven- and eight-year-old daughters, threw one of the girls' mattresses for us to sleep on in the truck bed of that old Ford pickup, and headed west. The girls rode with me as far as Nauvoo, Illinois, where they stayed with Marleen's parents. Meanwhile, our two sons remained in New York with their mom, who was finishing packing for the move.

Arriving at my sister-in-law's home, I realized I had no particular schedule or idea of what to do with my family, who were now spread out across the country in three separate states. All I knew was that I must land a decent job and find a place to live soon. There was no going back.

My interview with the church's welfare department went well. I enjoyed the people I met, and they assured me they would get back to me soon. I knew that was no guarantee, so the following week, I lined up several interviews with architectural firms I had contacted as a backup. On Friday of the second week, I was asked to come in and meet with welfare again, and I was offered the job. My new job would start in just over two weeks.

Earlier in the year, when we decided to move to Utah, I had opened our Rand McNally Road Atlas and asked Marleen in what area we might want to live. She had lived in Utah as a child and then again as a college student. Before she could answer, my eyes landed on a city name on the map, which seemed to be printed in boldface. The word "Tooele"(pronounced too-wíll-uh) captivated me as though I was looking at the Harry Potter marauders' map.

"What do you know about Tooele?" I asked.

"I've never been there, but we had family friends who lived in the Tooele Valley I visited once. It was nice but pretty rural," Marleen replied. I didn't say anything more about it at that time.

The day after I accepted the job offer was a Saturday. I had to quickly find a house to rent because I had already purchased a ticket back to New York. Following my instinct, I drove from West Jordan to the Tooele Valley. As I passed the point of the mountain and exited the freeway at the mouth of the valley, I had the powerful sense that this was our new home. Looking back, I do not know why I did none of the conventional things that should be done to find a rental house. I didn't visit an office or hire an agent, and I didn't even buy a newspaper. I felt no need to, even though I was in an unfamiliar city without any contacts. I drove up and down the city streets just enjoying the scenes and applying my eye of faith. I felt spiritually guided at each step of this journey and was confident it would continue as I looked and listened.

I had crisscrossed most of the city when I turned onto a quiet street then suddenly stopped. I was facing the 1960s-era Tooele stake center. I had seen LDS meetinghouses all around town but felt prompted to stop in front of this one.

An inaudible voice said, "Come to church here at 9:00 A.M. tomorrow, and you will find your house." Grateful to be done searching, I bought a sandwich, hiked up the canyon above the city and, with a sunset view of the entire valley, enjoyed my meal.

The following day, I arrived in the chapel just as the sacrament meeting of the Tooele First Ward started. I slipped into a pew in the back, which afforded me a good view of most of the congregation. As the meeting progressed, I thought about the prompting I had received the day before and was interested to see how it might be fulfilled.

At the appropriate time for visitor introductions during one of the smaller meetings that followed, I stood and introduced myself as an architect from New York who had just accepted a position at the Church Office Building. I was looking for a house to rent for me and my family. A handsome, older gentleman stood and declared the house next door to him was for rent, and he gave me the owners' names.

I contacted the owners right after church, asking if I could see the little three-bedroom, one-bath home that had been her mother's. They told me there was nothing else available to rent in Tooele, and that they were already reviewing ten applications, but they would take mine as well. I hurried back to West Jordan, confident I could convince them that we should be their tenants out of eleven families. I prepared the application and wrote a cover letter including a picture of our family and an explanation that, as homeowners ourselves, we knew how to maintain the property. We committed to returning their house and yard in better condition than when we rented it. I printed it all out, drove back around the mountain range, and hand-delivered the application before nightfall. The following Wednesday, which happened to be July 24 or "Pioneer Day" in Utah, I signed the lease and paid the first rent. The promise I'd felt was fulfilled.

Three days later, I boarded the plane back East to collect all our family and household for the return trip to our new life. Our move went as planned. We picked up the girls in Nauvoo, and the three older kids took turns riding in the cab of the moving truck with me. Upon our arrival at the little house in Tooele, we slept the first night on the floor. In the morning, the Tooele First Ward members came out in force to unload our truck. The following Monday, exactly one month after I first left New York, I was sitting at my new desk in the Church Office Building.

I would look back on this remarkable sequence of events with deep acknowledgment of the hand of the Lord in my life to move me in faith as soon as I was willing to yield my willful thoughts and trust. People we have told our story to have consistently shaken their heads and said it should not have been possible that it worked out so quickly and so perfectly for us. Because of that decision to move, I now tell my grandchildren, who are all growing up in Utah, that their pioneer ancestors "crossed the plains" not in a wagon or by pulling a handcart, but in an old Ford pickup.

13

A Church Architect and a Bishop

I began church employment in downtown Salt Lake City's Church Office Building in August 1996, as a project manager in the Welfare Services Department's technical and construction section. I arrived wide-eyed and full of hope for what my new career offered, both in terms of experience and what I could contribute to the worldwide church I loved.

My first assignment brought my enthusiasm crashing down. A project was underway to replace the aging Provo Deseret Industries (DI) thrift store—the church's largest—with a new facility on the same site without any downtime between. The contract architect's design effort was flailing, missing deadlines and lacking clear direction. My manager in Salt Lake City, who was also new in his assignment, asked me to insert myself into the project, determine why it was off-track, and report my recommendations. I invited myself to the contract architect's office in Orem, Utah. I soon discovered that the office was nearly empty of staff and that the architectural drawings were incomplete, poorly executed, and behind schedule. Embedding myself in his workflow to save the project led to several confrontations with the architect. In the final one, he threw me out of his office amidst a tirade of profanity. I wrote up my recommendation to my department's leadership to terminate his contract immediately and scrap his design. I also offered to hire a new architectural firm and guide a new design to completion.

My recommendation was bold. The contractor architect was politically well-connected in the church, and I was a newcomer from the East. Nevertheless, my proposal was approved, with the caveat that the project still be completed by the original date set and within the First Presidency approval budget. That put us a year and several hundred thousand dollars behind on day one.

I felt worn down when I read the fired architect's scathing response. The letter rattled me, and I wondered if I had made a terrible mistake in coming to Utah and getting church employment. I found the work far more complex than anything I had experienced in ten years of practicing in Albany. Marleen's father, who served in a stake presidency at that time, came to Salt Lake City for the church's October general conference and gave me a priesthood blessing. In it, he promised me that I would become an instrument in the Lord's hands to reform the church's physical facilities. That made me think of my patriarchal blessing that had inspired me to come to Utah. Hearing this new promise, I thought, "I am only a project manager in Welfare Services. I don't even work for the Physical Facilities Department. There ain't no way I will ever be a part of changing the whole system."

After church leaders approved my recommendation for the Provo Deseret Industries, department leadership reassigned my manager to another position and asked me to take his place as design and construction manager. This manager later told me he had hired me in anticipation of possibly becoming his replacement eventually. Because I was presenting as "male" at that time, my aggressive approach to solving the problem project in Provo showed department leadership that I was ready to run all their design and construction projects. I hadn't been aware that I was on a two-month job interview!

Today I recognize that had I been presenting as female, such an aggressive approach would not likely have met with approval. Exercising male dominance in conflict is something that I now regret and seek to purge from my character.

Empowered in my new leadership role, I found and hired a new architectural firm for the Provo DI. We got to work and had the successful hard opening as directed, on time and within budget, without a single day of lost sales.

Shortly before my hiring, the First Presidency had approved Welfare Services' proposal to complete a wholesale modernization of Welfare Square in Salt Lake City. These flagship welfare facilities, built during the Great Depression in the early years of the church's modern welfare efforts, showcased the church's principles of industry and thrift but needed an update.

As the new manager, I began attending all the design meetings for the Welfare Square renovation. I discovered severe concerns around the replacement of the Deseret Dairy milk products plant. The project leaders told me that here, too, the new facility needed to be built adjacent to the old one and must remain running until the new one could receive and process raw milk without a lost day because "cows don't stop giving milk." I wondered aloud where the cow's milk given on the Sabbath went. They gave me incredulous "don't ask questions" looks.

The church employed a nationally known engineer of milk processing plants from San Francisco. I knew nothing of such operations but quickly learned that typical milk industry facilities were enormous buildings that specialized in one type of processing only, whether it was liquid milk, cheese, powdered products, or other products. These different processes were never under one roof and never on a small scale. But our program for Deseret Dairy proposed putting all possible processes under one relatively small, 40,000 square-foot roof, operated by a skeleton staff of trained employees assisted by a constant rotation of volunteers who had never seen milk production before. Finally, the entire facility had to be visible as a showcase for the public to view on tours while still maintaining sanitary conditions.

As I probed our department's staff to test their commitment to such a matrix of conflicting requirements, they taught me the critical nature of what they called "priesthood purpose." The purpose of the facility we were creating wasn't simply to make milk products for the church—the church could buy those from the general marketplace. The purpose was to give members hands-on opportunities to serve and be a showplace of the church's welfare principles.

Armed with this understanding, I endeavored to resolve a design impasse that our talented consultant had been experiencing. By

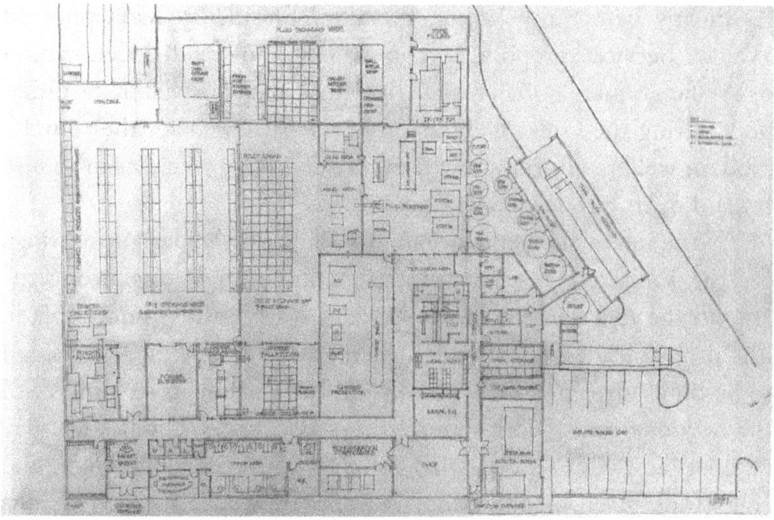

Laurie Lee's freehand sketch of design concept plan for the proposed Deseret Dairy Products building at Welfare Square, January 27, 1997. Courtesy Laurie Lee Hall.

this point, their engineers had created twenty-six different concept plans, each attempting to solve the impossible contradictions of requirements my colleagues had communicated. I had never seen twenty-six unsuccessful concepts on a single project. It was in crisis.

I called a meeting between our consultants and the department's stakeholders. Leading the discussion, I gave each of the twenty people in the room a chance to describe their view of the flow of people, goods, and services through the facility from beginning until completion and departure. As they talked, I diagrammed every step they described on whiteboards. By the end of the day, I had everything I needed to know. I went into my office the next day with photos of the whiteboard diagrams and a large sheet of drawing paper. I organized all the functions into a plan called "No. 27."

Within a few days, I presented "27" to the group, walking everyone through the plan according to their expressed needs. It was ultimately declared perfect and turned over to the professionals for completion. Later, a fellow church employee came into my office, saw the plan hanging on my wall, and mocked it for being a freehand pencil sketch. "The lines aren't even straight," he said, perhaps hoping to take me down a peg. So I explained how it came to be, and he sheepishly left.

Deseret Dairy Products opened on Salt Lake City's Welfare Square in 1998 and has continued to fulfill its intended purposes ever since. My experiences with the Provo DI and Deseret Dairy projects renewed my confidence and confirmed that I could succeed in this new work environment.

In those days, each church department was responsible for the care and maintenance of its own buildings. Without a unified church program, Welfare Services struggled to maintain its aging facilities. I was assigned to figure out how to increase our effectiveness. I learned that the leadership of Meetinghouse Facilities (the church's term for buildings where its congregations meet) was addressing the same concern, so I reached out to them for a meeting. I was profoundly impressed with what they described.

As I pondered how we might implement similar processes in Welfare Services, the answer came as a flash of inspiration. Driving home that night, I thought about how each department held its buildings close like independent fiefdoms, unwilling to share resources or responsibilities. The words came into my mind: "They are not your buildings, they're mine." We could do better than simply trying to duplicate what the Meetinghouse Facilities managers were planning to do. Instead, they should do what they already do best for *all* the church's buildings.

I met with the Meetinghouse Facilities leaders again and proposed that they maintain our Welfare Services buildings. They revealed that that had been their long-term plan, but assumed it would require a fight with us. They expected substantial pushback against the idea because they thought other departments would be reluctant to turn over their maintenance funding and control to them. They also admitted that their processes were not yet ready, so they were unprepared to take on other building types.

But I knew what was right and could not be dissuaded. They agreed to let me return to my department leaders and explain the concept. They assumed that would buy them time because they thought I would be initially turned down flat. But I had earned substantial credibility with my leaders over my first year, so when I explained how we could trust these facilities experts to do the maintenance work our department struggled to perform, my managing director was convinced. I brought the managing directors of both departments together to discuss the future steps, which included seeking the Presiding Bishopric and First Presidency approval of the changes.

Their approval came quickly, with a caveat: Welfare must relinquish my full-time-employee position and those of my staff to Meetinghouse Facilities so they could hire additional managers to accomplish their work. I had orchestrated a coup that left me without a position or workplace.

As soon as I found out, I went to see Carl Heinz, the managing director of Meetinghouse Facilities, with whom I had negotiated these changes. I asked Carl if there was any need for me in his department. His response was different from what I expected. His director of meetinghouse construction was leaving soon on a three-week vacation to his home country of France. Carl needed someone to run the US meetinghouse construction program in his absence. Though his confidence in me was shocking, I told him I'd do it.

The director briefly introduced me to his people and projects before he left town. The following Monday, I was sitting in his window office, receiving phone calls and dealing with problems I knew nothing about. Carl also invited me to sit in on the department leadership meetings as though I was one of them. These were no ordinary meetings. They went on for hours and included the best of the church's facilities leaders, who were overhauling how they would do physical facilities work for the church. They had worked over the previous year with Bain & Company, Mitt Romney's management consulting firm out of Boston, which had identified scores of inefficiencies and bottlenecks in how the church facilities program had operated. I was spellbound.

I also reflected on the blessing I had received from my father-in-law several months before, promising that I would participate in the overhaul of the physical facilities program. I now found myself sitting with the men who were doing just that. When the construction director returned, I had managed not to burn anything down, so I was kept on and given a six-foot square cubicle outside his office, among the secretaries, and tasked with completing whatever assignment came my way. I didn't belong there, but I got paid every two weeks. This situation continued for about six months until I was approved to be a new regional project manager, reporting to the man whose office I had initially occupied.

I often looked for opportunities to visit the Temple Construction Department in the twenty-six-floor Church Office Building where I worked. I hoped to work for this department someday. In the summer of 1997, I was chatting at the desk of Bob Dewey, one of the most senior temple designers. He surprised me when, in hushed tones, he pulled out a piece of paper with a simple pencil sketch on it. He whispered, "President Hinckley made this sketch. He has had a revelation to announce and build scores of small temples in places all over the world." At that time, the church had only fifty operating temples worldwide.

Though Latter-day Saints believe that God is unchangeable and never ceases to be God, the administration of the church is often tossed to and fro on the winds of what can be called "prophetic priorities." Such changing emphasis on what was critical significantly impacted the church's physical facilities, particularly regarding the design and construction of temples.

Students of modern Mormonism can observe these shifts in the different types of temples built during the different church administrations. One will soon recognize the personality fingerprints of top church leaders on the building program.

President Spencer W. Kimball emphasized growing and storing your food, modesty, and thrift. These emphases are apparent in the temples designed and built during his administration in the late 1970s and early 1980s. The initial wave of smaller (and thus, less expensive) temples are in Chicago, Boise, Dallas, Buenos Aires, and the Pacific Isles. Approximately thirty years later, nearly every one of the Kimball-era temples underwent massive renovations or expansions when the Temple Department deemed them too small or plain to serve well as temples.

In contrast, perhaps to emphasize the strength of the church in the United States, Kimball's successors, Presidents Ezra Taft Benson, Howard W. Hunter and, initially, Gordon B. Hinckley, built fewer but much larger temples like Bountiful and Mt. Timpanogos in Utah, as well as Boston, San Diego, and St. Louis.

But in 1997, President Hinckley appeared to be shifting back to President Kimball's emphasis on smaller, less expensive temples. Bob Dewey explained to me that to follow Hinckley's new plan, the Temple Construction Department would have to hire several more staff, and he wanted to know if I would be interested. I couldn't contain my enthusiasm at the prospect, and he promised to speak with his managing director on my behalf. He then gave me a copy of the sketch, which I was to keep confidential until President Hinckley officially announced the small temple program.

He did so at the church's next general conference, in October 1997. "There are many areas of the Church that are remote, where the membership is small and not likely to grow very much shortly," he said in his address. "Are those who live in these places to be denied forever the blessings of the temple ordinances? While visiting such an area a few months ago, we prayerfully pondered this question. The answer came bright and clear. We would construct small temples in some of these areas, buildings with all of the facilities to administer all of the ordinances," but without "extras" like a cafeteria or laundry facilities for rented temple clothing. The program would substantially reduce construction and operating costs of temples while bringing the ordinances closer to church members wherever they lived around the world.

Hinckley then electrified his audience by announcing his ostentatious goal to double the number of then-operating temples from fifty to 100 by the end of 2000—in less than three years. The church had built only 52 temples in the 167 years since it was organized in 1830! Almost overnight, new, locally-staffed small temples began popping up in nearly every state of the United States and numerous countries worldwide.

I followed up with Bob several times during this exciting period, but he eventually told me something about being unable to hire me from another department that needed me. My dream of working on temples was not yet to be.

As I embarked on my early years in church employment, I also grew in relationships and responsibilities in my personal and religious

Inspecting the progress of the Accra Ghana Temple in September 2003, one of the smaller temples President Gordon B. Hinckley announced. Courtesy Laurie Lee Hall.

life. After Marleen and I had settled into our first, rented house in Tooele, we realized we were in the original Tooele First Ward—steeped in history and lifelong existing relationships. Knowing it would take our best effort to be accepted and included, we decided to be very proactive in reaching out to others. This approach proved successful, and when we moved into our newly constructed house a year later in a different ward and stake, we continued with this attitude, setting an example for our arriving neighbors to follow.

Within several months of moving into our new home, our stake president called me to be the bishop of a new ward created from our recently developed subdivision. He explained that our former stake president had noticed us and recommended that he call me to be the bishop. Our new stake president said he received this recom-mendation with resistance because he preferred to obtain his spiritual confirmation of the choice. Sometime later, he pass house while out on his morning run and felt impressed that this was where the new bishop lived. Upon learning that I lived in the house, he acquiesced and immediately submitted my name to the Office of the First Presidency for approval of the call.

Marleen and I were attending the general conference in the Salt Lake Tabernacle that fall when we ran into our stake president from New York. I told him I had been called as bishop in our new ward, to which he replied that it made total sense. He told us that he felt grieved when we suddenly moved away because he was preparing to call me to serve as bishop back there, too. I felt amazed that three separate stake presidents identified me to serve as a new bishop just after coming off my traumatic breakdown over my gender identity.

There was no training for new bishops, so I felt clueless during my first year. I was painfully unaware of many social norms associated with Utah wards, and I often offended people in my ignorance. For example, I had never lived in a ward that sent off a full-time missionary and was unaware of the social traditions tied to such an event. Until one Sunday morning, when a missionary's mother stormed my office, leaving me no doubt about how disrespectfully I had treated her and her family. I had failed to assign someone to create a plaque recognizing this missionary, with his picture and area of service to display on a wall of our ward building. My counselors also struggled to fill their roles because I was so new at this that I was negligent in training them.

Our area was growing via new construction so quickly that the church approved dividing our ward to create two from one at the end of the year. I received a fresh start with added experience and insight. I became more effective in training leaders and caring for people. This growth, division, and creation of a new ward continued every year. The second version of being the ward bishop was far more enjoyable than the first, the third was even better, and so on. The advantage was that I could remake myself as bishop to a new congregation each time.

Those initial years as bishop took place in the twentieth century hile I was still in my thirties. I trusted my stake leaders implicitly. ught into every word that proceeded from them and our general h leaders. In trying to convey the peace I felt from being so locked in, I would tell other ward leaders in our council meetings, "If the stake president asked me to stand in the middle of Main Street, I wouldn't ask why. I would go do it." I believed that even if a leader asked me to do something wrong, I would be blessed for my obedience. I told them, "If the brethren came out and said peanut butter was now against the Word of Wisdom, that would be it. I would never taste it again."

Looking back, I know some who heard my words weren't as convinced as I was, but overall, ward members seemed to love my directness and clarity and came along for the journey. My willingness to conform and lead my congregation to do the same earned my ecclesiastical file leaders' trust, which led them to empower me to fill my role as I saw fit. It was a positive exchange. In the church, lay priesthood leaders were granted autonomy by keeping their file leaders out of trouble, staying within the lines, and solving our own issues.

14

A Temple Designer and a Stake President

Around the start of my service as bishop, Meetinghouse Facilities Department managing director Carl Heinz appeared in the doorway of my office at work. "I want you to be the director of the department's Technical Support Division," he told me.

"Umm, well, I'm enjoying meetinghouse construction," I replied. "I'd just as soon continue doing this."

Carl's voice became stern. "I'm not asking you. I'm telling you I need you to be the director of this division."

"Oh, okay," I conceded.

At barely thirty-seven, I became one of the youngest directors in church employment. Technical Support was a misleading name for the division. Its primary purposes were the design of the church's standard meetinghouse plans and reviewing and presenting for approval all meetinghouse projects for areas of the church outside the United States. My assignment came right as Bain & Company-inspired processes were implemented throughout North America. The plan was to roll out these processes worldwide in all the church's physical facilities programs during the year 2000—the same year as President Hinckley's goal to complete 100 operating temples.

To do so, the church needed new designs that made meetinghouses the same size worldwide. Previously built international church buildings were undersized and inadequate compared to those housing the same-sized congregations in North America. That assignment to standardize the designs fell to my new staff and me, and we had to move quickly to get the program developed and approved. When this worldwide program was approved and taught to leaders of the church facilities programs from throughout the world in December 1999, I felt gratified that I had seen the fulfillment of promises made to me in priesthood blessings that I would participate in the restructuring of church physical facilities and also serve those within the church in all the world. Only a few years earlier, I doubted these possibilities could ever have occurred.

Another heady, though at times nerve-wracking, responsibility of my new assignment was reporting directly to top church leaders. This responsibility included presentations to the Church Appropriations Committee, a subcommittee of the Council for the Disposition of the Tithes, which consisted of the First Presidency, the Quorum of the Twelve, and the Presiding Bishopric. My job in these meetings was to address any questions regarding church projects from everywhere in the world. I had a staff of several experienced facilities people who helped me prepare for this each week.

Once, President Hinckley stopped me when I mentioned the Buendia Ward's meetinghouse when I was presenting on more than twenty meetinghouses in the Philippines.

"Is that the one at the intersection of Della Costa and Soliman?" he asked. I had never been to metro Manila at that point, but he had been so many times he remembered the street names.

"How can we not know these things?" President Hinckley chided me when I confessed I didn't know.

"But I will find out and report back," was my attempt at a reply.

In the summer of 2002, Carl Heinz informed me that the Presiding Bishopric likely planned to have our Meetinghouse Facilities Department take over temple design and construction responsibilities. This would be a significant change since working on temples had long held an aura of nobility not found among the church's "lower" facilities programs.

By this point, all other departments with properties followed Welfare Services' example and used our Meetinghouse Facilities Department for their building care. Our department provided design, management, and care to all ecclesiastical church properties worldwide, except for the church's temples. President Hinckley personally managed the expansion of temple building, primarily through his legacy "small temple" program. He had handpicked those involved to accomplish his aggressive building objectives.

By 2002, that program was winding down. After achieving the President's goal of 100 operating temples by the end of 2000, those overseeing temple design and construction in the Temple Construction Department were weary from their hard-fought efforts to accomplish the president's objectives. Due to their frantic efforts, their work processes and controls were in shambles.

The notion of "opposition in all things," found in the teachings of the Book of Mormon, was apparent in the construction and operation of the church's temples. On one hand, the designers and builders of the Temple Construction Department had been consumed by the pace of building these newly announced small temples with unprecedented dispatch. Representing the "opposition" was the separate Temple Department. They were charged with operating the temples after they were opened or "dedicated," which included the sacred rites called "ordinances" performed inside them. The Temple Department had been caught off guard by the challenge of staffing and training so many volunteers to manage and run the daily work in the fifty new temples opened in less than three years. They preferred that temples come online at a slower, more measured pace. Many in the department also complained about the lack of amenities in the new small temple design, such as laundries and cafeterias. These buildings had cost little more than a standard LDS stake center.

Both organizations reported directly on temple matters to the First Presidency, which, as history demonstrates, emphasized conflicting priorities. Thrift and efficiency on the one hand, and the finest "celestial" experience for temple-goers on the other. Those in temple design and construction came to call the quandary the "temple pendulum." Furthermore, separate bodies of intermediate General Authorities interpreted the First Presidency's direction, communicating it to the employee level, namely the Presiding Bishopric in the case of Temple Construction or Physical Facilities and the Temple Department Executive Committee in the case of the experience inside the temple. Significant time and energy was spent unraveling and negotiating the tension between the two departments.

While the frantic and sometimes conflicting efforts of the Temple Construction and Temple Departments to complete and begin operating fifty new temples had left their work processes and controls in a state of shambles, our department's implementation of the worldwide meetinghouse program had rolled out smoothly, proving highly productive and significantly reducing the church's costs. It was probably for this reason that, in October 2002, Carl privately informed me that it was time for us to prepare to take responsibility for temple design and construction. At the direction of the First Presidency, the two of us began meeting confidentially with two subject experts from the Temple Department to craft improved temple design and construction processes. Carl guided the effort, but I felt alone in crafting the new work processes—steps to complete the work with consistent results, policies, and organization.

To assure confidentiality, I closed my office door and locked myself in when working on the new, temple-related project. I stored all the documents on a secure server and kept my notes in a locked drawer. Over the next six months, this exercise felt like nothing short of another well-executed coup, and I again was its architect.

By March 2003, I had completed writing the new work process, and the Presiding Bishopric and Temple Department approved the documents. The First Presidency asked for its immediate implementation. The mighty Temple Construction Department, which had built dozens of temples along with the church's 21,000-seat Conference Center over the prior three years, was dissolved and rolled into our Meetinghouse Facilities Department, renamed the Physical Facilities Department. This newly organized department was now responsible for *all* properties worldwide. Because I was the most familiar with the temple processes I had just written, Carl assigned me to train the temple architects and project managers who had joined us from the old department on how they would now do their jobs going into the future.

As I stood before those men assembled in the large training room on the twenty-sixth floor of the Church Office Building, most scowling at me and assuming defensive body language, I wanted to shrink before them. Some of these men had been building temples since I was in grade school. How audacious for a person as young as myself, with no experience designing or constructing temples, to stand up, show a few slides, and propose to tell them how to do their jobs. I completed this assignment without any validation that I had accomplished anything measurable in the minds of these venerable warhorses.

Afterward, I met privately with Carl to discuss the department's restructuring. He knew me as both a design leader in my current meetinghouse role and a construction manager in my previous role. He told me he needed to fill the design and construction director positions. Carl asked me, "Which would you choose?"

"I can do either, but I would like temple design," was my reply.

"I need you to take temple construction," he directed, letting me know he wasn't asking for my choice. And with that, all those scowling temple project managers were now reporting to me. It took a long time to gain their confidence. One day, in a staff meeting with them, I reached my breaking point of frustration. I exclaimed to them that I had overseen the construction or renovation of more than three million square feet in my ten years practicing architecture in Albany. I demanded they give me a measure of respect. Ultimately, by helping them be successful in their work, I earned their respect.

Meanwhile, at home, I was also taking on increasing ecclesiastical responsibilities. After five years of service as a bishop, I received a letter from the stake presidency. The letter explained that the church planned to divide our stake, necessitating interviews of key leaders, including me, by top church authorities visiting to select a new stake presidency. These are significant events in Mormondom. It was the second time in two years that our stake was divided. As a bishop, I participated in the process.

The visiting church authorities asked me and other local leaders privately to provide the names of three individuals we felt would do well as the new stake president. When I told Marleen this, I suggested that I could receive the call to be the new stake president, but I didn't know. We chatted about how the leaders might divide the existing fourteen wards. A line separating the old wards from the new ones made sense. It wasn't until several weeks later, as I was driving my little truck to work in Salt Lake City, that the Spirit's clarity revealed to me the dividing line between the old stake and the new. Rather than east/west as I imagined to be logical, the line would run north/south, extending like a flag to include my house again, just like my former wards often were drawn.

I also felt confirmation that I would be the president of the new stake. I began thinking of the people who lived in the wards that would belong to this new stake. As I drove, faces, names, and stake leadership positions they should fill came to mind. Once I got to my office, I took out a pad, wrote out the entire roster of stake positions, and filled in the names corresponding to nearly every position. That night, I shared the experience with Marleen without divulging the names, and all she could say was, "We'll see." Sometimes, the specificity of my spiritual insights was more than others could grasp.

I felt uniquely prepared when, six weeks later, Elder Earl C. Tingey, a leading General Authority, invited me to meet with him and called me to serve as stake president. In his next breath, he told me to pray about who should serve as my two counselors in the stake presidency and then let him know who they were as soon as possible so he could interview them and invite them to serve. He hoped to interview as many of the new stake leadership as possible that night so they could be sustained by the local members in our stake conference the following day.

I immediately told Elder Tingey I would not need to go away to identify counselors; I had already done so. I produced my pad with the nearly complete stake roster. He appeared shocked. But he took the two names and sent someone to call their homes to ask them to return for interviews. He then shared with me that in all his years of calling new stake presidents, he never experienced what he had that day. He had scheduled interviews with some thirty existing stake and ward leaders that weekend, but when the first fourteen recommended that I should be stake president, he called off the rest of the interviews and invited me in to extend the calling to me.

He also told me in passing that the following Sunday, he would be doing his next stake president calling in my former stake in Albany, New York. Just as was the case with being named as bishop in either New York or Utah, I feel I would have been called as stake president by this man regardless of which parallel universe I had chosen to live in.

After my two counselors accepted their calls, we met together, and they supported my list of people and the stake positions they would serve in. We added a few more. By the end of the evening, the new stake leadership was organized and ready to be sustained in the stake conference the following day.

When Elder Tingey set me apart as the new stake president, he explained that I would be like the church's president to the members under my care. Most of them would not know anyone in any leadership position above me. That might have held greater weight in more far-flung places than Tooele, Utah, only thirty miles from Salt Lake City, because many of our members had close connections to church leaders in Salt Lake, but I took it to heart. On the other hand, I knew many top church leaders because of my frequent meetings with them at work. I would successfully convey their goodness and love to my members.

Around the anniversary of my call to be stake president, we had a conference at which Elder Henry B. Eyring of the Quorum of the Twelve Apostles presided. It was my first experience hosting a visiting General Authority. Marleen asked me at one point why I looked so tense. I replied, "As soon as he leaves my church building, I'll be fine." I spoke first in the Saturday evening session for adults. When I finished my remarks and returned to my seat beside Elder Eyring, he leaned towards me and, in a droll whisper, said, "Fine *preaching*, president." I felt it wasn't a compliment but a challenge to do better in the future. Nevertheless, I thanked him.

From hearing other instructions from church leaders, I knew that they wanted us as local leaders to teach our people from our hearts rather than lecture them, as I had done that night.

It is humbling to serve as a leader in the church. I was always conscious of my need to watch myself and improve. Marleen frequently reminded me not to treat the church members like contractors. I knew what she meant. I demanded a lot from myself and had high expectations of others.

I felt a closeness of the Spirit while leading. It was a matter of feeling the ideas come to mind from a source beyond my logic and then saying aloud the things I was learning as they entered my mind. Often, as I was speaking, I would say something before I would think of it and learn from what I was saying as I said it, and in this way, I knew I was speaking by the Spirit.

Generally speaking, the work of the church in our stake I presided over advanced steadily and positively, well respected by those general church leaders who noted our efforts. In considerable measure, the members and families in our stake found joy in serving in the church, and our participation levels were high compared to other wards and stakes in the area.

Over my many years as a Melchizedek Priesthood leader, while presiding over priesthood quorums, wards, and finally the stake, I was asked to offer innumerable blessings in the homes of fellow members as well as in our own home. I loved doing so and was open to the opportunity of service it afforded. Marleen was never inhibited in telling the stories of our positive experiences with blessings. So much so that women who were neighbors or friends asked me to give them blessings, especially when they were experiencing problems with a pregnancy. Through it all, I felt that the Lord honored the blessings I offered, and my faith in the priesthood was unshakable.

As I matured in these experiences, my heart increased with sensitivity and compassion for those I ministered to in faith and by the power of God. I felt well-suited to the healer role and responded enthusiastically to the opportunity to administer blessings that I frequently saw my male counterparts shrink from or grudgingly accomplish. I witness that women generally are filled with the faith, concern, and empathy necessary for ministering to others, including through ritual healing.

In addition to ministering with priesthood authority, I also held "priesthood keys." As defined by the LDS Church's "Guide to the Scriptures," the keys of the priesthood "are the right of presidency, or the power given to man by God to direct, control, and govern God's priesthood on earth." The declaration that priesthood keys are "power given to *man* by God" is quite literal. Women do not receive priesthood keys. The church's governance is strictly a hierarchical patriarchy, with men who are given priesthood keys to direct the work of the church and preside over all other members within whatever jurisdiction they are called to, whether at the quorum, ward, stake, area, or general church level. Latter-day Saints give enormous deference to the presiding authority in the leadership councils of the church, all of whom are men.

This policy naturally leads to an imbalance of power in the lives of men, women, and gender minorities in the church. Recognizing this as a bishop and then a stake president, I did as much as I could in my jurisdiction to empower women. I used as my operating manual apostle M. Russell Ballard's book, *Counseling with Our Councils* (Deseret Book, 1997). I paid particular attention to everything he wrote regarding engaging the women leaders of the "auxiliary organizations" in our wards and stake as significant contributors in every feasible meeting. I encouraged each female leader that I called to serve to speak out and contribute. I taught everyone in our council meetings to value the voices of women. I doggedly ensured that every general discussion in these meetings began with the viewpoint of the women on the council. I watched with joy as those women, feeling empowered, flourished as strong and capable leaders. I began to study the importance of what had occurred as we enjoyed this brilliant, balanced leadership in our stake, filled with mutual respect and enormous creativity and energy.

I supported all the women of the stake by being present at every stake Relief Society meeting and activity. I also attended ward Relief Society meetings at every annual ward conference, totaling sixty or so times. I felt the Holy Ghost, belonging, love, and sisterhood in these meetings.

The women of the stake marveled that their priesthood leader was so devoted to them. To me, it only felt right, not just ecclesiastically but personally. I considered the stake and ward Relief Society presidents to be my equals in the administration of these units, standing beside me in just as important of a position as my two counselors. The women understood the families of the units like no one else. I learned their language, the language of the charitable heart.

I often stood up in stake priesthood meetings and taught the men what I had learned from serving alongside the women of the stake, sometimes taking them to task over things they needed to change to do better. Our general stake conferences almost always had more women and young women speak than men. They delivered powerful sermons and deeply touching experiences.

Sometime in the middle of my service as stake president, I attended a stake humanitarian quilting activity. Unbeknownst to me during the activity, each of the nine wards of the stake made an extra square to stitch together in a quilt for me. At the end of the activity, as I admired the many quilts the women had made to donate, I was overwhelmed with love when they surprised me with my own quilt—a fantastic representation of the combined faith of the nine wards of women I served. At the quilt's center was the beautifully embroidered Relief Society logo and motto, "Charity Never Faileth." That quilt hung prominently in the living room of my home for years.

15

Serving Under a Swinging Pendulum

In late 2004, Carl Heinz assigned me another group of projects to manage besides temples. The director of our department's Special Projects Division was retiring after leading the construction of the church's Conference Center and other one-of-a-kind construction projects. On this new special projects assignment, I was to direct both design and construction, which came as a shock but was also a source of excitement to me because the First Presidency had recently approved the renovation and structural strengthening of the famous "Mormon Tabernacle" on downtown Salt Lake City's Temple Square. Although it represented much more work, I felt thrilled and honored to have a design role in preserving such an iconic building, initially completed in 1867 under church president Brigham Young's direction.

There were times, however, when the pressure of guiding this and other extensive programs got to me. I felt I had to be highly aggressive to move things along to keep the assignment's pace. The contract architect for that project, my friend Roger Jackson, told me later that I could sometimes be a real "hard ass."

In the twenty-four months of the tabernacle project, we retrofitted it to withstand earthquakes, removed its underground baptistry and built three recording studios beneath the main floor, replaced its plumbing, reinforced and repaired its oval-shaped ceiling, built a music library and new dressing rooms for the famed Tabernacle

Choir, and remodeled the rostrum so that it could be reconfigured from choir seating to a performance stage as needed.

Over the months of this extensive renovation, the Presiding Bishopric and I frequently met with the First Presidency to provide updates. In one of these meetings, I showed a photograph of the new lath anchored to the enormous, nineteenth-century wooden roof trusses. As I described how workers would later re-plaster the lath ceiling, President Hinckley stopped me to ask, "What type of screw are you using on the lath? We don't want that ceiling coming down."

"That's right, sir. I don't know what kind of screw, but I'll be glad to find out."

"How can we not know these things?" Hinckley demanded of me once again, glowering.

The next time I was in the tabernacle, I spotted an open box of screws on the balcony floor. A nearby workman confirmed that these were the ones we used to attach the lath, so I pocketed a few in my suit jacket and carried them around for three weeks. At the start of my next presentation, I broke protocol, walked up to where President Hinckley was seated, and set the screws on the table before him. Returning to my spot, I reminded him he had asked me about the screws.

"Why, that's just the same grabber screw I used to install the wallboard in my home," President Hinckley exclaimed.

"Yes, sir, but we're using several hundred thousand of them," I quipped with a smile.

The president then made us aware of just how familiar he was with grabber screws.

After almost every report on the renovation process, Hinckley reminded us, "I just want my old tabernacle back, only strengthened." After two years of invasive construction, it was a great day when we completed the project and could finally walk the church president through the renovated tabernacle. I felt a mixture of pride and humility as I watched him walk up to the pulpit, grasp the podium, and gaze upon the refreshed, 3,500 seat hall. He was smiling with a gleam in his eye as he returned to this spot, from where he had heard and preached the word for nearly a century.

I then brought him down to the main floor and the first row of the new, oak pews. On my recommendation, he had decided to

The renovated Salt Lake Tabernacle (center), rededicated in 2007. From left to right in the background are the Conference Center, the Church History Library, the Relief Society Building, the Salt Lake Temple, and the Church Office Building tower.

remove the historic pine pews—dating back to the tabernacle's 1860s construction and artfully painted to look like oak by early Mormon artisans—and replace them with larger, actual oak pews of similar design. Sitting on one of them, he exclaimed, "They're just as hard as the old ones."

"Yes, but now there is no chance of anyone getting lead paint poisoning, and they will require far less maintenance," I replied, repeating these points from our original proposal.

Though he was in his nineties, President Hinckley continued vigorously pushing forward his ambitious building program. To revitalize an aging downtown Salt Lake City, in late 2006 he announced the construction of the City Creek Center, a for-profit, mixed-use, shopping, living, and dining development on two church-owned blocks adjacent to church headquarters. The design and construction of this massive project caused significant personnel disruption to our Physical Facilities Department. Several church architects and project managers were transferred to this project for its five-year undertaking, including my colleague, the director of temple design.

To fill the now-vacant position, I proposed to Carl Heinz that that role be added to my duties, making me the director of the temple construction and design divisions. Organizational tension had existed between these two divisions, and I hoped that if I oversaw both of them, I could unify all the staff and thereby increase collaboration and efficiency. I had long desired to be on the design side of temples. The Presiding Bishopric approved this recommendation, and my workload doubled.

Almost immediately after the Salt Lake Tabernacle's rededication in April 2007, the Presiding Bishopric assigned our recently combined division a new special project. For many years, the offices and archives of the church's enormous Church History Department were located in the East Wing of the Church Office Building. The department was outgrowing this limited space, and the historical archive needed to be updated to modern preservation standards. The First Presidency approved the construction of a new Church History Library across the street from the Conference Center and the Church Office Building. The facility would house state-of-the-art archival space, a public-friendly research library, and departmental offices. The massive undertaking included an underground tunnel connecting the new building to other office buildings at church headquarters. At its 2009 dedication, Presiding Bishop Burton first referred to me as the "chief architect of the church."

All my success certainly didn't mean that I was without flaws. On one unfortunate occasion, I committed to a completion date for a temple under construction that the Office of the First Presidency would use to schedule that temple's dedication date. Once scheduled and announced, these dates were fixed. When my project manager learned of the date, he and his file manager came into my office and described how the completion could not occur by the date I had given for completion. Losing my composure over our communication breakdown, I shouted at him, berating and accusing him of lying and misleading me. None of which was true. I severely overreacted to the challenge this created. In hindsight, I realize I was responding in a manner modeled for me by men of authority I had known, including my dad and former boss in Albany.

I had to report the mistake to my file leaders and eat crow, knowing the temple would not be ready as I committed. I eventually apologized to my guys in all sincerity for how I reacted. I was wrong and genuinely regretted the injury I caused these good men. I vowed not to let work pressures make me do that to someone again. I kept the experience close to my heart. Years later, when I would closely examine the flaws in my makeup, this incident burned brightly on my conscience.

A few months after the completion of the Salt Lake Tabernacle renovation, I did examine one thing that, at the time, I saw as a personal flaw. I sought the courage to rid myself of my periodic temptation to dress in female clothing secretly. I don't think I was even actually dressing at that time. I just knew I still had the desire to do so, and I wanted to forsake or "cross myself in all these things," as the Book of Mormon prophet Alma taught. I determined, as awkward as it was, to go to my ward bishop (whom I supervised as his stake president) and, for the first time, confess my long-term struggles with what I then only referred to as "dressing." At that point, I was not aware of the terms "transgender," "gender identity," or "gender presentation."

I entered my bishop's office and sat across from him, where he was now sitting in the chair I had previously occupied when I was bishop. I had confidence in this good man. I had called him as a bishop and trained him accordingly. He was also a licensed therapist, so I hoped he would have insight into what drove me to feel and think as I did.

I described my situation as best I could, summarizing my childhood and teen experiences, my determination at eighteen to stop forever pretending that I could ever be a girl, and then my occasional slipping back into these desires throughout my adult life. It was the first time I had mentioned these things to *anyone.* It felt good to finally say it aloud to someone. When I concluded, he sat there stunned, almost without words. He fumblingly admitted that he had no answers to offer me. I recognized he was in a problematic place. He couldn't confer with his stake president about what to do in such a situation because his stake president was me.

I never considered reaching out to a higher-ranking church leader at that time. Through my professional and ecclesiastical years of service in the church, my trust in the general leaders had become jaded. I returned home from my bishop's office satisfied on only one level. I had finally told another human being of my inner struggle, my bishop, but I still felt alone in my concern about my desire for the feminine.

In that same summer of 2007, as I worked to get my bearings in temple design and to overcome the perception of architects and designers that I was "just a construction guy," I received an invitation to meet with Presiding Bishop H. David Burton. He explained that President Hinckley met with him privately and asked for work to resume on the standard plans for small temples. Since the completion of the 100th temple in the year 2000, temple designs had drifted away from Hinckley's original concept of smaller, more spartan temples, again becoming more extensive and complex.

President Hinckley wanted us to incorporate the lessons learned from the first set of smaller temples into new plans for use worldwide. But this time, we were to proceed deliberately and not in haste, and the Temple Department must not know anything about what we were doing. We had learned their concerns before and could adjust without their influence. Once Bishop Burton was satisfied with our new design, he would share the plans privately with President Hinckley for his approval. We dutifully agreed and returned to our offices to figure out how to be covert, even though our colleagues from the Temple Department frequently met with us at our desks.

I proposed a design competition amongst my staff to create concepts for four temple configurations, each adhering to a list of limited rooms and functions, with an eye to optimum efficiency. When we reviewed all the proposals as a group and selected the four strongest, we awarded each winner the responsibility of leading the team to develop further the concepts to present to President Hinckley. This effort brought my staff together in collaboration, unlike what they had ever experienced in the Church Office Building, and won me their respect as the leader of the design division.

Once President Hinckley approved our plans, he asked us to beta-test our ideas on the next temple he planned to announce, which would be in Gila Valley, Arizona. We knew we needed to measure and report our quality, cost, and timeliness metrics compared to recently completed temples.

I was excited about what we would accomplish for the church president. But Gordon B. Hinckley died at age ninety-seven in January 2008, four months before the Gila Valley temple was announced. Completed in 2010, the temple was built at one-third of the cost and in one-third of the time required by other recent temples of the same capacity. It was a huge success, and the Presiding Bishopric congratulated us. We proved we could build three temples for the price the church was paying for one and in much less time.

However, the new church president, Thomas S. Monson, showed no interest in our results. Instead, he began his leadership by explaining his conviction that the church would always have enough funds to build temples. The message was clear. Our designs no longer needed to be particularly economical or efficient, and no two temples were required to look the same.

"What moron made that decision?" President Monson had boomed indignantly when he was told about the reduced specifications for the Gila Valley temple. *I* was that moron, along with my staff and consultants, acting under the explicit direction of President Monson's predecessor, and our choices were appropriate given the criterion President Hinckley assigned to us. As I opened my mouth to respond, to his credit, Keith B. McMullin of the Presiding Bishopric spoke up and shouldered the responsibility for the decision. As we sat through Monson's scathing lecture, I was grateful for a church leader who protected his staff.

We walked back to Bishop McMullin's office in silence. After we got there, he looked down at his desk for a while in contemplation, then, looking up at me, said, "David, my boy, sometimes in this church, you can be right and still be wrong."

Building larger, more elegant temples wasn't the only position that President Monson was vigorously taking. In that same summer of 2008, he and other top church leaders called on Mormons in California to donate their time and resources to campaign for the passage of Proposition 8, which would overturn the California Supreme Court's recent ruling ensuring the legality of same-sex marriage in the state. The church's efforts to help pass Prop 8 became a full-court press and a bonafide loyalty test for its members, especially those in California. Although I had not yet accepted my

LGBT identity as a transgender individual, I believed firmly in justice for all and equality before the law.

We in Utah were not exempt from both the negative media coverage and hostile rhetoric from the church associated with Prop 8. At our quarterly Coordinating Council Meetings—a gathering of the stake presidents to coordinate activities, mediated by an assigned regional church leader called an "Area Seventy"— Prop 8 was the focus. Rather than a collaborative discussion amongst stake presidents, as we had previously enjoyed, our Area Seventy now lectured us for ninety minutes. He parroted what top church general leaders said regarding the need for the church to support Prop 8 and safeguard the "sanctity of marriage" as explained in the 1995 Family Proclamation.

I did not feel the Holy Spirit in this and other meetings like it. Instead, I felt grossly offended. The Seventy told us it was our solemn duty to return to our stakes and repeat all of this as we had received it, convince our members to donate money generously to this cause, and call any of their friends and relatives in California to persuade them to do everything they could to pass Prop 8.

Unlike any meetings I had attended before or since, I felt physically ill during those brutal lectures. I wanted to run from the room to avoid hearing the hate but didn't because it was in my nature to absorb the bad but not pass it along.

I found myself leaning on what Elder Tingey taught when he called me as stake president three years before. I held all the authority to direct the church's work in my stake. I felt a deepening responsibility to be guided by personal revelation to do what we did in our stake. I rarely called headquarters for advice, and I never sought direction from whichever Area Seventy had oversight of the stakes in our valley. I didn't need anyone to report to. I understood that no one else held the authority to know what God wanted to be done in our corner of Tooele. I wasn't afraid to ask God, to listen closely, and to act accordingly.

I determined I would never utter one word about Prop 8 to anyone in my stake, to my counselors, or even to my wife. I would not stain our stake's pulpits with this venom. And I never did.

California voters passed Proposition 8 in their elections that fall, but it was overturned less than two years later after a federal judge ruled it unconstitutional. I was satisfied that Prop 8 was never a topic of discussion in our stake. By following my conscience and directly disobeying a charge, I kept myself and our people unsullied and our stake safer for queer folk, at least for a while.

But at work, I strove to follow President Monson's direction regarding temple building. I discovered a quotation from the church's second president, Brigham Young, when he contemplated building other temples in addition to the Salt Lake Temple, which was then under construction. It essentially said he enquired of the Lord, who responded that he made the flowers and grasses of the fields in all their varieties. Therefore, no two temples need to be the same, either.

Our design teams interpreted Brigham Young's statement to mean that each temple could take its general styling cues from prominent architectural, artistic, and cultural motifs. This was professionally stimulating, and we relished the opportunity to build in contextually appropriate ways. We also wanted to create temples that appeared to have always existed, conveying a sense of timelessness and permanence.

The most obvious example of the difference between Presidents Hinckley and Monson's approaches can be seen in the development of the Philadelphia Pennsylvania Temple. Announced by President Monson six months after he announced the Gila Valley Temple, Philadelphia could have been a repeat of the Gila Valley standard model, constructed on a modest suburban site owned by the church. Instead, the new First Presidency directed us to find a downtown Philadelphia site where the temple could be prominently featured.

After a lengthy search by our real estate and design teams and working closely with the city government, the church purchased two large urban redevelopment sites on Vine Street across from Philadelphia's downtown Catholic Cathedral. The location was fraught with numerous constraints, including a requirement for a historically sensitive design and a mandate that the Angel Moroni statue that tops the steeple of most LDS temples could stand no higher than the cross that topped the cathedral.

The resultant temple we designed is a masterpiece of classically inspired architecture. The church also purchased a site opposite the temple to prevent the area from being developed in a manner incongruent with the temple's spiritual nature. On that property, as director of the Special Projects Division, I led the design and construction of two neighboring buildings—a new stake center and a 264-unit residential tower.

The Philadelphia temple had the same capacity as the small model originally planned for the rural site and served a similar number of church members. Ultimately, the church spent much more funds on this entire downtown development. President Monson's philosophies were music to the ears of the leaders of the Temple Department, who were insulted that we had developed the new small temple standard floor plan without their input. They took every opportunity to influence President Monson to increase their role in interpreting the First Presidency's mind and will regarding temples. Their department despised the Gila Valley Temple due to its origin story. With the passing of the church president who had directed its creation, we were defenseless against challenges to our capability to do the design work which church leaders had entrusted to us. Temples developed under President Monson's tenure grew ever more extensive and elaborate. There was continual pressure to increase each temple's exquisite beauty. President Monson's years represented the extreme of striving for the highest temple design and appointment level. We entered the era my colleague Roger Jackson of FFKR Architects referred to as "the golden age of temple design" because more gold was expended than in any previous season of temple building.

There would be only one more attempt to apply the valuable lessons tested in Gila Valley. In the late summer of 2008, discussions were underway in confidential circles about the site selection for a temple to be built in Kansas City, Missouri. This would be a singularly sensitive project. The church's founder, Joseph Smith, established the church's headquarters or "Zion" in that area in the 1830s, declaring that Jackson County, Missouri, was the center place for gathering the Latter-day Saints before the second coming of Jesus. The sign of these events would be the construction of the temple Smith planned to build there.

Although mob violence forced Smith and his followers to abandon their land holdings in Missouri, the origin prophecies regarding the eventual return of church members to western Missouri have remained the stuff of legend among the most ardent of LDS faithful.

In 2008, the First Presidency was concerned that the announcement of a new temple in Western Missouri might trigger an unintentional furor of gathering to "Zion" and prepping for the end of times. They directed our department to research all former land records and report to the First Presidency that the anticipated site for the new Kansas City Temple had never been a part of Jackson County, lest some of the church's most zealous members would misinterpret this as the fulfillment of prophecy.

As I sat in my office one afternoon with one of my temple architects, discussing the design approach for the Kansas City Temple, he suggested we adopt and modify the recently completed Twin Falls, Idaho, temple plans. I felt impressed that there was a better answer. A different solution was needed in Missouri. Over the previous year, he and I had led a team looking at creating period-appropriate new buildings for a planned expansion of church educational and public-use facilities in Nauvoo, a prophetic priority of previous church president Hinckley. We carefully analyzed every possible archetype of early LDS architecture to influence our potential designs.

With that background in mind, I turned to my whiteboard. I traced out the silhouette of a multi-story temple with two towers, one front and one back, based on the footprint and proportions of the nineteenth-century LDS temples like Logan and Manti in Utah. I told my colleague that no reuse of a modern design would do here. We would propose the historic two-tower form for this historically significant location. This temple form hadn't been used in over a century.

The completed Kansas City Temple demonstrates the effort's success. In the following years, many adaptations of the two-tower form, such as the Philadelphia and Rome temples, were used.

Despite President Monson's heightened expectations for elegance and historically authentic design, the lessons I learned from President Hinckley's Gila Valley-type standard plans to maximize the value of the structure and mechanical systems of the temples, those things Bishop Burton often called "The Invisible Arts," remained with me. I also profoundly believed what President Hinckley had taught, that the temple exists to provide the ordinances. Nothing about its design or appointment should cause a feeling of dissonance or distract from the focus on the spirit and teachings of the ordinances. There was a great deal to balance within our work. I decided that to do so successfully, our design and construction division had to learn to work collaboratively with our counterparts in the Temple Department and do away with the adverse effects of organizational tension between us that had previously hampered the work.

To achieve this, I initiated what became a vital component of the temple design process. I held design team meetings every Tuesday around the conference table in my office. The meeting functioned like a church council in which we prayed to have the guiding influence of the Holy Spirit, with me serving as presiding officer and two men from the Temple Department as my counselors.

Each temple design team presented their sketches and visuals for review and discussion. This meeting might last four to six hours, depending upon the volume of work to review. Each design team received clear, coordinated, and approved direction they needed to advance their projects. By doing this, I significantly leveraged my impact on each project, ensuring they were progressing efficiently and in a direction that met the expectations of all our church leaders.

We set and tracked aggressive design schedules, from the First Presidency's announcement of a new temple to their approval of its exterior and plan design, closely monitoring and reporting our progress. The quantity and quality of design work produced during those five years are incredible.

A year after construction of the Kansas City temple started, President Monson announced a temple for Brigham City, Utah, on a city site across from the historic Brigham City Tabernacle. The announcement of this particular temple raised another complex dynamic. Oversight of temple design and construction rested solely with the First Presidency. Members of the Quorum of the Twelve Apostles, who had other specific duties, did not participate in the temple process. But in this case, the president of the quorum at the time was Boyd K. Packer, a Brigham City native who, as a youth, attended school on the grounds where this new temple would be built.

I attended an early planning meeting of the First Presidency when the concern came to light. President Henry B. Eyring, one of President

Monson's two counselors, asked him what role President Packer might have regarding this particular temple. The tension in the room mounted. Everyone knew of the long and somewhat strained relationship between Monson and Packer, two very different church leaders. In a lovely act of grace, President Monson asked several of us to arrange to visit with President Packer to seek his input regarding the temple.

"Your assignment in being there is to listen to President Packer and only take notes. You are not to speak." The commanding tone in Bishopric Second Counselor Keith B. McMullin's voice conveyed the importance of his instruction to me. "I understand," was the only acceptable response. By this point in my roles of working with senior church leaders and directing temple design and construction (I had worked with Bishop McMullin for ten years), the "Brethren" had enough confidence in me to allow me to be present in such a meeting.

The unique circumstance of my role was soon reinforced when I received a phone call in which a woman on the line asked if I would hold for President Henry B. Eyring.

"Brother Hall, you are aware that the design and construction of temples is the sole purview of the First Presidency?"

"Of course, President," I replied.

"Fine, so you will report all direction you may receive from President Packer to the First Presidency immediately."

"Yes."

My role was tightly constricted: listen, take notes, do not speak, receive direction but don't implement it, and somehow return and report to both parties, even if the ultimate direction from the First Presidency was contradictory to President Packer's. The only chance for success was a truly inspired design solution that all would agree upon.

President Packer was known for loathing modern architectural design. He was a strict historicist and classicist, not only in architecture but also in his worldview. He was outspoken and strongly influenced church policy and practices over the previous fifteen years.

Bishop McMullin instructed me to bring photos of a handful of existing temples he planned to show President Packer. I was worried that all the pictures of the temples McMullin asked me to bring were modern designs.

As I prepared this packet of photos, I felt impressed to slip into the

Dedicated in 1999, the Columbia South Carolina Temple (top left), is representative of the dozens of nearly identical temples built as part of President Hinckley's small temple program. The historically designed Kansas City Missouri Temple (top right), and Brigham City Utah Temple (bottom left), both dedicated in 2012. The Philadelphia Pennsylvania Temple, dedicated in 2016.

back of my folder one that McMullin had not asked me to show—a rendering of the then-under-construction Kansas City temple, purposefully designed with proportions and characteristics reminiscent of nineteenth-century Mormon temples. I knew logically I would not have the chance to show this one, but I brought it anyway.

The First Presidency assigned Bishop McMullin; Elder William R. Walker, Executive Director of the Temple Department (also a neighbor and former stake president of President Packer); and me to meet with President Packer. I felt my senior colleagues' heightened anxiety as we walked from the Church Office Building to the nearby

Church Administration Building, where President Packer and other top church leaders have offices.

It was immediately apparent how intimidated these two seasoned General Authorities were as we met with the man who, based on his seniority, was next in line to be the church president. The eighty-five-year-old Packer was sitting in his wheelchair at a small, round table in his spacious, wood-paneled corner office, and they each took a chair on either side of him. Last to sit down, I was in the chair directly across from President Packer. Strangely, this put me in the position to lead the meeting, not just take notes.

As McMullin and Walker introduced the subject of the Brigham City temple, they seemed more than just respectful, but even fearful of their host. They asked me to produce the assigned photographs one at a time as they described each temple. They were pretty common temple forms, with end spires and a center spire, all detailed in something I'll call "Mormon Moderne." The presentation went quickly, without President Packer uttering a single word. But the look on President Packer's face and his body language as he slumped uncomfortably in his wheelchair spoke volumes. He was not impressed by our current temples at all.

The men whom I accompanied sat in embarrassed silence. At that moment, I had to decide if I possessed the courage to follow the impression I had and violate the specific instructions I had been given not to speak. Catching Bishop McMullin's gaze, I whispered, "May I show one more?" Out of options, he nodded almost imperceptibly.

I pulled out the rendering of the Kansas City temple and handed it across the table to President Packer. He hadn't touched any of the other temple photos but picked up this one and studied it intently, holding it close to his eyes. As he set it back on the table, on top of all the others, he began speaking to me as though we were alone. He talked with me about how nearly perfect this design was for Brigham City. A smile came across his face as he said, "This will do nicely but with nine bays of windows instead of these seven." He took a pen from his coat pocket and sketched on the image an extended side wall of the temple by two additional bays. "Can we do this?"

"Yes, of course, President," I answered. He continued to discuss his thoughts regarding the temple with me while the two General

Authorities sat on either side, silently listening. In conclusion, Packer requested that I be permitted to return and share with him the design as it progressed.

Walking back to the Church Office Building, I apologized for going contrary to specific instructions. But these two relieved and humbled General Authorities assured their newly empowered architect that no apology was needed. The meeting was successful beyond their expectations.

We reported back to members of the First Presidency, who were also appreciative. They assigned me to continue periodically returning, unaccompanied, to share the temple's design and construction progress with President Packer. I met with him numerous times, which was a unique, additional step for this particular temple. When I shared with him the final images that we had prepared to go forward to the First Presidency for approval, he excitedly called out to his administrative assistant in the next room, "Sister Thompson, please ask Russ, Dallin, and the other Russ, Tom, and Jeff, to come to my office now."

I rose to my feet as Elders Russell M. Nelson, Dallin H. Oaks, M. Russell Ballard, L. Tom Perry, and Jeffery R. Holland—the next five apostles in seniority—entered the room and gathered around me, admiring the presentation boards I held. President Packer described each room of the proposed temple to them, and they were all very complimentary.

During the temple's construction period, as I continued to meet with President Packer to share progress photos, he never let me finish without asking if it would be completed before he died. It was obvious that he viewed the completion of this temple, in his birthplace and youthful home, as one of the crowning events of his long life. I assured him we were proceeding with all dispatch. Near the end of construction, he grew contemplative when he saw photos of the nearly completed building. Finally, he offered with reverence, "This temple is to the Great Salt Lake Temple as the Son is to the Father." This was the most sacred compliment that President Packer, author of the book, *The Holy Temple,* could have ever made to me.[1]

Ultimately, we completed the Brigham City temple on time. In a second great kindness, President Monson assigned President Packer to preside over the temple's dedicatory sessions. Usually, the church president bears that privilege.

Coincidentally, it was during the time of these meetings with Packer that I would finally come out as transgender to myself and many others. I often wondered what perceptions President Packer, whom I had worked so closely with, might now have about me. One month after the Brigham City temple dedication, he led a discussion in a joint meeting of the First Presidency and Quorum of the Twelve in the temple to decide whether to release me as stake president. President Packer then went on to live nearly three more years. The Church History Department asked me for an oral history of my experience working with President Packer on the design of this temple. It was initially available online, but I can no longer find it.

However successful I was as a church architect, church leaders did not always heed my insights. As we were nearing completion of the design of the Rome Italy Temple, I took a team back to Europe to conduct a construction manager/general contractor search. We had previously conducted a similar search across eleven major cities in five different countries to locate the construction manager who was then completing the Kyiv Ukraine Temple, which was reportedly the most corrupt place to do business in the world. In repeating the process for Rome, we revisited many of the same firms, including those working for us in Kyiv, along with a pair of Italian companies.

Our team sought proposals from those interested in building the temple in Rome. In the end, three submitted proposals representing a wide range of bid costs. An Italian firm came in lowest. The next lowest, but still substantially higher, was a bid from the Kyiv temple's construction manager, an Austrian firm. The third proposal was even significantly higher than the second.

Immediately upon learning the identity of the low proposal, several of our trusted colleagues in Italy recommended that we carefully investigate this contractor on suspicion of issues surrounding unethical and unprofessional practices. We did so, and I shared some red flags with my managing director and the Presiding Bishopric. After lengthy discussions, I strongly recommend that the church not hire the low bidder but instead go with our successful and proven Austrian firm. They were outstanding to work with and performed with the highest integrity despite the corrupt conditions in which they worked in Ukraine.

The Presiding Bishopric pushed back because of the sizeable difference in the bid cost. Ultimately, I refused to implement their final decision with more energy than I had defended any previous proposal. The difficulty of working with the low bidder would likely eradicate any difference in the first cost. I was caught off guard by what happened next. My managing director informed me that after eight years, I was no longer the director of temple construction. One of my staff was assigned to take that role. The Bishopric specifically directed him to put the low bidder under contract and get the Rome temple started, which he did. I retained directorship of temple design and watched what occurred in Rome from the sidelines.

It was far worse than I could have imagined. Work began slowly, but the temple construction experienced several failed inspections, and complete tear-outs and rebuilds were needed. Financial challenges arose and progress ground to a halt. Then a protracted battle ensued to remove the contracted construction manager from the project, requiring the church's project manager to take over the Italian subcontractors. However, few subs were interested in working for a foreign manager.

Eventually, in desperation, the church hired several full-time personnel to relocate to Italy as expatriates to supervise the languishing project until completion. Construction of the Rome temple took nine years—three times as long as we needed to complete that responsibility in Ukraine in an arguably more challenging business environment. I never knew the final cost of the Rome effort, but I know the second bid had been exceeded even when the church severed ties with the original constructor.

It remains incredibly frustrating to have known what was best and to be ignored. To count the cost in excess funds, years, and lives impacted, all of which could have been avoided.

I learned that the pendulum of church leader policy and decisions swung above our heads like the sword of Damocles. I put my head down and focused on my assignment until the next swing came.

Notes

1. Boyd K. Packer, *The Holy Temple* (Bookcraft, 1980).

16

From Ashes to Authenticity

"A massive fire destroyed the Provo Tabernacle, a historic building that has been a landmark in Provo for more than a century."

Hearing this news report on the radio made December 17, 2010, a day I'll never forget.

Marleen and I were driving to Snow College in southeastern Utah to pack up our daughter Liz, who had just completed her associate's degree. Liz was leaving in January to serve an eighteen-month mission at the Los Angeles Temple Visitors' Center.

"What do you suppose happened?" Marleen asked as we listened to the news story.

"I really can't imagine," I thought aloud, thinking of my colleagues in the Meetinghouse Facilities Department (MFD) who were stewards over the building. "I hope this wasn't a mistake on MFD's part."

Curious, we stopped in downtown Provo on our way south to check out the fire. Though Provo City safety officers prevented anyone from getting too close to the tabernacle, we could see the heavy, dark smoke roiling into the sky.

"Did you ever attend meetings there when you were at BYU?" I asked Marleen.

"We attended a stake conference there and a Christmas concert around this time of the year," she replied.

"From what I can see, the fire has destroyed the tabernacle," I said sadly.

Provo LDS Tabernacle engulfed in flames, December 17, 2010.
Courtesy *Provo Daily Herald*. Laura Rowley, photographer.

We continued to Snow College, where we packed up Liz's things. On our drive home the next day, we went with her to the nearby Manti temple so she could receive her temple endowment rites in preparation for her becoming a full-time missionary.

Our time in the temple with Liz was delightful. As was often the case, I was as focused on the temple's historical murals and architectural details as on the sacred religious ceremony. The temple was not busy, so after the ceremony, one of the temple workers escorted us on a relaxed tour of the rest of the venerable, historic building, which Mormon settlers built in 1888.

I received surprising news on the Monday morning following the fire. The Presiding Bishopric asked my Temple Design Division, instead of the Facilities Management Division, to take stewardship of the remains of the 1898 tabernacle, stabilize the shell of what was left, collaborate with city officials, and determine if the remains of the building could be saved. The assignment made sense because my workgroup had led the reconstruction and seismic stabilization of the Salt Lake Tabernacle on Temple Square just a few years earlier. I felt a thrill and a sense of confidence at the opportunity to work on another iconic and historic building. In 2004, when the Presiding Bishopric assigned me to oversee the renovation of the Salt Lake Tabernacle, I lacked confidence. That assignment seemed to present a much higher chance of being a career-ending project than a career-building one. This time, it would be different.

Within days, our construction personnel erected the scaffolding-like framework to stabilize the brick walls of the Provo Tabernacle. A shell of the building was all that remained. There was legitimate concern that any seismic movement or strong winds could cause even more loss. Once the contractors stabilized the walls, various teams went to work to investigate the remains. The Provo City fire marshal's office searched for the cause of the fire. Insurance adjusters were anxious to know the extent of the loss. Our team hoped to salvage and document any existing elements that might aid our design process. Church historians were desperate to observe what they could before the remains were gone. The public clamored for answers about the fire's cause and what the church intended to do with the remains of the beloved building. All the while, church leaders anxiously waited for our team's report on the viability of preserving what was left.

My first walkthrough of the tabernacle's ruins came on a frigid, bright morning just after the New Year. By then, the fire marshal had determined that the lighting, which had been left on overnight, had overheated and sparked flames in the attic structure. The inferno caused the roof to collapse, crushing the mezzanine balcony, organ, and rostrum below. A beautiful, sacred building, now hollow, was all but lost.

The winding stairway in the southeast corner turret was the only one of four still usable, so we ascended it and looked out across the scene from what would have been the attic access door. The smoldering debris had been soaked with hundreds of thousands of gallons of water for several days to extinguish the fire completely. January's freezing temperatures turned the debris pile into a solid block of muddled ice ten to twelve feet high. Deep within the ice lay the answers to all our questions.

Simultaneously, in my personal life, I was embarking on a new quest to find answers frozen deep within myself, hoping to rediscover what brought me peace and joy.

The previous month, I had suffered from an awful stomach virus that led to a series of life-changing events. Unable to keep anything down for several days, I became dehydrated and realized my bowels were not moving. Excruciating pain forced me into the local hospital, where I remained for four days. The doctors could find nothing wrong with me and sent me home without answers.

Back home, I attempted to eat a little to regain my strength, but whatever I ate only brought more severe abdominal pain. That weekend was our stake conference, and I was still serving as stake president. I arranged for my counselors to cover the afternoon meetings, but I dressed and attended the evening session of the conference, where I was scheduled to speak.

Sitting on the stand as the presiding officer, I was in agony. When it was my time to speak, I stood and white-knuckle grasped the pulpit, resting my forearms on it to maintain my balance. I was cramping so severely as I spoke that I feared I might pass out. Such was my devotion to my church service. When I finished and sat down, I felt satisfied that I had given my full measure of strength to accomplish my assignment.

The next day, when my condition only worsened, Marleen decided I needed to go to Salt Lake City's Intermountain Medical Center. "We're not sure what's going on, but we're going to start you on an NG tube," an ER doctor there told me. I had no idea what an NG tube was, but I was glad they were taking some action, unlike the doctors at the smaller hospital back in Tooele. "We'll just insert this tube into your nostril and down your throat into your stomach so we can empty you. As you feel it enter your throat, try to swallow several times to help lead it down."

I tried to hide my terror with a joke. "Then I suppose NG stands for 'No Good,' right?" The nurse told me I took it well, but the insertion made me gag and was horrible.

I found myself confined again to a hospital bed for the next five days. Only this time, I was attached to an IV and the NG tube linked to a vacuum line, which removed my stomach and upper intestines' contents into a quart-sized, clear canister mounted on the wall above my bed. "Our scans cannot see anything besides your colon tissue," a doctor told me. "There is no physical blockage. Our hunch is that your colon collapsed. We won't know for sure unless we take a look via surgery. But first, let's wait a few days and keep you emptied. Then perhaps the colon will relax and open back up independently."

That was the best these doctors had. I needed to stay put and give it time. So I was frequently left alone in my hospital room to rest, think, and contemplate if surgery was my next step.

I thought a lot. I had been rather grumpy while in the Tooele hospital, which I regretted. I have always believed that though we seldom choose our challenges, we can choose how we respond to them. Even though I now found myself as miserable as I think I have ever been, I decided I wanted to be the best, kindest, and most patient person I had ever been.

I spent the next several days in the hospital peeling back, like the layers of an onion, my attitude toward everything in my life. If I could choose to be my best self even in these extreme circumstances, I could commit to doing so every day. My task became clear. I needed to identify and remove all harmful elements of my character while safeguarding the good, performing a deep assessment of whatever should be repaired, strengthened, or rediscovered.

Confined for days, I had ample time and space to look inward. I realized there was a lot about myself I did not like. I admitted I was often angry, prone to speak harshly, unduly demanding, generally ill at ease with myself and others, and frankly without peace. I reflected on the many times I had treated others poorly.

I did not know at that time where my self-assessment would take me. When the doctors finally pronounced me free to leave, I went home only with the conviction that inner changes had to come. I committed to finding the root causes behind my untoward demeanor and doing the work to become a new me and live in peace. I was ready, if necessary, to burn down to the ground any part of my life. Should I have been asked at the time, I could not have said who or what the new me was. Would I have had the courage to say the words even if I had known what they were?

Journaling helped me recognize things about myself that felt wrong, such as how I dealt with conflict or pressure, which were unhealthy and which I needed to mitigate. I looked deep into the contents of my personal "shell" to discover what characteristics I wanted to keep and which I could build upon.

I also began writing a "fictional" narrative. The protagonist was a talented young designer named Laurie Corridoio. (The Italian family I worked for at the pizza parlor during high school had given me the nickname of *Corridoio*—Italian for "hallway.") The story unfolded details of Laurie's childhood and teen years with family, followed by college and young adulthood. Although I pretended to myself that I was writing fiction, several chapters in, I had to admit that I was writing my own fantasy story of my life if I lived it as Laurie. Like falling bricks, it hit me that Laurie's life was much happier than mine, even though the context of her story was the same as mine. She grew up free from the sadness and anxiety of hiding her true self and struggling with constant gender conflict. I envied her peace.

In writing this story, I had inadvertently exhumed my female gender identity from where it had been buried, laid it bare in front of me, and walked through her life for several months as she revealed her story. I felt a powerfully peaceful connection to the Laurie in the story. This female identity I then knew so little about seemed to be the new me I was seeking.

Though I had convinced myself for three decades that I had forever buried my awareness of being female, my true self was surfacing again as I gave it permission to.

While traveling on work assignments in 2011, I started using my off-hours time in my hotel room to explore my female identity. Initially, I tried to understand what that even meant.

On a work trip to Winnipeg, I experienced an adrenaline rush when I went shopping in a local Walmart and purchased a few feminine clothing items. I traveled for work nearly once a month and looked forward to experimenting with different outfits for a few hours in my room each evening. Some outfits hung awfully on me or didn't fit, but others seemed passable.

Over time, my inventory of female clothing grew until I was packing as much for Laurie as I was for David. I neatly hid the feminine things on the bottom. Once when I was going through airport security with my work colleagues, we were all stopped as TSA agents thoroughly searched our bags. I felt mortified when, as everyone watched from a distance, all my clothes came out, male and female. I frantically debated in my head whether I should lie and claim that my wife must have left some of her clothing in the suitcase, or fess up and say, "They're mine. What of it?" Whether the agents or my traveling companions noticed or not I'll never know, but no one said a thing.

On one trip I brought a tube of lipstick I discreetly borrowed from Marleen's drawer of castoff makeup. Never in my life had I used makeup. It was a little thing, but something transformational happened when I stepped back from the mirror after applying her deep-red lipstick. It's difficult to describe, but it was so much more than just lip color. Whereas I had only ever seen versions of "David" in the mirror, now he was gone. For the very first time, I *saw* Laurie Lee! At that moment, I felt a spiritual joy. My heart raced and leaped with happiness as I saw this expression of my femininity. It felt like coming home to myself after wandering lost for more than half a century. Staring at my reflection, I drank in the feeling as my eyes and cheeks became wet with tears. I advanced toward the mirror and rubbed a little lipstick onto my cheeks.

In the following months, I experimented with different makeup. But nothing ever replaced that life-changing jolt I received when I saw myself wearing lipstick for the first time and felt entirely affirmed in both body and soul.

A favorite transwoman author of mine, Jennifer Finney Boylan, described the feeling this way: "For me, it has meant having a sense of myself as a woman, a sense that no matter how comfortable I was with [just] being feminine, I was never at ease with not being female. When I was young, I tried to talk myself out of it, telling myself, in short, to 'get over it.' But I never got over it.

"I compare it to a sense of homesickness for a place you've never been. The moment you stepped onto those supposedly unfamiliar shores, you'd have an understanding of overwhelming gratitude, solace, and joy. Home, you might think. I'm *finally home.*"[1]

But at work, I continued to present as male. After five months of investigation of what remained of the Provo Tabernacle, our team completed our assessment and report. I submitted the results to the Presiding Bishopric for them to present to the First Presidency. We reported that the building's shell was not a total loss but salvageable and could be preserved similarly to what we had done for the Salt Lake Tabernacle. We also offered new-build alternatives if church leadership decided not to reconstruct. Then we waited out several weeks of silence.

On June 26, 2011, I was in the midst of a week off at home when I received a phone call from Presiding Bishop David Burton. "The First Presidency is pleased with your report regarding the Provo Tabernacle," he told me. "They have a special request, which you must keep confidential, engaging only the smallest number of your staff possible. They want you to return and report if the tabernacle remains can be rebuilt into a *temple.*"

"Absolutely," was my response. I hung up the phone, awash with awe.

I was sitting at my bedroom desk, a solid maple table my grandparents used to provide breakfast to their bed-and-breakfast cottage guests on the coast of Maine in the 1950s and 60s. As I contemplated this new assignment, thoughts flooded my mind as they often did when challenged with a new project.

This time was different, however. I was sitting at my desk dressed as Laurie when I took the phone call! Marleen and our youngest daughter, Tatyana, were visiting our oldest son, Isaac, and his family in Idaho. I had taken advantage of the empty house, perhaps for the first time during daylight hours, to dress or "present" as Laurie as part of my effort to find my true self. At that point, I was still unsure if I was sinning by wearing women's clothing and making myself up this way. I feared I was cutting myself off from the companionship of the Holy Spirit, but I was about to discover that was not the case.

Unable to pause the rush of ideas, I found some drawing paper and went to work. The report we had submitted on the tabernacle was in my computer bag, giving me plenty of base drawings. The idea of putting the modern temple program into a historic LDS building was familiar. Our team had previously worked on several project ideas for the church's properties in Nauvoo, Illinois, for President Hinckley. I also led the designs of the new temples in Kansas City, Brigham City, and Philadelphia based on historic building forms. This latest assignment would be my first opportunity to apply all this

Discussing a design idea with a colleague at the groundbreaking ceremony for the Provo City Center Temple, May 12, 2012. Courtesy Laurie Lee Hall.

acquired knowledge to design the modern temple program into an already existing, historic structure.

I envisioned the layout of the rooms on three building floors. Though the tabernacle had a two-story façade, its interior had only been on one level, with a mezzanine balcony. I thought through how the temple support areas like dressing rooms and mechanical systems could work, as well as how temple patrons would symbolically and physically move through the temple. At the same time, I also committed to the principle that there would be no visible building additions to the original, historic form of the tabernacle.

Like our design plans for the renovated Salt Lake Tabernacle, I produced quick sketches describing the three levels of the new temple. We would excavate several levels below the former main floor, with additional underground spaces created beneath a park adjacent to the tabernacle. In less than a couple of hours, the layout was clear and ready to develop. I determined the handful of people I would trust to show these sketches to who would develop the design into a full presentation to the church's leadership.

I did all this while sitting at my grandparents' table as Laurie. The paradigm shift at that little table was the self-acceptance of my female gender identity, even though it conflicted with my physical biology. I did not understand then, as I do now, the affirming experience it was for me to create the design of such a unique project while being my authentic self. Doing so stripped away decades of guilt and shame regarding my identity and my finding authentic self-expression. I found the confidence to move forward with my investigation of truth. As I sat and designed this new repurposed temple, I was redesigning and repurposing myself. I find it hard to describe how this experience changed me. Over the next five years, as circumstances at work and church compelled me to continue to present myself as male, I knew inside that I was female—knowledge I once possessed as a child and teen but suppressed for so long. My anger, anxiety, and frustration, which I was working to overcome, were directly related to my denial of my true self. Finding and never burying again my gender identity was the key.

Energized by this truth, I studied what I came to know as transgenderism. I felt profound relief to know I was not alone in feeling gender incongruence and conflict. The proper term for this was gender dysphoria, which, through therapy and treatment, could be mitigated. This information opened my eyes as I studied online transgender healthcare issues and the protocols associated with medical transition. I also read many stories of social transitioning—or dressing, grooming, and using names and pronouns that align with one's gender identity.

The complete design of the new Provo temple took three months to prepare. No more than five or six people outside church leaders were even aware of the design's existence when President Thomas S. Monson announced, to audible gasps from the congregation in the October 2011 general conference, that the church would rebuild the burned-out Provo Tabernacle to become the Provo City Center Temple.

A month following this dramatic announcement, I was on an overnight flight from Salt Lake City to Lisbon, Portugal. Unable to sleep on airplanes, I used the time in the dimly lit quiet to record my thoughts on my smartphone. I documented the case I made for myself that I was transgender. By the time I arrived in Lisbon, I had prepared something of a personal treatise.

Our team separated and went to our hotel rooms to rest before

This photo appeared in a March 2012 newspaper article celebrating Laurie Lee's work on LDS temples and her ecclesiastical service as one of seven stake presidents in the Tooele Valley. Courtesy *Tooele Transcript Bulletin*. Maegan Burr, photographer.

we began the next several days' efforts of documenting architectural precedent to guide our design of the future Lisbon temple. Once in my room alone, as I frequently had over the past several months, I used the time to dress and make myself up as Laurie. Just like when I was a teen, doing this brought an enormous sense of relief and wholeness of self. I lay on the bed, re-reading my journal from the flight coming over, reinforcing to myself that, right or wrong, I was genuinely transgender.

For several months, my personal experiences and study continued to eliminate the guilt and shame of this admission, yet I was still unsure of where God was regarding the issue. Having guided all aspects of my personal and family life, pastoral service, and project work for the church using personal prayer and revelation, I was confident I could learn God's mind concerning me if I but asked.

For the first time in my life, I knelt while still presenting as Laurie, unsure of what response I would receive as I prayed, "Dear Heavenly

The Provo City Center Temple was completed in March 2016. Courtesy Laurie Lee Hall.

Father, this is me, Laurie Lee, this is who I am. I have studied a lot about what it means to be transgender, and I identify as female."

I was amazed by the response. A peaceful assurance and sensation of joy revealed to me that I had finally come to accept myself as Deity had *always* known me, just as God had created me to be. I sat and pondered this answer for a long while.

I now had knowledge and assurance that my gender, my eternal spiritual identity, was not only acceptable to God but was previously known by God. And that mattered enough that heaven felt joy over me catching up to this knowledge. Understanding this cemented my truth! I had, after fifty years, finally accepted myself as God knew me. The thought brought joy, which penetrated deep within me. My real work of change began, but my true identity still lay deep under the rubble of the choices and trappings of my adult lifetime of attempting to present as a male, contrary to my nature.

Notes

1. Jennifer Finney Boylan, "To understand biological sex, look at the brain, not the body," *Washington Post*, May 1, 2023.

17

Esther and the King

After feeling heaven's acceptance of my identity during my life-changing prayer in Lisbon, I knew I needed to prepare to "come out" to Marleen. Thinking through how to do that, I anticipated the whole conversation would be very emotional for both of us. I wasn't convinced I could successfully say what I needed to say before I would be in an incoherent mess of ugly tears. My solution was to write her a letter, explaining directly and briefly the critical points of being transgender and expressing my love for her and my continuing commitment to our family. I asked for her support even though I did not know what the future would look like for me, but I also acknowledged that she might not want to remain with me.

I wrote and saved the letter, planning to sit down and have her read it and talk it through just after the New Year. Then, remarkably, as I was driving home from work on the first Friday of January 2012, I got a phone call from Marleen, asking me about the women's clothing she had just found in our closet—clothes that were not hers. It was fortunate I had a plan in place because I never imagined how hard it would be to answer her question by coming out to her on a phone call. I asked her to trust me and wait for me to get home, and I would explain everything.

By the time I arrived, she was sitting on our bed sobbing. The women's clothes she had dumped from the plastic garbage bag containing my entire stash were scattered around her on the bed and the floor. She mumbled something about me having an affair as I walked past her to our computer to print out the letter. I handed it to her as it emerged from the printer and asked her to read it before discussing it. And, I said, the clothes are mine.

Completely unfamiliar with transgenderism, she had no idea what to think.

"Does this mean you are leaving me?" she asked after reading the letter. "Does this mean you want to be with a man instead of me?"

Her questions helped me realize how complex and confusing this news was for her. We both cried as we talked for a long time, sometimes holding each other, sometimes pulling away to breathe. To not overwhelm her with information, at this point I shared very little about my past struggles with my gender, nor did I tell her all I had recently learned about being transgender. She immediately struggled with the thought that I had intentionally lied by not disclosing any of this during the past twenty-five years of marriage. Finally, after gaining her composure and strength, she told me I had to swear that I would never use women's clothing again. If I wanted her to stay with me, I had to cease thinking about it entirely.

I felt crushed under the weight of her demand. As ecstatic and hopeful about my future as I'd been in Lisbon, I now felt the walls of the box I was in closing even tighter, growing all the more inescapable. Coming out did not lead to more freedom as I had hoped but to greater scrutiny and restriction.

I told Marleen I needed to consider her demand. I went to Liz's empty bedroom across the hall to ponder, pray, and read scripture for the rest of the evening. When I finally returned to our room, I told my wife I would do all I could to honor her request and deny myself of my true gender identity yet again, as I had done since I was a teen. I kept this promise with exactness for the next six weeks.

But once the human spirit knows the truth, it refuses to be denied living it. I was more miserable than ever as I again attempted to live in denial of my true identity. I did not want to go on.

Marleen saw it, too. She watched the toll it took on me as I morosely moved through each day. Finally, she asked how I was doing, allowing me to speak freely. I explained how I couldn't live like this when I knew what God had confirmed to me about myself. Relenting a bit, she suggested that if I wanted to dress in a nightgown at night, it might help mitigate my feelings. We went shopping, and she picked one out for me. For the first time in my life, I had a partner—albeit a reticent one—in my gender presentation transition.

One June morning in 2012, I dressed in my suit and tie for work while Marleen lay asleep in our bed. As I prayed to prepare for my day, my mind reviewed concerns about the day's work. Suddenly, amid an unrelated thought, the voice of the Holy Spirit came powerfully into my conscience. "You are a beloved daughter of Heavenly Parents." The sweetest and fullest expression of divine love I had ever experienced engulfed me beyond my ability to describe. I wept, repeating in my mind what I heard and felt. It was not an answer I had been asking for. Instead, the Spirit freely offered the gift of this experience, one that I would soon need to support me through what was coming.

I had another affirming experience like this the following month. "Read Esther," the Spirit's voice spoke to my waking mind. We were on a family vacation at our little house near Bear Lake, Utah. Marleen and all the kids were still sleeping. The day before, we'd been on the lake in the hot sun, then stayed up late playing board games. We were all tired, but the voice in my mind let me know I had something I needed to do. As I shook the last bit of sleep from my consciousness, I wondered when I had previously read the Book of Esther. I only vaguely remembered the Esther story.

I got out of bed, found my scriptures, and sat in the big chair in our front room. I opened the Old Testament to the Book of Esther and obediently began reading. The story takes place during the Jewish captivity in Babylon. The king of the Persian empire, Ahasuerus, was looking for a new queen because the previous one had been "disposed of" after disobeying him. Esther was presented to the king by Mordecai, her uncle and guardian. The king chose Esther as his new queen. He loved her but did not know she was a Jew. Esther kept her true identity secret.

The story continues through various episodes of intrigue until the king's closest advisor, Haman, wanted all Jews executed because they offended him. Haman convinced the king that because the Jews were a different people from the general population, he should send forth a decree that all Jews throughout the empire should perish on a specific day.

When Mordecai learned of this, he urged Esther, the queen, to go before the king and speak on behalf of her people. Esther initially refused, knowing she risked death if she approached the king uninvited. And if the queen spoke against the king's decree and he discovered Esther was a Jew, she too would likely be destroyed.

But "who knoweth," came Mordecai's answer to Esther, "whether thou art come to the kingdom for such a time as this."

The moment I read those words, I knew why the Spirit prompted me to read the story of Esther. The message was clear: I had been brought to the "kingdom" and found favor with the church leaders, but I was secretly transgender. It would become my responsibility to come before these leaders, who loved and trusted me, to change their hearts and save my people, the gender-variant Latter-day Saints.

Though terrified, Esther became convinced of her role and was ultimately able to change the king's mind, saving the Jews. I had faith that if Esther could do it, so could I. I focused on this role and found strength in the foreknowledge I received. I wasn't surprised when the opportunity came, and it arrived quickly.

From then on, I started coming out more as transgender. Marleen helped me find ways to dress more androgynously at home and away from work. With this strong tailwind at my back and an internal hunger to feel more fully like Laurie all the time, I began to dress androgynously in all my spare time at home. For some reason, I found it easier to shed some unwanted weight and keep it off. Our marriage relationship, though, became strained. My highs often corresponded with her lows, and her need for her husband, whom she saw slipping away, produced my lows.

When Liz returned home from her mission in Los Angeles, Marleen and I decided it was time for me to come out to each of our kids and their spouses. Until now, I hadn't come out to anyone besides Marleen, but she had outed me to most of her family and her closest friends so she could have the moral support she needed from others. My protests at her outing me without my permission, when it was my identity and my story to choose to share, seemed to mean nothing to her. With our kids, though, we decided we would sit with each and tell them together.

Our oldest daughter, Alissa, and her husband, along with our second son, Wade, and his fiancée, were understanding and accepting.

We worried how Liz, as a recently returned missionary, might feel about such news. Her daddy, the stake president who had just officially released her from her missionary service, was about to describe going way off script. As we had the others, we reassured her that I wasn't going anywhere, that her parents' marriage was intact, and that I loved her and would always be her dad. Liz responded that she "was good with it." Her time in LA had opened her eyes, she said. Her favorite convert baptism was a lesbian who had previously been in a long-term same-sex relationship.

It is typical to fear the worst before coming out, especially to loved ones. Having these three adult kids receive my news with acceptance and love was a great relief to me and their mother.

My heart broke when our oldest son, Isaac, and his wife, Violet, had an adverse reaction. I barely got out the words, "I am transgender," before Isaac jumped up and ran out of our room where we were speaking. Violet pursued after him. There was no talking to them. They packed up their children and went home. My close relationship with Isaac ended that day, and I haven't been with him or his family in many years. Losing him was, and still is, incredibly painful. I know better now that I am not responsible for their peace or reaction to who I am. But the loss of my relationship with them still feels raw. We held off on talking with our adopted daughter, Tatyana, who was still a young child and had special needs.

I began meeting with Terri Busch, a trained gender therapist and a true gem of a find in Salt Lake City. Together, we strengthened my resolve and excavated deep within myself to discover the best path forward. Her efforts with me helped mitigate my gender dysphoria and cope with the new challenge of familial and social rejection of my truth. At times, weekly therapy sessions were all that supported me and kept me from crashing down.

During this time, I saw a parallel between my work on myself and the work I was leading to transform the burned-out Provo Tabernacle into a strong and beautiful temple. Both thrilling and terrifying.

Along with thousands of others, I attended the groundbreaking ceremony for the new Provo City Center Temple on May 13, 2012, where Elder Jeffery R. Holland of the Quorum of the Twelve Apostles officiated. Everything was moving at a dramatic pace. We had started construction on an incredibly complex project less than a year after my assignment to determine if it was even possible. Meanwhile, there was so much about myself that I was learning and adjusting to.

The morning of October 25, 2012, was going as usual at work until my assistant told me that Elder Don R. Clarke's secretary was on the phone. When I picked up, she told me he wanted to see me at 11:00 A.M. Because Elder Clarke was serving on the Missionary Executive Committee, I thought through the various projects underway for the Missionary Department as I headed to his office. I had previously worked with him and his staff when he was the Area President of Central America and our department was building temples in El Salvador, Honduras, and Quetzaltenango, Guatemala. I also wondered if something was lingering from one of those projects.

When I reached Elder Clarke's office, he asked, "Do you know why you're here?" I thought I was getting some new work-related assignment, or perhaps a new ecclesiastical assignment, as my tenure as stake president was drawing to a close. I wondered if I should feel some inspiration at that point, like when I was called to be the stake president. But no, I wasn't feeling anything like that.

"You must know why I've called you here. Why don't you explain it to me?" Elder Clarke continued to pepper me with questions for about twenty minutes, hoping to break me down into some sort of confession. The truth was I did not know why he had called me to his office, and I had done nothing wrong to feel guilty about. Yet he seemed to think I was stonewalling him. He was growing impatient, so I finally suggested he just tell me why he had called me to his office.

"You consider yourself *transgender*, isn't that correct?" The words seemed repugnant to him. I immediately relaxed, thinking, "Oh, is that all?" Being transgender was not sinful, and I no longer felt ashamed of it.

"Yes, I do," I replied.

I was now to the point of being willing and able to be open about my identity. I was looking forward to the discussion we were about to have until Elder Clarke accused me of everything from questionable to downright filthy behavior that I was supposedly guilty of. I spent the next hour talking him down from believing everything awful he had been led to think about me. In the end, I helped him understand that yes, I considered myself to be transgender, that I was "out" to some family and friends, that I sometimes ventured out in public with my wife dressed androgynously, that I wrote some blog posts about my feelings and experiences under a pseudonym, and that I was part of an online support group. I was confused and could think of no reason why he was interrogating me on this subject, especially because we had no ecclesiastical relationship.

Before our discussion ended, Elder Clarke revealed to me that our oldest son Isaac, who received the news that I was transgender with disgust, had shared this information with his stake president. The stake president then told his file leader, an Area Seventy, who reported it to Elder L. Whitney Clayton of the Presidency of the Seventy, which serves directly under the First Presidency and Quorum of the Twelve Apostles. The seven men of this body preside over dozens of other General Authorities or "members of the Seventy."

Clarke explained that Elder Clayton was away on assignment. Clayton wanted this matter addressed immediately and so instructed Elder Clarke to meet with me and obtain a confession. The phone chain had inaccurately magnified my story to nearly unrecognizable proportions.

Elder Clarke told me he would report our discussion to Elder Clayton. "Oh, and one more thing," he wanted to meet with my spouse that afternoon. She should come in as quickly as possible. I left his office and, rather than returning to my own, went down to my car in the parking garage to make a private call to Marleen. I explained what I had just experienced and that this General Authority required her to come immediately to his office. It was upsetting to her and not at all convenient. She scrambled to find a substitute for her elementary school crossing guard job and pulled Tatyana out of her sixth-grade class early to come in.

I sat with Tatyana in the Missionary Department lobby while Marleen met Elder Clarke in his office. Our daughter entertained the administrative assistants and surprised them with her knowledge of Book of Mormon stories.

The interview went far longer than I expected. My head was reeling from the unexpected events of the day. I could not imagine where this course was taking us. I felt like we were being swept by a current down a dangerous river. When the door finally opened, Elder Clarke asked me to come in. Tatyana was to sit patiently outside.

Marleen's face revealed that she had been crying hard. Elder Clarke presumptuously asked her if she would receive a priesthood blessing from him and if it would be okay if I assisted. We proceeded to do so. I honestly don't remember what he said.

I then walked with Marleen and Tatyana back to the parking garage. Horrified and angry, Marleen said she had never felt so dirty in her entire life. Elder Clarke's words to her in that office were patently wrong in attitude and content.

Given the turmoil and misunderstandings in both of our meetings with Elder Clarke, I concluded it would be best to help set the record straight by sending him a courteous letter clinically explaining my gender dysphoria, which he could then add to his report to Elder Clayton.[1]

Upon his return to Salt Lake City, Elder Clayton called me into his office in the Church Administration Building, where the church's top authorities work. We would meet together many times over the next two months.

Elder Clayton acknowledged he had read my letter and asked me several questions. Throughout our interview, he repeatedly connected me to my role in temple design.

First, he wanted assurance of my belief in the church and its teachings. He then wanted to know about my relationship with Terri Busch, my therapist. I repeated that although she was not a church member, she worked with me within my spiritual context, which she understood and appreciated.

He asked about my involvement in support groups or meetings. I explained my experiences in North Star, the online LGBTQ support group for Latter-day Saints, and our dinners with other members. He asked about my sexual orientation, specifically if I was attracted to males. I clarified my commitment to my covenant, monogamous relationship with no other interests. He wanted to know if I had ever been *physically* unfaithful to Marleen. He asked if I had ever used pornography. I explained I liked looking at photos of well-dressed women because I wanted to emulate them, but he clarified that he needed to know if I ever viewed images of people engaging in sexual intercourse. I assured him no, pornography had never been of interest to me.

Elder Clayton talked with me about the doctrine of gender and the resurrection or afterlife. He summarized that the 1995 Proclamation on the Family emphasized that gender is eternal and that humankind's universal resurrection, made possible by Jesus Christ's resurrection, will make everything right. I agreed with him, explaining that I had a spiritual witness that my spirit is female, which I consider my eternal identity. I believe the resurrection will make my physical body congruent with my spirit.

I also pointed out that many of my struggles at work now stem from social and emotional issues within me from my feelings of gender dysphoria. When I explained in detail my clinical diagnosis of what was then called "gender identity disorder (GID)" and the secondary effects of depression, anxiety, and panic disorder, he countered with his experiences with depression and how he had successfully studied, fasted, and prayed them away.

When I sought to help him understand the science behind gender identity and the difference between it and sexual orientation, he responded by quoting General Authority training he had received regarding "same-sex attraction" and that it was all right to have "feelings" so long as individuals never "acted upon them."

Though his demeanor was more at ease and gracious than Elder Clarke's, our conversations seemed just as unproductive. However, nothing he said made me feel the least bit censured, judged, or criticized. He did not mention worthiness issues nor indicate that my actions could affect work, but he was loving and understanding, and his posture was genuine interest. He offered no recommendations for change and did not condemn or withhold anything from me.

Elder Clayton explained that he would recommend that I be released from my calling as stake president since I had already served nearly nine years, and it would not appear punitive in any way. Though I loved my calling, the good we were doing, and the almost nine years I had spent working with wonderful people, the toll of the priesthood role was taxing my female-gendered soul. I had been struggling with dysphoria for so long and now faced the challenge of poor social and cultural acceptance. The release would be welcome so I could take better care of myself.

I testified to him that I had received a sure witness from God, sealed with divine love and the power of the Holy Ghost, that I was a beloved daughter of Heavenly Father and Heavenly Mother. He responded by charging me to reread the Family Proclamation, which seemed pointless to me. I nearly had the whole thing memorized.

When I met with Elder Clayton the second time four days later, he told me that he and President Boyd K. Packer had reported my situation to the First Presidency and Quorum of the Twelve in their weekly meeting in the Salt Lake Temple. This meeting occurred just two months after President Packer had dedicated his beloved Brigham City temple, on which we had worked so closely for months.

In their meeting, the Brethren determined that since I had served as a stake president for almost nine years and had done nothing that required church discipline, I would be released honorably from my term as stake president at a special conference on December 9, 2012. The conference would be positive and complimentary to my service, so there was no need to worry. All three members of the First Presidency expressed admiration and appreciation for me as an architect. Elder Clayton summarized his feelings by saying I made quite a name for myself here at church headquarters and was highly thought of and loved. President Monson wanted to be sure I received a priesthood blessing, so Elder Clayton promised to do so after the stake conference where I would be released.

On the appointed Sunday morning, Elder Clayton presided at our special stake conference and released me as stake president to a vote of thanks from our congregation of close to 1,000 in attendance. My former second counselor, Gregg Stillmann, was called as the new stake president. After the meetings, Elder Clayton asked if he could visit Marleen and me, so he followed us back to our house to talk and ultimately give both of us a priesthood blessing. In my blessing, he made some reference to wearing appropriate clothing.

Once he was through, he told me I needed to get out of my white shirt and tie after he left and finally relax. Afterward, as I did so, I felt a strong impression from the Holy Spirit, "It mattereth not what clothes you wear." I had never felt the Spirit so strongly contradict what I heard in a priesthood blessing, but I was grateful for the allowance!

The Thursday following my release was the monthly temple design and construction meeting with the First Presidency in their council room, where I would share my presentation as usual. This meeting was my first with the First Presidency since they had learned I considered myself transgender. They had met regarding my fate twice over the past few weeks. Knowing this, I was more nervous than usual, not knowing what they might say or do during the meeting. I always arrived early at these meetings to ensure our AV equipment was functioning correctly. On this occasion, I was unduly early.

I stood nervously behind my chair, awaiting the arrival of others.

President Dieter Uchtdorf, one of President Monson's two counselors in the First Presidency, soon walked in, also quite early. An immigrant from Germany, he is a tall, fit, handsome man with thick silver hair. He looked directly at me as he entered the doorway, paused momentarily, then effortlessly circled the table to reach me. He extended his right hand to take mine and, instead of shaking it as I expected, pulled me into a tight hug.

"Vee are so glad that you are here vith us!" he said deeply and loudly in his distinct German accent. I melted into his embrace, my nervousness erased. In tears, I gently thanked him. I was among friends.

Esther had bravely spoken before the throne—and was found acceptable.

Notes

1. See letter to Elder Don R. Clarke, October 28, 2012, Appendix B: "General Authority Correspondence."

18

Following the Dictates of My Conscience

A few weeks before my release as stake president, Presiding Bishop Gary E. Stevenson, who oversaw the Physical Facilities Department and thus my employment, called me to meet with him and the church's Human Resources managing director, Ben Porter.

They told me they had met with Elder Lance Wickman, general church counsel, to review the legal issues about my case so they could make an employment recommendation to the First Presidency. Bishop Stevenson had then met alone with the First Presidency, telling them he found no reason why my employment should be terminated. The Presidency agreed and reiterated that they wanted me to continue my present assignment, acknowledging the great good I had done in designing temples.

But Bishop Stevenson then explained to me that he needed to communicate the constraints of my behavior if I wanted to remain an employee. He emphasized that church employees are to "maintain the highest level of conduct" and warned that others might construe my gender-variant behavior to be outside that definition. Concerned there could be adverse workplace ramifications, like potential sexual harassment risk should other employees be offended by my transgender thoughts or actions, Bishop Stevenson directed me to talk with no one at work about my feelings. As he detailed these concerns, I sensed they came from human resources and legal counsel rather than constraints imposed by the First Presidency.

Stevenson and Porter told me I must avoid any behavior "that could harm the church's reputation." This included never again wearing any women's clothing at work or home, ceasing participation in all "online group therapy," and no more blogging. Such participation represented negative communication behavior that could come back to discredit the church.

Finally, Bishop Stevenson advised me to seek therapy to help me control my feelings and behaviors rather than express them, and only from those who are "doctrinally aligned" with the church. He again admonished me to study the Family Proclamation, which he said would bring me comfort and peace. When he asked me if I could follow each of these constraints, I told him I would try, but I knew there would be negative impacts on me emotionally. "Then let's be open with each other about the challenges you might face," he told me, which I agreed to do. Over the holiday break of December 2012, I used my time off to compose a letter to Bishop Stevenson, explaining why the constraints would be difficult, if not detrimental, for me to follow.

The constraints, I explained in a letter, were primarily aimed at restricting behavior, even in my home and personal life, that had already proven helpful to me in mitigating the harmful effects of gender dysphoria. By the time I returned to work in the new year, I had prepared this explanation and was ready to defend it. I gave Bishop Stevenson my letter, stating that because "I have a diagnosed and actual medical, physiological, and emotional condition, *I formally request accommodation* necessary to mitigate its effects in my life and allow me to continue functioning effectively as an employee in my current job assignment." I explained that restricting all my options to mitigate my condition even while away from the office constituted an overreach that would harm me, including my ability to perform my assignment at work.

Not long after I hand-delivered this letter, I met with Stevenson again, this time without Ben Porter. I recorded my notes on our discussion. He broke the ice by describing his recent trip to Brazil and talking about the several temples he visited, complimenting me on how lovely they are. To move the conversation along, I offered to read aloud the letter I had given him. I did so at a deliberate pace.

He responded that he appreciated how professionally, thoughtfully, and studiously I approached the issue.

We then slowly went back over several points. Bishop Stevenson had gained some understanding of gender identity disorder (as it was then called) and gender dysphoria, but acknowledged he needed to learn more about this from professional sources. I sensed his sincerity. As the chief temporal officer of the church, he felt it was his responsibility to have a better grasp of the matter.

Bishop Stevenson asked whether I was still receiving help through therapy. He also asked how my wife and each of our children felt about my wardrobe and wondered if my actions were unsettling to any of them. I noted that my oldest son and his wife were still quite upset with me. I explained that I had made some incremental adjustments to my wardrobe, more successfully finding pieces from the men's side of the aisle that mostly met my needs, and I had refrained from wearing women's clothing at home since we last met. He seemed pleased with this explanation. He said he appreciated my efforts to live in conformance with the conditions set by the First Presidency, implying that they wrote the requirements instead of him and Ben Porter.

He asked if I felt the constraints placed on me were overly onerous or harmful, saying that the church's intent was not to harm me but rather to support me. I answered by reinforcing my need for accommodation that would allow me to manage my gender dysphoria. Although we never got into the details of what that accommodation would look like, I wanted to be able to dress in ways that helped me feel comfortable when I wasn't at work and to have the freedom to meet others like me online and in support groups to discuss our experiences with dysphoria.

Bishop Stevenson reiterated that he wanted me to remain an employee. Regarding my accommodation request, he said, "We will accept where you're at." I took that to mean that he was granting me latitude in my wardrobe when I was away from work, which would mitigate my dysphoria so I could feel well enough to fulfill my assignments at work. He referred to the exception or latitude as an "amendment on clothing" and wrote that phrase on his copy of my letter. He asked again that I seek a professional LDS therapist with knowledge of gender identity disorder and make an appointment to "broaden my perspective." He would also like to speak with them if I found such an individual. I looked but never located such a person.

After this somewhat positive meeting, I felt aghast and dismayed by a follow-up letter I received from Bishop Stevenson.[1] It bore little, if any resemblance to the tenor of our meeting or my understanding of the accommodation he granted me. Instead, it seemed to be authored by someone else for Bishop Stevenson's signature as a direct rebuttal of my letter to him. The letter contradicted nearly everything I understood from our meeting, calling my request for accommodation "moot" and reinforcing instead of relaxing each of the constraints levied before that meeting. The letter concluded, "Brother Hall, I sense this issue has become a dominant concern in your life and may be displacing other concerns of greater eternal consequence. I would advise you look more beyond yourself and work toward identities that are more Christ-centered such as your identity as a husband and a father, a priesthood holder, a child of God, and as a fellow Saint, and the anxieties you are experiencing that you relate to gender issues will temper."

I was stunned to read such a pejorative reversal, which entirely disregarded my points regarding coping. Regarding my clothing, the letter unequivocally stated, "First, let me summarize my recollection of the conditions you accepted as you met with Ben Porter and me. You would not wear any women's clothing, visibly or otherwise, at any time, whether at work, home, in public, or elsewhere, nor would you groom as a woman." With the constraints came the warning, "Your continued employment will depend on your successful adherence to them." Gone was any sense of latitude or an amendment to the constraints that Bishop Stevenson and I had discussed when just the two of us met in our last meeting. At the time of these conversations in 2013, the church had very little written policy (other than counseling against "elective transsexual operations") to guide decisions regarding transgender members and employees, which may explain why our conversations lacked clear direction and why decisions and opinions seemed to be all over the map.

I remembered my impression after Elder Clayton released me as stake president: "It mattereth not what clothes you wear." I had always strived to be obedient and faithful, but I decided to no longer submit to counsel that went against what I knew to be true. I was born transgender. I felt blessed to be able to contribute to the church at a high level, and I knew that I did so with heaven's full support. I wanted to continue to dedicate my time and talents to designing beautiful, sacred spaces for the benefit of church members, but I could not do that if the church would not allow me the privilege of following the dictates of my conscience.

The situation at work had become a distressing fight to retain my employment in an environment once highly appreciative of my efforts but now hostile to who I was. I did not know how long I could continue. At home, I faced the reality that although at times Marleen had supported some steps I needed to take to mitigate my gender dysphoria, she could not accept where we both knew my gender transition was going—that I needed to live full-time as a woman.

Seeking validation of my growing hope to eventually fully transition, I asked Marleen, "How do you see my gender expression in the future when the day comes that I am no longer working for the church? What does it look like?"

"You've said you want to change completely," she responded.

I confirmed that but also affirmed my love for her. My need to transition did not mean I was leaving her in any way.

Our friend Joanne, the wife of a fully transitioned spouse, had written a letter to Marleen the previous day. Joanne, I later learned, told Marleen to "get with it" and support her transgender spouse as she was doing. That did not sit well with Marleen, and the letter contributed to her responding to me with emotion-filled statements and rhetorical questions that continued long into the night.

"Will you go see the doctor for testing? Will you not try to get this fixed? Are you so determined to be a woman that you won't fight your feelings? Am I not worth fighting for?" she asked.

"I do not want to be seen with you as a woman, with you in a dress. Do you think we could publicly hold hands? I would be embarrassed to be seen with you. You do not look like a woman. Doesn't that embarrass you? If this is how you have always felt, why did you marry me and have a family?"

My need to live my female identity authentically had come into conflict with her heterosexual identity. "I cannot stay married to you with you as a woman. I will not touch you if you are a woman. Do you think we would have sex, with you as a woman? I will not be a lesbian. Two women are not supposed to be married, precisely like blacks and whites are not supposed to marry," she said. "I deserve to have my husband back."

While Marleen's homophobic and racist statement shocked me, I recognized that it was impossible to ask anyone to change their sexual orientation. She didn't ever intend to be with a woman. I had changed the rules, and she didn't get to choose.

"I do not understand how you could do this to me," she continued. "You do not know how much you have hurt me. I want to hurt you as badly as you have hurt me. I should probably just leave now and care for my parents. You have left me no choice but to either deal with your changing or being forced to go."

In the end, there was nothing I could say in retort or defense that I hadn't already expressed many times. I concluded that at this point, to salvage our marriage and keep working to find a way to make it work together, I must abandon my hope of transition for as long as I could.

When I didn't wear my nightgown to bed that night, she asked why.

"This is how you could hurt me as badly as I have hurt you—by forbidding my gender expression," I answered.

"Then we have both lost and given up so much."

A while later, she asked me what I was thinking.

"I hope my life is short," I said.

"You're having suicidal thoughts again?"

"Maybe more rationally this time. I'm not planning to end my life, just wishing it would end, that somehow there was a way to find relief from this pain."

One of the last things I remember her saying before I entered a fitful sleep was, "I don't understand why we cannot agree on this." She wanted unity where there was none.

The next day, Marleen left me a voicemail at work, apologizing. She knew we needed to be together and that we could figure out how to make this work.

But in our next conversation, she asked me yet again if I was willing to see a doctor for testing so that I could be "cured." Repeating futile conversations like these nearly every night was exhausting. When we prayed together, sometimes Marleen pleaded with Father in Heaven to give me the faith and strength to overcome my gender dysphoria and return to her as her husband. I could not conclude these prayers with a concurring "Amen." I would then explain to her again that asking God for something I knew was contrary to his knowledge of my true identity was wrong. Sadly, we went around in circles like this for years.

At work, I allowed my feelings to ferment for several months before I decided to take action again. With my eventual transition now clearly my intention, I obtained a treatment summary from my therapist, Terri Busch, confirming that I needed to begin gender transition as the medically recognized resolution of my health problems. I wanted to formally request that the church support my continued employment in designing its temples—only now I would do so as the woman I truly was. I sent a new letter to Bishop Stevenson, outlining the steps I would be taking to accomplish my transition.[2]

I soon received an email from my managing director, Brant Robbins, telling me that I was no longer the director of Temple Design but the director of Special Projects—a lateral move. It was late Friday afternoon and I was already home for the weekend, so I called Brant on his cell phone to learn what happened. He responded that he did not know. The Presiding Bishopric had just called him and specifically instructed him to inform me that I was off temples entirely as of that day. They gave him no reason and no room for questioning.

The news devastated me, but how the Bishopric handled it hurt even more. I knew the First Presidency had expressed their full support and appreciation for me several months before. I did not believe this change originated with them. I wondered if the Bishopric was trying to keep me from directly working with the First Presidency—as was required for the director of temple design—before I went too far in my transition. Whatever the case, I had no doubt that I was forced off Temple Design after six years because I considered myself transgender and had now expressed my determination to live authentically as the woman I truly was.

One of Bishop Stevenson's counselors in the Presiding Bishopric was Dean M. Davies, who had been my colleague when he, too, was an employee in the Physical Facilities Department. We were both serving as directors when the Bishopric chose between the two of us to replace Carl Heinz as our department's managing director. Since I turned down the position, preferring design to administration, Dean received the promotion and became my boss. We traveled the world together for several years, identifying new temple sites and proposing concept site designs.

At times, I enjoyed working with him, but occasionally we disagreed and I went toe-to-toe with him to defend my point of view. He could be vindictive and selfish, capable of inflicting significant harm on those who opposed his opinions or who might impede his upward mobility in the eyes of the senior Brethren.

He was called as a General Authority to serve in the Presiding Bishopric just a few months before my interviews began with Bishop Stevenson. In this new ecclesiastical assignment, Bishop Davies oversaw temple real estate, design, and construction, which put him in the position to direct such a change to my assignment. I worried that his actions were personal toward me.

At Brant's direction, I attended one more round of temple-related meetings with church leaders in September in order to help provide the handoff to my successor. Brant told me later that Bishop Davies chastised him for letting me anywhere near temples again, contrary to his explicit direction.

I felt depressed and beaten down and useless for the next several weeks. I was not emotionally able to engage in my new assignment and seriously considered leaving church employment far sooner than I had ever expected. The workplace no longer felt safe to me.

Then, a tremendous blessing occurred. The principal client of my new Special Projects assignment was the church's Missionary Department, contemplating a significant expansion of the flagship Missionary Training Center in Provo, Utah. This was the same educational facility I had lived in during the fall of 1982 as I prepared for my missionary service in Buenos Aires. The church had not updated it much since then.

I stopped thinking about myself and became spiritually driven to figure out this exciting new assignment. This change felt like what happened to me during my interview with my mission president many years ago. I went into that interview downtrodden but found myself spiritually prompted to tell him I would figure out how to connect with the city's people and, as a result, built the highly effective exposition.

The effort of master planning the expansion and designing the new buildings was very similar to the effort I had led seventeen years earlier at Welfare Square. From that experience, I knew I needed to fully understand the "priesthood purpose" of such facilities and think like those who administered the Missionary Training Center (MTC).

Once again, I sequestered myself in my office with the door locked and read from cover to cover the *Preach My Gospel* manual missionaries used in their preparation at the MTC. I became focused on discovering the principles that would describe the nature and spirit of a facility for missionary training.

Because our lead architectural consultants were not LDS, just as was the case at Deseret Dairy, I knew I needed to help them understand the spiritual purpose of our facility, not just the static requirements. I produced on my whiteboard the list of principles I gleaned from my study, prioritized them, and called them "MTC Design Guidelines."

I took them to the leaders of the Missionary Department, explained their origin, and received their full endorsement. We then presented the guidelines to the Missionary Executive Committee, chaired by Elder Russell M. Nelson of the Quorum of the Twelve Apostles, who approved them with appreciation. Elder Nelson then presented my guidelines to the First Presidency, who endorsed them. We now had an inspired way to guide our work. I was deeply humbled to receive the blessing of knowing how to move this project forward and invigorated to see what the results of our team efforts would create. Over the next three years, our design team constantly referred to the guidelines as we developed the beautiful buildings and grounds of the new Provo MTC.

Notes

1. See Gary E. Stevenson to Brother Hall, February 19, 2013, Appendix B.
2. See Hall to Bishop Stevenson August 6, 2013, Appendix B.

19

Some Things Must Change

Following my release as stake president and coming out as transgender to family, friends, and church leaders, a sister I knew well in the stake approached me. She said she had decided to serve as a surrogate mother for a couple who were unable to have a baby, an act discouraged by church policy. She wasn't asking for my advice, though I suddenly had much to offer—she was already three months pregnant. I suppose she needed to tell someone she respected and was seeking support. I was initially anxious for her over such a choice and continued to feel this for several days. But when I saw her again, I asked if she wanted a blessing associated with this pregnancy. Though she wasn't actively participating in the church, she still had a strong faith in the ministering power of the priesthood, so she said yes.

Though I felt angst about this pregnancy and the hardship and risk it placed on her, as I placed my hands on her head and pronounced her name, my concerns melted away, and my heart filled with God's love for her and the sacrifice she was making for another family. After the blessing, I told her of those powerful feelings I felt. In time, she delivered a healthy baby girl to the new parents. Only several years later did she reveal to me that the little girl was being raised by two dads, two gay LDS men who married and created a beautiful family with her help. Then I knew the whole meaning of the witness I received: God loved this young surrogate mother for what she did for this child and loved and approved of her parents—two loving, devoted dads!

In late 2013, Marleen was diagnosed with high-grade breast cancer for the second time in six years. While staying at her side and comforting her through five surgeries over the following six months, I delayed taking any further steps in my gender transition.

The secretary to Presiding Bishop Gary Stevenson set up our next meeting for February 7, 2014, three days before Marleen's first scheduled surgery. He didn't identify a topic for the meeting, but I was sure it was for my accountability check he had stipulated in his letter to me a year before. As Marleen and I discussed it, we concluded it would be wise for her to join me. She wanted to be sure I was not mistreated or misunderstood and, if required, speak her mind that employment leadership had no right to dictate the affairs of my private life.

I knew that if Bishop Stevenson chose to take a hard line regarding the content of that previous letter, the result would be my termination, especially if Ben Porter from Human Resources was present. I prepared myself for that possibility, which caused me severe anxiety layered on top of the concern I already felt for Marleen because of her cancer. The possibility of losing employment with Marleen's health issues made me feel less bold about requesting an accommodation to transition gender presentation at work at this time. It felt like a time to stay below the radar for another season.

I contacted my therapist and received a signed version of her treatment summary letter, along with her faith and encouragement. I described the situation in detail in emails with an attorney at the Transgender Law Center (TLC). Based in Oakland, California, they are the largest trans-led national organization promoting the rights of all gender-variant people. I asked how direct of an approach I should take, including having a letter from TLC. The attorney counseled wisely that while still an employee, I should keep the discussion limited to medical conditions and the need for accommodation and treatment and not raise the specter of discrimination or legal actions. The attorney advised that it was important not to show disloyalty to the corporation that employed me.

Marleen and I went to the meeting with Bishop Stevenson prepared with my therapist's letter and definitions of gender dysphoria from national health organizations. Marleen's being in the meeting was beneficial. The bishop acknowledged the significant stressors we had experienced over the past year—my release as stake president after serving for nearly a decade, the divorce of one of our children, an important job reassignment, ongoing care of our special needs child, and now Marleen's cancer. He asked how we were holding up.

In answering, I did not mention gender issues but focused only on the challenges he raised. I wanted to let him start talking about gender if he chose to. He asked if the counseling we received was helpful to us. I stated I was still seeing Terri but had also met with Justin McPheters from LDS Family Services, as he had asked. Marleen and I both found Justin had no experience with transgender care.

Bishop Stevenson brought up my role at work over the past year, noting how valuable my ten years of service on temples had been, and joked that I left the frying pan and entered the fire by moving to Missionary Department projects. He noted several times how significant my contribution was to "several major initiatives" and that I was very well recognized around church headquarters.

He said the most important thing he and his colleagues could do right now is support us as a family as we go through the trial of Marleen's surgery, treatment, and healing. He cut me plenty of slack for not getting back together within two months, as his last letter had requested. He seemed tentative and awkward instead of direct and specific when discussing the topics of our prior conversations about my gender dysphoria.

When Marleen stepped out of the meeting to take a phone call, Bishop Stevenson used her absence to be slightly more to the point and asked about my apparel. I put him off by saying he did not have to worry about my clothing. Marleen reentered, and he sheepishly told her we were discussing my clothes. Marleen merely responded there was no problem with that.

The bishop seemed satisfied, almost grateful he heard what he wanted to hear, and asked nothing more about my being transgender. He saw Marleen and I both getting along well and at peace. I wondered if the meeting was mainly to prepare him to give a favorable report regarding me should anyone ever ask. Having accomplished his purpose, he suggested we meet again in about four months but did not specify how that should occur. I sensed his gentleness toward my issues, which I had always felt during our in-person interviews, was still intact. I hoped that foretold an additional season of grace towards me and my employment.

Marleen and I left feeling we had dodged the bullet. Her involvement had been critical, diverting attention to her health and reinforcing that we were okay as a couple. We discussed our lack of full disclosure regarding what I was doing contrary to the church's constraints, including my wardrobe outside the office, my continuing therapy with Terri, and my online activity, in addition to my long-term intent to fully transition, but we felt comfortable that we had been as open as he had asked us to be. We knew we had done nothing wrong that merited his or the church leaders' concern.

When Marleen had largely healed from her treatment near the end of the summer of 2014, I began talking with her about taking my next step in the gender-affirming healthcare process—hormone replacement therapy (HRT). I reconfirmed to her that there were no medical tests that doctors could run to "prove" whether I was or wasn't transgender or that could "fix" my gender identity the way she wanted. The only medically supported path forward was HRT. I had been her support through her illness. Now I needed her support with my treatment as I, too, needed healing and change.

August 24, 2014, was the day I received my first prescriptions for HRT—two testosterone blockers and estradiol. With the medications, I felt grounded in a way I never had before. My gender dysphoria was swept away, along with its secondary effects of depression, anxiety, and panic disorder. I came to appreciate how sensitive our brains and bodies are to hormones and how both rely on the stimulus of hormones. Getting my hormones right felt like I had been trying to run a diesel engine on regular gas, and now, after fifty-three years, I was finally supplying it with the correct diesel fuel. I found the next level of change and peace I imagined might be possible while I lay in my hospital bed four years before.

Marleen also noticed the difference. Though she had been adamantly against my starting hormone therapy, within weeks of observing the change it brought in me, she changed, too. She surprised me when she said, "I have talked with some of the wives in the North Star support group whose husbands have been struggling with their gender, and I told them what a difference being on hormones has made for you. You are calmer now and less angry and frustrated. I told them they must stop waiting and get their husbands on hormones, too." Marleen's about-face from an HRT denier to a promoter was also life-changing, increasing my hope that she would walk this journey with me.

But HRT didn't solve all my physical challenges. I grudgingly realized what most adult transgender women do. Suppressing testosterone and boosting estrogen does wonders for eliminating unwanted male body hair but does little or nothing to reduce one's facial hair. Only semi-permanent treatments like laser hair removal and the far more painful electrolysis are effective. Because laser hair treatments are ineffective on light-colored beards like mine, I conceded that my only real option was electrolysis. I asked around in the support groups and found an electrologist named Ann who, though a devout Latter-day Saint, had experience with facial hair removal for transgender women.

I fearfully approached Ann's small brick rambler and walked around back to the kitchen door as instructed. Ann answered the door and seemed as shy and nervous as I was. She led me into her basement to a small, windowless room with her treatment table and equipment set up. Ann briefly explained the procedure. I would hold a steel terminal in one hand while she inserted an electrified needle, attached to the terminal by a cord, into a hair follicle. The stronger the current Ann sent into the base of the follicle, the more effective the "killing" of the follicle in limiting the hair's regrowth. She said we would try a few, incrementally increasing the power until she discovered my tolerance level.

After several experiments, we found the top of my pain threshold, which we discovered was on a less sensitive part of my neck. So, she zapped me approximately every four seconds and plucked the now-dead whisker out with stainless-steel tweezers. My job was to hold still through all this while never letting go of the terminal in my left hand. I could not feel the current in my hand, but occasionally I found myself holding onto the terminal so tightly that my hand fell asleep.

Ann tried calming me by engaging in casual conversation and

playing relaxing music. It still hurt like the dickens! Partway through the session, she began dabbing my face with a tissue and noted I was bleeding far more than most of her patients. That did little to mitigate my tension. Ann also warned me that electrolysis was not permanent and that I'd have to go through this process more than once for each follicle. I told her that if this torture was what it took to remove my beard, I was on board for the duration.

At the end of the hour, Ann daubed my affected area with a soothing cream and declared we had addressed the first 751 of my thousands of whiskers. She dutifully recorded the figure in a notebook. I was surprised to learn that her equipment gave her a precise count.

I checked the treated area in the rearview mirror when I climbed into my car. It was pure road rash, looking like somewhere between my ill-fated slide into second base wearing only gym shorts in PE and the appearance of raw ground beef. Fortunately, I had taken a sick day for this first foray. I just hoped I might look less damaged for work the following day. When Marleen saw me that afternoon, she openly questioned my sanity for wanting to go through such a procedure. She wondered what else I would submit myself to.

I got into a rhythm of meeting with Ann every Monday morning for double appointments—two non-stop hours of jabbing and plucking. I became accustomed to the pain as she worked across all areas of my neck below the jawline. Filling our appointments with conversation and relaxing music, we nixed more than 2,000 hair follicles each week. After several months, she began working on my cheeks, and I learned that different areas of my skin had various levels of nerve endings and sensitivities. The most painful places were around my lips and under my nose. I would tear up and writhe on the table, allowing only a few upper lip zappings every half hour.

We often joked about Ann's secret dark side, conducting evil experiments in her basement by inflicting pain on her victims with jolts of electricity. It was all very Mary Shelley's *Frankenstein.* Yet I was still grateful for it, gladly paying Ann out-of-pocket at the end of every session.

In time, I realized this effort would take far longer and cost more than anticipated. After exhausting the residual funds I had budgeted initially and not wanting to impact our family budget, I told Marleen

I would sell my beloved classic Ford pickup to continue my treatments. She was shocked. I had owned and tinkered with a succession of old Ford trucks over the years, and this one was my favorite. It was my favorite color of green inside and out, built around the time of the first Earth Day in the spring of 1970. I had period buttons and stickers on the interior representing the seventies ecology movement and dubbed it the "eco-ranger" truck despite its gas-guzzling V8 engine. I loved taking our oldest grandchildren for rides around the valley, with them all strapped down across its big bench seat. How I would miss that experience.

I soon sold it to its new owners and set the proceeds aside, eventually spending every bit of it and then some in Ann's basement torture lounge. I honed my process to get electrolysis done each Monday by routinely shaving Thursday morning for work, going in Friday unshaven—which became less and less noticeable—and not shaving over the weekend so the whiskers would be long enough for Ann to pluck by Monday. I attended church meetings on Sundays with three days of beard growth. Being so scruffy at church only served to magnify my church-related gender dysphoria.

I would go to each Monday's treatment in soft, casual clothes to help me relax. After each treatment, I headed to the Church Office Building, parked my car underground, and entered one of the basement's unisex restrooms. I would take my estradiol, do what I could to treat my sore and bloodied face, and put on a white shirt, suit, and tie—the church's expected work attire for men. By the end of the day, I often had blood stains all over my shirt collar despite my efforts to avoid it. My swollen and brutalized face and blood-stained collars every Monday must have been a pattern that did not go unnoticed. Yet it continued for more than two years without anyone mentioning it. I accomplished all this while, as a church employee, I was working with the Missionary Department Executive Committee, chaired by Elder Russell M. Nelson.

The money for these treatments eventually ran dry. According to Ann's records, we treated some 60,000 follicles. Some regrew, but most did not. She was wise to treat the darkest hairs first. It was largely successful, though some darker hairs have returned over time. I still shave because I prefer to feel as smooth as possible. As time wore on and I dealt with skin cancer on my face and arms caused by sun exposure, along with areas that heal very slowly due to age, I have chosen not to return for additional treatment. I am satisfied with where I am.

Looking back on the myriad of reasons no one would ever choose to transition on a whim, submitting to the cost and torture of endless electrolysis treatments has to be among the top.

I began this journey feeling deeply that some things must change. In time, I saw nearly everything change. I changed, yes, but I was still me, a much better representation of myself than ever before.

20

Policies of Exclusion

The years 2013 through 2015 were a crossroads of conflict in the LDS Church over issues of gender and sexuality. In early 2013, a group of Mormon women organized under the name "Ordain Women" and urged church leaders to change policy so that women and girls could be ordained to the priesthood like their male counterparts. I was in a Physical Facilities Department meeting when the director of our Headquarters Facilities Division, which managed ticketing for events on the church headquarters campus, informed us that Ordain Women had requested 150 tickets to attend the male-only priesthood session of that October's general conference. Their request was denied, but I quietly rejoiced when he reported that instead, the First Presidency had approved the Presiding Bishopric's request to broadcast the priesthood session of the conference session live on television and online for the first time in history, making it possible for all church members to watch the proceedings, not just men and boys in attendance. This decision appeared to be made to sidestep conflict with Ordain Women, but dozens of women still lined up to request admittance into the in-person priesthood session on October 5. They were denied entrance, and the demonstration made national headlines.

A few months later and exactly three weeks after my February 7, 2014, meeting with Presiding Bishop Gary Stevenson, Ordain Women again took action, this time requesting 250 tickets to attend the priesthood session at the church's next annual general conference in April. Again denied tickets, they once more organized a walk in which even more LDS women requested admittance to the in-person priesthood session.

The following month, Elder L. Whitney Clayton—the same church leader I had met with in 2012 and who released me from my calling as stake president—was training local church leaders in Virginia, where Ordain Women founder and leader Kate Kelly was living. In a May 17 meeting, local leaders asked Elder Clayton what to do about the Ordain Women group. Clayton reportedly answered that public advocacy of female priesthood ordination is an act of apostasy. Kate Kelly's bishop excommunicated her in June.[1]

When I later came out publicly in 2016, my being a woman who had exercised priesthood authority and presided as a stake president struck a chord with LDS feminists, including those of Ordain Women. I frustrated many who asked me to share what I thought about the ordination of women. I had no immediate response to a subject I had yet to consider carefully enough to benefit others. I was so wrapped up in my struggles at that point that I could not look beyond my journey to articulate an opinion.

That fall of 2014, a few months after Kelly's excommunication, I met with a group of transgender people, their spouses, and some parents of transgender youth. We had connected through North Star, a Latter-day Saint LGBTQ support group. In our discussions, we identified a need for an online group for transgender Latter-day Saints and their families. About twenty-five of us formed a Facebook group called the TransActive LDS Support Group, which continues to grow and provide support nearly ten years later. I was not yet on Facebook, so one of the group members helped me set up a profile for the new name I had already chosen for myself, Laurie Lee Hall. At that point, only a few family members and members of this Facebook group knew of my new name. I soon discovered that being connected on social media as dramatic events unfolded gave me a deeper appreciation of the battle that lay ahead of me.

The year 2015 began with a historically significant step forward, followed by painful setbacks for LGBTQ communities in Utah and in the worldwide church. On January 27, 2015, less than a year after my last meeting with Bishop Stevenson, LDS Church leaders held a jaw-dropping press conference. In it, they supported and called for statewide and national legislation to protect vital religious freedoms while at the same time supporting legislation to provide housing and employment protections. The move was significant because most LGBTQ Utahns did not have those protections at the time.[2] The church supported a similar approach in 2010, but it was made law only by the city of Salt Lake that year.

People on both sides of the aisle hailed the church's pronouncement as a critical step forward in Utah. State Senator Jim Dubakis (D-Salt Lake City), the only openly LGBTQ member of Utah's legislature at the time, said, "I know that together, we can build a community that strongly protects religious organizations' constitutional liberties and, in addition, creates a civil, respectful, nurturing culture where differences are honored, and everyone feels welcome."[3]

Two days after that press conference, the *Salt Lake Tribune* broadcast a rare interactive interview with apostles Dallin H. Oaks and D. Todd Christofferson to respond to the public's questions on LGBTQ issues. One member of our TransActive LDS Support Group sent in a question about her transgender son. "I just told my bishop two Sundays ago," she wrote. "I hate having to fear what retaliation I might have for supporting [my son]. Some bishops are awesome and loving, and some people get the threat of being excommunicated. I think we as members need th[e] assurance that we can indeed have our own opinion, support our children, and still follow our beliefs."

Watching the online event live, I was jolted by Elder Oaks's reply.

"This question concerns transgender," he said, "and I think we need to acknowledge that while we have been acquainted with lesbians and homosexuals for some time, being acquainted with the unique problems of a transgender situation is something we have not had so much experience with. We have some unfinished business in teaching on that."[4]

I was excited to have a senior church leader publicly utter the word "transgender." I felt reinforced again in my belief that I, like Esther, had "come to the kingdom for such a time as this." I hoped I could help the church grow in understanding and compassion towards transgender people. I hoped I could broaden its teachings on eternal gender in inclusive ways that would enable me and so many others to live and worship according to our true natures. It was an exciting moment.

But while it was thrilling to consider that my community was on church leaders' radar, it was also frightening that their "unfinished business" might eventually mean taking aim at us.

In March 2015, the Utah State Legislature followed the church's lead and passed SB 296, amending the state's 1997 Antidiscrimination Act to include sexual orientation and gender identity as protected classes in housing and employment. But the new law exempted "religious employers." The press dubbed it the "Utah Compromise."[5]

My careful study of the new law convinced me that my recent request for accommodation as a transgender church employee sat squarely at the center of the compromise. While I rejoiced with my transgender friends across Utah whose housing and employment rights were now assured, I openly mourned on Facebook that as a trans employee of the Corporation of the Presiding Bishopric, the new law did not protect me or others like me from discrimination by my religious employer. My employer had placed me on probation in 2012, and with this new law, my employment was in even greater jeopardy. Still, I could not help but hope that my years of service, sincerity, and courage before the church leaders would somehow bring positive change.

Issues of gender and sexuality reached a crescendo again in July 2015 when the United States Supreme Court made a landmark decision in the *Obergefell v. Hodges* case. The court ruled that the Fourteenth Amendment guaranteed the right of same-sex couples to marry. Four months later, on November 5, 2015, after my day at work at the Church Office Building, my Facebook feed lit up with news that the church was making a statement on a new policy directed at same-sex couples. I devoted the evening to understanding what was happening. The church had quietly added its latest policy to its official handbook of instructions for stake presidents and bishops, which someone had then leaked to the public.

The policy labeled same-sex LDS couples, including those now legally married, as "apostates" requiring church discipline. Even worse, minor children of these couples could not receive the sacred ordinances of baby blessings (which placed the infants' names on church records) or of baptism (typically received at the age of eight), which makes the recipient an official member of the church. The First Presidency had to approve any exceptions. Children of same-sex couples could be baptized when they reached the age of eighteen, but only if they disavowed same-sex marriage and cohabitation. Since baptism was a requirement before being ordained to the Aaronic Priesthood, the new policy also meant that twelve to eighteen-year-old boys who had parents in a same-sex marriage could not participate in the rituals of blessing or passing the sacrament as their other male peers did. I felt shocked as I learned of the policy. I could not believe that this cruel stance could come from my church.

The next day, Church Public Affairs Managing Director Michael Otterson conducted what appeared to be a hastily assembled televised interview regarding the new policy with Elder D. Todd Christofferson of the Quorum of the Twelve. The awkward interview made me feel sorry for those men I knew and respected, whom I later learned from the apostle's openly gay brother, Tom Christofferson, had been assigned by the First Presidency to voice the church's position. In the interview, Elder Christofferson described why church leaders felt the policy change was necessary. "We regard same-sex marriage as a particularly grievous or significant, serious kind of sin that requires church discipline. It means the discipline is mandatory," he said. It "doesn't dictate outcomes, but it dictates that discipline is needed."

Concerning the new policy's restrictions on the children of parents in a same-sex marriage or relationship, Elder Christofferson stated that the exclusion of these children came out of compassion, that church ordinances and participation were "likely not going to be an appropriate thing in the home setting, in the family setting where they're living as children where their parents are a same-sex couple."[6] Elder Christofferson failed to acknowledge that excluding these children from receiving the ordinances and ordinations would single them out as different from their peers and possibly even mark them as "unworthy."

In church meetings the following Sunday, the new policy was *the* topic on everyone's minds. Some were shocked and outraged by the prospect, while many others were apologetic or vehement in defending any stance the Brethren took. Marleen and I talked the issue through at length. She knew I was already deeply in support of the LGBTQ community. Neither of us could imagine what this might mean concerning us and our marriage. We knew the day was coming when I would present full-time as a woman, making us appear to be a same-sex couple. At Marleen's encouragement, I emailed President Stillmann, our stake president, inquiring what he knew about how church leaders would interpret the new handbook language regarding our particular situation. He replied that he did not know. Stake presidents had not yet received training on the subject.

Continuing to feel stunned, I could not look away over the following weeks as reports circulated regarding the trauma, harm, and increase in youth suicide. People in my LGBTQ community that I cared about were losing family and friends at an increasing and alarming rate. These innocents were young people who struggled to reconcile their faith in an institution that had so repugnantly turned on them. In the eyes of the church that many were still trying to embrace, the person they inherently were had become irrefutably repulsive to God, unworthy of his love and blessings.

As such harmful, destructive rhetoric on the part of senior church leaders continues today, I continue to focus on the fear, disillusionment, and abandonment of the vulnerable. As a result of the church's positions, many precious people have lost relationships, families, homes, and even their lives. I would soon discover for myself what it felt like to be targeted by my faith community.

What I came to call the "Big Lie" occurred on January 10, 2016, when Russell M. Nelson, then president of the Quorum of the Twelve Apostles, spoke to a worldwide devotional for young adults. President Nelson called the policy an inspired revelation from God.

"This prophetic process was followed ... with the recent additions to the Church's handbook, consequent to the legalization of same-sex marriage in some countries," Nelson said. "Filled with compassion for all, and especially for the children, we wrestled at length to understand the Lord's will in this matter. Ever mindful of God's plan of salvation and of His hope for eternal life for each of His children, we considered countless permutations and combinations of possible scenarios that could arise. We met repeatedly in the temple in fasting and prayer and sought further direction and inspiration. And then, when the Lord inspired His prophet, President Thomas S. Monson, to declare the mind of the Lord and the will of the Lord, each of us during that sacred moment felt a spiritual confirmation. It was our privilege as Apostles to sustain what had been revealed to President Monson. Revelation from the Lord to His servants is a sacred process."[7]

I immediately recognized that it was highly unlikely that a revelatory process like the one President Nelson described had occurred. Based on my meetings with President Monson two years earlier, I doubted that he was well enough mentally to have had such a profound experience. The eighty-eight-year-old president's mental faculties were failing him. And, working at the director level for the church, I had witnessed the machinations of the highest councils of the church and participated in committees that wrote, wordsmithed, presented, discussed, and eventually approved church policy. Revelation from God was not in the process.

This so-called revelation from God, rather than being formally announced or shared with the church's membership, was quietly added to the electronic handbook of instructions for stake presidents and bishops, a handbook then not available to the public. After it was leaked, immediate and substantial chaos ensued. Within a week, the church had issued adjustments to the language associated with excluding children as pertaining only to those young people who had same-sex parents as their primary caregivers.[8] To me, it was unimaginable that a divine revelation from on high needed to be updated immediately after the fact.

Concerning Nelson's description of the policy's supposedly revelatory origin, Nelson's colleagues did not subsequently testify to the origin story he shared. Instead, they were silent. One General Authority member of the church's Presidency of the Seventy told a small group, which included a worried, gay father whose young children were church members, that some in the Quorum of the Twelve were upset with this policy. "I guarantee you that this policy will not last," this General Authority said.[9]

I felt stunned to see the president of the Quorum of the Twelve Apostles, a man with whom I had worked closely on the Missionary Executive Committee and the design of the new Missionary Training Center, call such a destructive policy a revelation from God, given in love and compassion. The policy, which came to be known colloquially as the "Policy of Exclusion" or the "PoX," could not have represented the mind or heart of a loving Redeemer. President Nelson's saying it was God's will felt blasphemous to me, a gross misappropriation of ecclesiastical authority. On that day, church leaders lost moral authority in my life, which informed my journey going forward.

Notes

1. Cristina Flores, "Discipline," kutv.com, July 26, 2014.
2. "Leaders Call for Laws That Protect Religious Freedom," Church Newsroom, churchofjesuschrist.org, January 27, 2015.
3. "Reaction to LDS Church announcement on LGBT, religious protections," *Salt Lake Tribune*, January 27, 2015.
4. Peggy Fletcher Stack and Robert Gehrke, "Balancing LGBT, religious rights won't be easy, Mormon leaders concede," *Salt Lake Tribune*, March 2, 2015.
5. For more on SB 296, see Gregory A. Prince, *Gay Rights and the Mormon Church: Intended Actions, Unintended Consequences* (University of Utah Press, 2019), chapter 23.
6. "Church Provides Context on Handbook Changes Affecting Same-Sex Marriages," Church Newsroom, churchofjesuschrist.org, November 6, 2015.
7. Russell M. Nelson, "Becoming True Millennials," *The Church of Jesus Christ of Latter-day Saints 2016 Devotionals*, churchofjesuschrist.org, January 10, 2016.
8. Cimaron Neugebauer, "LDS Church adds more clarification to same-sex marriage policy in Handbook 1," *KUTV2 News*, November 13, 2015.
9. Interview with Bryce Cook, January 31, 2016, and August 24, 2024; Prince, *Gay Rights and the Mormon Church*, 267.

For more on this tumultuous time, see: Taylor G. Petrey, "A Mormon Leader Signals New Openness on Transgender Issues. This Could Be Huge," *Slate*, February 13, 2015; Kiersten Nuñez, "About 1,500 resign from LDS Church at event prompted by policy change on same-sex couples," Fox 13 Utah, November 14, 2015; Marion Edmonds-Allen, "Suicides or Not, LDS is Harming LGBT Youth," *Advocate*, February 13, 2016; Michael Barker, Daniel Parkinson, and Benjamin Knoll, "The LGBTQ Mormon Crisis: Responding to the Empirical Research on Suicide," *Dialogue: A Journal of Mormon Thought* 9, no. 2, Summer 2016; and Elizabeth Dias, "Mormon Church to Allow Children of L.G.B.T. Parents to Be Baptized," *New York Times*, April 4, 2019.

21

Beginning My New Life as a Woman

"I'm glad to finally get to talk to Laurie."

It was March 2016, and my long-time assistant, Susan, was sitting across from me on her last day before retiring after forty-four years of working in the Church Office Building. Her smile was more coy than usual, and her eyes twinkled. In our time together, she survived cancer and chemo treatments twice and often looked tired and weak, but that was not the case today. During her multiple illnesses, I aggressively protected her position with me. She frequently reiterated that she wouldn't work for any other "man." We developed a deep and primarily unspoken loyalty to each other. Her use of my true name, for the first time, in my church office was entirely out of context, and I reeled from the surprise of it.

My gaping expression conveyed my unspoken, "How did you know?"

Susan was delighted to finally reveal her long-guarded secret. "I monitored your email while you traveled in case something time-sensitive needed your immediate attention," Susan explained. "Sometimes you wrote emails to yourself containing your journal entries. Many of them described your gender dysphoria and coming to terms with your true identity as 'Laurie.'" This happened for many years, including coming out to myself and God during that work trip to Lisbon.

"So, you read them ... *all* of them?" I was initially aghast at the apparent invasion of my privacy and the liberties she had taken.

Susan's smile spread even broader, giving me my answer.

I marveled that she never let on what she knew about me all that time but waited until the day before she retired to tell me. During our years together, Susan had two difficult bouts of cancer and chemotherapy. Throughout the entire experience, she worked as often as she could. When I received pressure from Human Resources to replace her with someone who could work daily, I aggressively protected her and her position. She told me frequently she would never work again for another man. Now I understood her dry humor.

Susan explained that she knew she was protecting *me* at every turn. She covered for me during each therapist and doctor appointment, which at times were several per month. She never said a word when I came into the office late every Monday, with my poor face and neck raw from electrolysis treatments and the untreated whiskers showing sloppy, four-day growth. Susan kept my schedule clear on Monday afternoons so I could hide in my office and heal unseen. When my appearance started changing—I grew my hair longer, and my face and body became softer and more feminine through HRT—and colleagues came by her desk to question what was happening with me, she feigned that she had no idea what they were talking about.

As I comprehended this new revelation of all Susan had done for me, my heart overflowed with gratitude for her. I realized I had benefited from her loyalty far more than she ever had from mine.

We sat together for quite a while and cried as I filled in the blanks of my transition journey. I told her I did not expect to be employed by the end of the year, either. Over time, it had become incrementally less viable to present as male as doing so became increasingly offensive to my soul. The time was coming fast that I needed to live full-time as Laurie, which I figured would never be acceptable at work, despite my hope to the contrary.

My younger sister Debbie was the first person I came out to in my family of origin. Coming out is almost always accompanied by pre-conversation anxiety and views of worst-case scenarios, but I trusted her to treat me with respect. Rather than take the risk of a phone call, I emailed her about my feelings and lifelong experiences with dysphoria. Her response to me was better than I could have imagined. The opening line of her email back to me was, "Wow, wow, wowee!!" More poignantly, she wrote of how she now understood why I was always so sad as a youth, realizing that I carried the constant burden of identity conflict. After things went so well with Debbie, I wrote to my high school friend Mike, who still lived in Detroit. I described my experiences with dysphoria from the time we knew each other as teens. Like Debbie, Mike responded that he knew I was always sad but didn't know why. I also told Mike he was my first real "schoolgirl crush." He replied that he was glad he hadn't known that back then.

I decided not to come out to my sister Sandra. As adults, we had lost connection. I would text her a short birthday greeting each April, to which she would only reply with a brief "Thank you." It felt too awkward to try to create a relationship as Laurie with someone I didn't even have a relationship with.

When it came to my parents, I would say aloud and mean that I would not come out to them "in this life." I could not bear the thought of the expected judgment and word daggers that might come, especially from Dad, should the news of my truth come to them. I had stood up to Dad on many issues before, but this was so close and personal to me that I dared not risk crossing a boundary into a painful minefield.

Once I began hormone replacement and taking steps to transition, I knew the time would come when they would no longer know me as their son. I thought I would have to withdraw from my connection with them, including regular notes, emails, and occasional phone calls on special days throughout the year. I didn't want that. We'd experienced temporary disconnections before, and I can't say I liked it. I wouldn't even be able to tell them *why* I'd withdrawn. I did not want to expose myself to the harmful words and energy I feared, even if I only made a single call.

But over time, I began to be more thoughtful about it and felt I needed to repent of my determination never to tell them. I wrote Debbie, knowing she would understand perfectly what I was up against.

Her reply was so full of wisdom that it blew me away. She validated my fears but told me I "needed to give them the chance to love me for who I am." Whoa! Wow, wow, wowee! I asked her when she, my younger sister, became so wise. With that concise teaching, I resolved to come out to our parents. But how? I decided to write them via email, too. I had learned that was the only way to express all I needed to and afford the recipient time to process the message. Knowing Dad was highly reactionary, I took it one step further. At the end of my letter, I asked my parents to think carefully about what I shared with them and told them I would not read a reply or answer a call for seven days to give them time to process and decide what they wanted to say to me.

I included in my explanation many things I felt and did growing up. I told them I planned to legally change my first name from the one I shared with Dad. Knowing that could be painful for them, I also explained that I planned to use Laurie Lee as my new name, the very name they had chosen for me had I not been assigned male at birth. I felt they reserved the name for me, having not given it to either of my younger sisters. I have always kept the name in my heart since Mom told me forty-five years ago. I hoped that might provide a balm to the blow.

My parents honored my request to wait before contacting me, but I still panicked when I saw their number on my phone the following week. To my profound surprise and joy, they spoke very tenderly about my news and graciously extended their complete love and acceptance. I cried a lot then and after. I became so grateful for my parents' reaction, the courage Debbie afforded me, and the blessing it was to retain my parents' love on my journey forward.

My parents expressed their happiness with the name I accepted, which they had chosen so long before. In each of these cases with people who were the closest to me in my childhood and youth, my revealing my gender identity brought them a measure of peace. In the twenty-first century, there were finally words to describe what they had always sensed in me growing up, but was not yet publicly defined.

At work, timing was critical, so I held off on coming out to all my colleagues for as long as possible. If I could wait until I was fifty-five and completed twenty years of service, I could retire with some of my retirement benefits protected. I would turn fifty-five in June 2016, and August 3 would mark my twentieth anniversary as a church employee.

One morning in April 2016, a group email popped up on my phone while I was preparing for work. The subject line read, "Gender-neutral restrooms." The author was a colleague who directed temple construction in North America. He had sent it to our managing director and all the department's division directors. He shared a photo of a gender-neutral restroom sign he had photographed at the San Diego airport.

Coincidentally, I had flown through there recently and photographed the same sign. Gender-neutral restrooms are far more common today, but in 2016, they were more of an exception, so I joyfully posted my photo and positive comments about it on my private social media. However, my colleague's emailed comment accompanying his picture were deriding and offensive. I collapsed onto the toilet in my bathroom, unable to believe my eyes. It was highly unprofessional and prohibited by policy to send out such emails in the first place, given their potential for harassment.

Far worse for me was that he had targeted the transgender community with his comments. I considered my options. If I ignored the email, I was sure some colleagues would reply with lighthearted comments, which might further reveal the bias of my fellow department leaders and hurt me even more. Or I could answer, push back, and tell him to stop and retract it. Doing so could jeopardize my employment just a few months before I could receive my retirement benefits. Despite the risk, I decided to stand up for my community and who I was. I needed to take this opportunity to speak out. I replied quickly before anyone else could, pointed out how ignorant and wrong his statements were, and concluded by saying, "Perhaps you think you don't know someone who is transgender, but now you do!"

I had now violated the last of the constraints placed upon me by the Presiding Bishopric: I had spoken of being trans in the workplace. When I arrived at work, all eyes were on me. My supervisor, Brant Robbins, summoned me to his office, where I met with him and the department's Human Resources director. Brant seemed to be doing damage control to determine what level of militancy I planned to take on the issue and whether I was a threat to the department. He calmed down when he learned I was not a threat. Brant, who was a stake president in Orem, Utah, then explained that just the previous Sunday, he had met with a returned missionary who came out to him as transgender and intended to transition their presentation to male. The two of them had a good discussion, and his heart had softened towards transgender people. I offered quiet thanks to another good trans person who set the example. I later learned that the individual was none other than my friend Emmett Claren, now actor and singer-songwriter Emmett Preciado. We had been to transgender support meetings together and shared ideas on our TransActive LDS group.

Later that morning, each of my staff and many friends from our Temple Design Division came into my office to express their concern and support for me. It was a lovely and unexpected outpouring of kindness. That day's outcome relieved my fear of being terminated on the spot, and for the next several months, I served as an "out transgender" senior architect for the church. Having the courage to come out at work seemed to fuel my desire and readiness to be out in all my circumstances.

If the church's leaders over the Physical Facilities Department allowed me to remain employed as I transitioned gender presentation, including my legal name and gender marker changes, it would set a critically positive precedent and opened up church employment and church participation for gender-variant people. I was convinced I was in the best possible position to make such a bold request and put it to the test. My employment record had been laudable. At the time, I directed the design and construction of several projects for the Missionary Department, including expanding the flagship Missionary Training Center in Provo. I also directed the church's real estate investment group's most prominent current project, the Alexander residential tower, adjacent to the recently completed Philadelphia Temple, near the city center. I had also explained to the Presiding Bishop three years earlier that my transition to living authentically as a woman was forthcoming.

But despite my involvement in critical projects and overall track record, I also knew that chances were slim that my employer would accommodate my request. I needed to have a backup plan. I had a strong relationship with several architectural firms and construction managers whose contractual services I had coordinated for the

On the Provo Missionary Training Center construction site, April 21, 2016. Courtesy Laurie Lee Hall.

church for years. I contacted the principal of one of the architectural firms, which I highly respected, for a private meeting while I was in their Portland, Oregon, offices for project meetings.

He may have supposed I had some performance-related issue or a new project to discuss. Instead, I raised something I had never spoken of face-to-face before in a professional setting: I came out as transgender. I explained the pros and cons of how that might affect my employment with the church. Together, we explored the possibility of my coming to work for his firm as a project design manager, and his interest in my services was evident. We agreed to keep the dialog open and confidential and watch how things played out with my employment over the summer. I repeated this process with other selected firms with equally positive responses. It was an odd experience to have long been their employer and now seek employment. But in each case, the conversation was held as professional colleagues, equal with the opportunity to benefit the other mutually.

On the last Sunday of May 2016, as I stood in front of the bedroom mirror attempting to tie my tie for church services, my spirit finally cried out: *enough!* I could no longer keep up the ruse of presenting as male in those places that required it of me. I collapsed from emotional pain and did not attend my meetings. Concerned for my welfare when I didn't show up, Bishop Darrell Cotton came by our home that afternoon. Bishop Cotton was a remarkable man and the right person to lead our ward at this critical juncture. Full of enthusiasm, with beaming eyes and a smile to match, Darrell Cotton was a friend to all but took particular notice of the marginalized and unfortunate. He was uninterested in "going by the book," including anything in the church handbooks that seemed unfairly and unnecessarily restrictive. His ministry demonstrated pure, unbounded love for the Lord Jesus Christ and his fellow man. His energy and drive to do more good infected everyone.

I told him I was at the breaking point and that it was time for me to come out and finalize my transition. I could no longer swap gender presentations multiple times each day to make others feel comfortable. He agreed to help me.

We didn't know it then, but our timing was not good. Less than two weeks later, in a June 10, 2016, "correlation meeting" for church leaders, General Authority Seventy Larry Y. Wilson trained the Area Seventies who oversaw the stakes in Utah. The training was to prepare the Area Seventies for the "Coordinating Council Meetings" they would hold the following week with the stake presidents they advised.

This preparatory meeting began with the announcement that three of these Area Seventies—all attorneys by trade—would "assist stake presidents with disciplinary situations" that "may become public or involve media attention." Requests for their involvement in disciplinary action against a church member could "come at the request of a General Authority, Area Seventy or Stake President." Issues requiring discipline included "same-sex marriage, ordained [*sic*] women, apostasy, transgender issues, or other items" that might not be addressed yet in the church handbook of instructions. The three attorney Area Seventies would "walk through procedures with the stake president and help him design a measured way to deal with the situation." Elder

Wilson concluded the meeting by sharing the New Testament story of Jesus driving the money changers, the unholy, out of the temple.[1]

Not knowing that these meetings were taking place, Bishop Cotton and I developed a plan for me to come out. We chose the first Sunday service in July for me to come out as transgender to the ward and stake, removing the last barrier to public social transitioning everywhere outside of work. Bishop Cotton would be conducting Sunday's "Fast and Testimony Meeting," the monthly "open mic" meeting where church members are welcome to share their faith-promoting feelings and experiences. Bishop Cotton would use his opening comments to set the stage by emphasizing inclusion, compassion, and acceptance. I would then walk to the mic as the second speaker, piggybacking on his remarks and announcing my coming out.

When that Sunday arrived, I felt a little anxious but more euphoric about finally sharing my truth. As the bishop concluded his words and turned from the pulpit, I sprang up from our second-row pew to the podium. I stood at the pulpit of our neighborhood meetinghouse, where I had conducted the ward's first sacrament meeting fourteen years earlier. I looked over the congregation filled with the faces of friends, neighbors, and fellow servants, many of whom I had known and served for nearly twenty years as their bishop and stake president. Taking a deep breath, I described in simple terms how I had struggled with gender dysphoria all my life but had finally found spiritual acceptance as a transgender woman. I explained that I would soon socially transition to presenting as my female self. Leaning on the bishop's comments, I pled with our ward to exercise patience with me and compassion for me and my family.

Many women in the ward approached me after the meeting, offering support and hugs. Some said it was the most spiritual meeting they had attended in a long time. I later learned that other ward members complained to the stake president and church headquarters that it was the greatest abomination they had ever seen in a chapel.

After chatting with several women in the chapel (no men greeted me), I headed to the Sunday School class for adults, which I had been teaching for some time. This Sunday, I noticed that several who typically attended the class weren't there. I also noticed many came to class whom I had not seen before.

As I attempted to teach the class the following Sunday, authentically presenting as Laurie Lee, an enormous amount of animosity filled the room. Even Marleen, who had seen me as Laurie for years, was on edge to watch me teaching the gospel while wearing women's clothing. At one point, Don, a friend whose family I had ministered to for several years, stood bolt-upright, looked at me angrily, and then brusquely left the classroom without a word. Others followed him and "held court" in the hallway outside the classroom for the rest of the lesson time.

I later learned that significant contention broke out elsewhere in the building. Before my class started, Stake President Gregg Stillmann demanded that Bishop Cotton get to the classroom and prevent me from teaching. Instead, the bishop supported me as I gave the lesson. At the end of the class, he stood and addressed those who remained, imploring everyone to extend grace and kindness toward me. Then, privately, he told me how the stake president had objected to my teaching that day. He released me from my calling to teach the following Sunday at the direction of the stake president. The release left me sad and forced me to realize that I might not be able to serve in the ways I had in the past, in the ways that I loved.

In a subsequent conversation with President Stillmann at the beginning of my social transition at church, though he seemed thoughtful and kind towards me, he asked me to hold off on attending weekly meetings of the Relief Society—the church's organization for women—until he could be sure there would be no disruption if I participated.

I was now dressing and living as Laurie Lee everywhere except at my job. One day, as I was driving home after onsite construction meetings at the Provo MTC, it occurred to me that now that I was presenting at church as a woman, questions about my holding the male-only priesthood would surely be raised. I decided to be proactive and show my willingness to conform to current norms. I emailed President Stillmann, explaining why I thought that he, as my priesthood leader, should ask me to forego using the priesthood. He replied with his agreement and told me to stop exercising the priesthood. I offered this solution so my transition would be perceived as something other than a threat. Astonishingly, President Stillmann would later cite my offer as grounds for church discipline against me.

At work, General Authorities were on their summer break, which they take every July. Church employees who worked with these senior leaders often took advantage of the month to spend their annual leave, causing work in some headquarters departments like mine to fall to a low ebb. This July lull gave me more time between my transition and what I knew was coming at work. Early in the month, my supervisor Brant Robbins told me in an email to cancel planned, out-of-state business meetings so I could meet with him instead, though he wouldn't say why. His tone showed me that there was no negotiating this, so I canceled the meetings. But when the day came that I was supposed to meet with Brant, he didn't even come to work. I never heard why our appointment didn't happen. Although I was annoyed about canceling my work trip for no reason, I felt relieved that I had avoided what might have been a confrontation with Brant.

The reprise was short-lived. Two weeks later, Brant sent me another email asking for a Friday meeting in his office. Since his tone was the same, I knew he would now address the topic he had previously avoided. I had done all I could to plan for this eventuality. At the appointed hour, I entered his office and sat. Brant had been in charge of our department for four years, and I had served with him as a fellow division director for many more before that. When the position he now held had come open for the second time due to Davies' call to the Presiding Bishopric, I was serving the department as acting managing director, and everyone expected me to be appointed full-time. But in my interviews with the Presiding Bishopric, I declined to take the assignment for the second time, to their visible dismay. I explained that the position required a generalist, and as an architect, I was a specialist. Besides, I was starting to come out to some family and friends and knew I could not accept the position with the challenges of gender identity that I was beginning to face. So Brant was assigned the role and performed it well.

We respected each other and enjoyed a friendly relationship. He was a big man with an equally big, deep voice. He usually greeted me with a generous smile and a crushing handshake, but today his heavy brow was tightly knit and descended low upon his ordinarily kind eyes. In the interview again was the department's human resource director, Jerry Moody. Jerry tried hard to fill his role in the department, but time had shown he understood nothing about our business and usually managed to land on the wrong side of most topics.

"Where is this going?" Brant began. I will never get used to church leader interviews starting with a pointed question without context, leaving me to figure out the topic or seek clarification. Jerry shifted nervously in his chair as Brant waited for my response. He knew me to be someone who could argue a point successfully until all opposing sides cried "uncle." He looked concerned about what would happen next.

I had no genuine belief that my employer would permit my social transition. But before I left the Church Office Building for the last time, I knew I had to ask. I committed myself in early 2016 to do so not only for my benefit but also for future queer employees.

"I need to know if I will be allowed to retain my employment if I socially transition here." There, I asked it! But I didn't stop there. I didn't want just a middle manager's opinion on the issue. "And I need to know what the decision of the Church Human Resources Committee is." All of us knew that the First Presidency chaired the Human Resources Committee.

I then explained that social transition is a medical and mental health accommodation benefiting the employee without harming the employer. I linked struggles I had long experienced at work to ongoing dysphoria, which I was sure would be mitigated if I were only permitted to transition.

I pointed out that the great "Utah Compromise," passed thanks to our church's support, guaranteed housing and employment protection for transgender employees. State law now requires every large employer to allow employees to transition without fear of retribution. I acknowledged that the church had successfully built in their religious exception to that law, but pleaded that the church grant an exception and follow the spirit of the law they advocated because it was the ethical thing to do.

Jerry became flustered and started to chime in with a list of excuses, but Brant cut him off. "I'll get you your answer," he said with a sense of finality.

My answer came in the form of a phone call four days later. My stake president, Gregg Stillmann, called me at work and asked me to meet him at his office at church that evening for an undisclosed purpose. I decided to go to the meeting, presenting authentically as Laurie. When I arrived, I was surprised to see my friend and bishop, Darrell Cotton, sitting on President Stillmann's right. Both of them were wearing dark suits, white shirts, and ties. It was uncommon for a church member to meet with their bishop and stake president simultaneously. I sensed this was going to be anything but a friendly visit.

President Stillmann—whom I had called to serve as a bishop and then as one of my counselors when I was *his* stake president—seemed distraught. I couldn't tell if it was because it was the first time he'd seen me presenting as Laurie or the reality of what he was about to do.

"I need to take your temple recommend away."

Stillmann was subdued and had difficulty making eye contact as he spoke the words to me from behind his desk.

Church members are taught that a current temple recommend is a sacred symbol of membership in the church. It enables the holder to enter and worship in the holy temple. And, like all other church employees, I was required to have a temple recommend because it assured that the holder maintained specific standards of "worthiness." If I lost my recommend, it meant I was disqualified ecclesiastically and, in the eyes of the church, morally unfit to remain in its employ.

"You have separated yourself from the priesthood and the blessings of temple attendance," President Stillmann said to justify his action. He referred to my determination to present as a woman as the cause, even though nothing in the church handbook of instructions said that transitioning social presentation was grounds for canceling one's temple recommend.

I knew I needed to push back. "Surely this is not your decision alone," I replied, feeling higher church authorities were directing him. His calling me in for this meeting—just four days after I asked for a decision from the Church Human Resources Committee as to whether I could retain my employment if I socially transitioned—could not be a coincidence.

"This decision is mine alone," he countered. I still didn't believe him.

"President, we both know that holding a recommend is based solely on a person's properly answering the fifteen temple recommend interview questions," I began. "You and I have memorized these questions, so let's review them together."

This was a bold approach, but I knew I could back it up. Even though it had been three and a half years since I administered a recommend interview, I had conducted hundreds of them in my lifetime and received them quite a few times, too. I knew that if I recited and then answered each of these fifteen prescribed questions as if I were conducting my own interview, I could determine the meeting's outcome. My stake president leaned back into the chair that used to be mine as if resigned to what he knew was about to come.

"Do you have faith in and a testimony of God the Eternal Father, His Son Jesus Christ, and the Holy Ghost?" I began, then sincerely answered that question by expressing my faith. For an hour, I asked and subsequently answered each of these questions in detail, demonstrating that I was living up to every commitment the church requires of its members to be considered in good standing and worthy of a temple recommend.

"Do you have faith in and a testimony of the atonement of Christ and of His role as Savior and Redeemer?"

"Do you have a testimony of the restoration of the gospel in these the latter days?"

"Do you sustain the President of the Church of Jesus Christ of Latter-day Saints as Prophet, Seer, and Revelator, and as the only person on earth who possesses and is authorized to exercise all priesthood keys?" I had resolved in my mind at that point that although I no longer ceded these men's moral authority to guide my life, as a church member, and one who understood the challenges of striving to be an inspired leader with human frailties, I could continue to offer them my sustaining support.

"Do you sustain the members of the First Presidency and Quorum of the Twelve Apostles as prophets, seers, and revelators? Do you sustain the other General Authorities and local authorities of the church?"

"Do you live the law of chastity?"

"Is there anything in your conduct in relation to members of your family that is not in harmony with the teachings of the church?"

"Do you support, affiliate with, or agree with any group or individual whose teachings or practices are contrary to or oppose those accepted by the Church of Jesus Christ of Latter-day Saints?"

"Do you strive to keep the covenants that you have made, to attend your sacrament meetings, and to keep your life in harmony with the laws and commandments of the gospel?"

"Are you honest in your dealings with your fellow men?"

"Are you a full tithe payer?"

"Do you keep the Word of Wisdom?"

"Do you have financial or other obligations to a former spouse or children?"

"Do you keep the covenants you made in the temple?"

"Do you wear the garment both night and day as instructed in the endowment and in accordance with the covenant you made in the temple?"

"Have there been any sins or misdeeds in your life that should have been resolved with priesthood leaders but have not been?"

When I came to the last question, "Do you consider yourself worthy to enter the Lord's house and to participate in temple ordinances?" I said, "Yes!" and then sat back, believing I had answered the fifteen questions more thoroughly and affirmatively than perhaps any of us in the room had ever witnessed. I glanced at Bishop Cotton for the first time in the meeting. He was smiling with what looked like a tinge of gratification.

"Considering this information," President Stillmann said, "I see no need to take your temple recommend."

Exhausted but satisfied, I rose from my chair, thanked the two men, and excused myself.

When I awoke the following day, the previous night's experience of defending my spiritual worth had so emotionally drained me that I was too exhausted to go to work. I spent much of the day thinking about the critical juncture I now found myself in. When I returned to work the following day, I received another phone call from President Stillmann, nearly at the same hour, again asking me to meet him in his office for an undisclosed purpose. It was telling and a little creepy how repetitious the request felt.

When I arrived at our church building, President Stillmann was sitting behind his desk with Bishop Cotton to his right, both in dark suits, white shirts, and ties, as though neither had moved since I left there forty-eight hours before.

"I need to take your temple recommend away," the president said.

It was beginning to feel like Groundhog Day. Only this time, I said nothing. What more could I say? It was apparent what was happening: Because I asked Brant if the church would continue to employ me after I transitioned as a woman, someone had instructed my stake president to cancel my recommend, which church employees were required to have. Because President Stillmann had not done so, whoever was advising him reiterated the demand, and he had called me here again. There was no option and no local discernment for my stake president.

My conclusion was based on a hunch, but minutes of a January 8, 2016, council meeting of church leaders, later leaked to the public, supported it. In that meeting, like the one held in June 2016, General Authority Seventy Larry Y. Wilson provided training on "church discipline" to Area Seventies, who supervised Utah's stake presidents. Wilson taught the Area Seventies that "stake presidents and bishops who are unwilling to address disciplinary matters are subject to being released," and that "those who will not apply the appropriate discipline have misunderstood what compassion is."[2]

My ecclesiastical leader was forced to be the one who would disqualify me from church employment by canceling my temple recommend. If I no longer held a recommend, the church could legally terminate my employment and avoid dealing with the ramifications of a transgender employee asking for accommodation to transition.

I sat in utter silence, glaring as the president squirmed uncomfortably. Unable to stand the long pause, he began to speak, rambling on for nearly twenty minutes in a nervous blur of words that yielded nothing of value. Finally, he stopped and said, "Aren't you going to say anything?"

I stood up from my chair, rising to my full six feet so that he and the bishop would take in my entire presentation as Laurie, which I hoped they would never forget.

"President, your judgment is unjust," I said, then turned and left the office.

I knew it was time to take the next step. As soon as word reached church headquarters that my stake president had rescinded my temple recommend, they could immediately terminate my employment. I needed to act first. I had already drafted a letter to Brant indicating my intent to retire from church employment. I arrived early at the office the next morning and placed the letter on his desk. My days as a church employee were coming to an end.

Any fear I felt about the fallout from suddenly announcing my retirement was without justification. Instead of retaliation, department leaders and my staff offered only goodwill to me over the next two weeks leading up to my final day. Gender transition, particularly, was never mentioned again. Even though I was departing in the middle of a significant project—the multi-building expansion of the Provo Missionary Training Center—there seemed to be nothing but support, though mingled with a sense of relief. I was leaving without a major confrontation, without a fight.

On my last day, Brant and the other directors treated Marleen and myself, presenting as male for the last time, to lunch at the Cheesecake Factory, where he gave me various letters and gratuities related to retirement. Typically, there would have been a retirement social for someone employed for twenty years like me, held on the lovely and open top floor of the Church Office Building, with everyone in the department and a member of the Presiding Bishopric invited. Brant used the private luncheon to keep my departure lower-key and out of the general view.

Following the luncheon, Marleen and I had an unusual appointment with the Presiding Bishopric and their executive secretaries. I had worked closely with these men and their predecessors for most of my twenty years there. Each knew I was leaving to complete my social transition to presenting as a woman. I suspected that their office had orchestrated removing my temple recommend to avoid having to answer my question of whether I could remain employed after transitioning.

Their conversation with us was most gracious, considering the circumstances. They each talked about me glowingly, recounting my contributions to the work of church Physical Facilities throughout the years. They emphasized the obedient and respectful attitude I always showed the senior Brethren. They reminded me to maintain the same attitude towards the church leaders after my departure. I was informed what was still expected of me. This was the last hour of my church employment.

Upon returning home, I loaded all my male-presenting suits, shirts, and ties into my Ford Explorer, drove to my local Deseret Industries thrift store, and made a sizable donation. I thought of how, fifty years before, my parents had not given me a colorful Easter dress, but a clip-on bow tie and made me wear it. I would never again give others authority to tell me who I was and how I should look. I had finally severed my last tie with those who would dictate how I presented myself. I would no longer be compelled to look differently from how I identified just to make others comfortable.

Although it is often called "gender transition," my gender had always been female. Mine was a transition from presenting as an inauthentic gender to the one I have always profoundly felt was me.

On this day, I began my life full-time as my authentic self, Laurie Lee Hall.

Notes

1. Utah Areas, Area Seventies Correlation Meeting Minutes, June 10, 2016, mormonleaks.io.
2. Utah Areas, Area Council Meeting Minutes, January 8, 2016, mormonleaks.io.

22

Closed and Opened Doors

After my forced retirement in September 2016, I moved quickly on legal changes associated with my transition—my court-ordered name change, updating my identity documents with both name and gender marker changes, and all the financial organizations like banks and credit card companies that required my new name.

Now living full-time as Laurie Lee, I reached out to my contacts at other architectural firms to seek formal employment interviews. For them, it was their first time to get to know me as a woman. I had multiple in-person interviews with two firms, who had long been church consultants and were still engaged in ongoing significant projects. We mutually agreed that as they brought me on, although I had a wealth of experience with church projects, at least initially I would not be assigned to work directly with my former colleagues at the Church Office Building. By December, I felt confident that I would receive offers of employment right after the first of the year. I was excited to get to work and finally practice architecture openly as my authentic self.

Now that I was living full-time as Laurie, I experienced what it felt like moving through the world as a woman. It's true that many people only saw me as a transgender woman, or worse, a man in a skirt, rather than just simply *as a woman.* But I was becoming more familiar with how it felt every day to wake up and be me without planning when I would present as who. I reveled in the serenity and joy I now felt.

Name tags Laurie Lee wore while cooking Thanksgiving dinner for her in-laws' family, November 24, 2016, after her court-ordered name change was finalized two months before. Courtesy Laurie Lee Hall.

In December, the Provo City Center Temple design and construction team invited me to join them for an annual luncheon commemorating the fire that nearly destroyed the Provo Tabernacle six years earlier. I had attended this luncheon for all the previous years but came as Laurie this time. Only some people on the team knew of my transition, and I could see it was hard for several men in attendance to accept me. I walked past where they were seated and joined some of the women of the team, including several designers and the church historian assigned to the historic building project. They were delighted to see the new me and catch up. It was as though they had always known me as me, and it was so affirming.

Later that winter, the City Center Temple project received a prestigious Historic Preservation award at Utah's State History Awards dinner. My friends from FFKR Architects, the consultant architects for the temple, invited me to the event and to sit with them at their table. We were seated in a ballroom at large, round tables of eight. Looking around the ballroom, I noticed that my former Physical Facilities Department colleagues had a table where Brant Robbins and my other peers were seated. Occasionally, I noticed them looking over at me. They had not seen me out as Laurie, either. None of them said hello or acknowledged me in any way. There was also a table for our construction manager contractor, Jacobsen Construction. Some looked my way nervously, but a couple of these former associates ventured over to say hello and ask about my well-being. When the time came for the award presentation, the emcee asked everyone who had worked on the temple project to stand. I felt proud that I, as Laurie, was among those who stood to be recognized.

Everything was going well with my new life until January 2017, when all communication from potential employers abruptly stopped. Suddenly, no one would take my calls, answer my emails, or respond to my texts. I had naively assumed that if I stayed away from contractual work on church projects, no one would have a problem with my working for companies that happened to have contracts with the church. But now I questioned that assumption. Over the years, I had seen the Presiding Bishopric's Office turn on other professionals and service providers, refusing to use the services of contractors who had done something to offend someone in power at the church. In a few of these cases, I even saw the Physical Facilities Department, at the direction of the Presiding Bishopric, pay off contractors so they would not make waves publicly. Frustrated, I concluded that someone at the church must have told these companies who contracted with the church not to hire me.

By this point, the church was developing its position on transgender rights. Exactly two years had passed since apostle Dallin H. Oaks, a former Utah Supreme Court Justice, had said in the *Salt Lake Tribune* broadcast that the "transgender situation is something we have not had so much experience with. We have some unfinished business in teaching on that." Since then, the church has begun clamping down on any permissiveness of individuals' rights of self-identification of gender. On January 16, Salt Lake City's Kirton McConkie law firm filed an amicus brief to the US Supreme Court in the case of *G[avin] G[rimm] v. Gloucester County School Board,* on behalf of the LDS Church and other religious organizations. Gavin Grimm was a transgender boy at a Virginia high school who sued his local school board after it dictated that he must use the girls' restrooms based on his sex assigned at birth. Kirton McConkie's amicus brief stated that the participating churches held the scriptural description of "male" and "female" found in the Bible's creation story as their core tenet, and refuted any self-determination of gender identity on the part of an individual. Although I didn't immediately know that the church was taking this action, I would become keenly aware of it later. What I did know at that time was that I could find no work in architecture as a socially transitioned woman.

Devastated, I was forced to look outside my profession to support my family. I looked into ridesharing, which had recently come to Salt Lake City, and became a Lyft driver. I learned the best times and areas to stay busy with riders through experimentation. I had a big Ford station wagon that could take seven or eight passengers or a lot of gear. It was prime ski season in Utah, so many groups needed rides from the Salt Lake airport to any of the several ski resorts in the nearby Wasatch Mountains. I drove around the university housing areas and upscale Salt Lake neighborhoods every Thursday, Friday, and Saturday evening to find people to bring to bars and restaurants downtown. After closing time, I stayed busy running the same folks back to their homes. Occasionally, I had a drunk person get sick in the car, forcing me to end my night early. Most nights, I kept driving until 2:00 or even 4:00 A.M., working eight- to twelve-hour shifts.

It felt bizarre to have been a stake president just four years before, now driving people around to bars and parties. But I also discovered an unforeseen advantage: I met hundreds of total strangers each night and interacted with them as my true self, as Laurie Lee—the only way any of them knew me. After being closeted, this constant public exposure built my confidence and thickened my skin. I also learned what it feels like to be vulnerable as a woman. In a few detestable incidents, patrons in my car made sexual advances on me. "Don't touch the driver!" I shouted at them in a deep, low voice, outing myself while striking fear into their hearts!

Being a Lyft driver was a temporary solution while I worked on other ways to use my expertise and talents. I occasionally met with transgender people and their family members to provide support, helping them find understanding, address the intersection with their faith, locate service providers, and so on. I discussed my ideas for a more formal means of providing useful information to these folks with Terri Busch, the gender specialist who had been my therapist.

Terri was very enthusiastic about lending her professional insights and support. She introduced me to Nicole, another licensed social worker, and Colleen, a child psychologist who was also queer. The four of us began meeting in Nicole's offices to develop a seminar to each contribute from our unique perspectives to support transgender people and their loved ones. By April 2017, we had produced material for a three-hour seminar and held our first "Families and Gender Variance Project" workshop at the Salt Lake City YWCA. It felt like a great accomplishment and contribution to the community. We had every intention of enhancing the presentation and holding it regularly. Although I used some of the material in other productions for various organizations, we never returned to offer the workshop again in the same way.

Nicole became impressed with my organizational skills and asked me to provide professional *business* coaching to her and her associates as they expanded their therapy practices and created other programs and seminars. I was glad to take on assignments with them. Initially, I just worked in their meeting room on their projects. However, when word got around that I was providing beneficial consulting services, Nicole rented a tiny office in their suite, and I hung my sign on the door. Before I knew it, I had started a formal business coaching practice called LLH Pathways. I was unknowingly on my own "pathway," full of unexpected turns and surprises. It was good work as I drew on my experience managing offices, employees, and programs worldwide for the church. Soon, I had several clients beyond Nicole, including design professionals, other clinicians, and practices. Meanwhile, I also continued to provide pro-bono support to transgender individuals in navigating the name change and gender marker process in Utah. For a while, I thought that business coaching and consulting would be my permanent new career since I'd found no other opportunities to work in architecture.

In my religious life, even though I was still an active member of the church in every way, Stake President Stillmann forbade me from holding a calling, attending the temple, or even formally visiting members in their homes—all things that were a central part of my life for thirty-six years. I understood firsthand the painful ways church leaders can intentionally remove even the "altar of service" from the reach of those they choose to marginalize or purge. I responded by offering whatever informal acts of service I could. One of my neighbors served as the ward librarian, providing classroom materials to teachers before they gave their lessons each Sunday. She and her assistant were elderly, single sisters who seemed fond of me in my new presentation as Laurie Lee. I routinely checked in with them as the sacrament meeting was out every Sunday to see if they needed my help. Soon, they began phoning me in advance if one of them couldn't make it. Providing library assistance to ward members, especially those opposed to my social transition, became gratifying. I wasn't officially called or sustained. I didn't need to be. I just wanted to find an altar on which to give my offering of service, even if it was limited.

Bishop Cotton started a Book of Mormon class on Tuesday evenings, designed to teach those new to the faith or returning to participation in the church. I attended as well, even though I had studied the book for decades and had practically memorized it. I befriended the folks in the class and helped them gain essential insights into what we were learning. After asking my librarian friends and the women in our Tuesday class if their visiting teachers (women in the ward assigned to be aware of the well-being of each woman and their families) were visiting them, and finding most were not, I befriended them as a fellow sister and became aware of their unique needs. The ward Relief Society president was thrilled to receive my regular updates on the welfare of these sisters my friends. I found satisfaction in serving my ward family this way, and I wanted to continue to do so until the church clarified and opened up its policies on attendance and service on the part of transgender members like me.

About a year after I came out to my parents, I was visiting them in their home for just the second time as their daughter when a National Geographic TV Special, "Gender Revolution," aired. It was a thought-provoking look at the social, medical, and scientific issues surrounding gender identity. We sat together, our eyes glued to the show. Mom turned to me in tears and expressed how she wished she'd understood this before so she could have helped me and protected me from the pain I experienced. It was an incredibly tender and healing evening for us that, a short time before, I could have never in my wildest imagination dreamed possible. Though he didn't express it, I sensed that Dad felt relief as he understood his oldest was never a son. I did not represent some failure on his part to raise a "manly son."

During that visit, I accompanied my parents to several doctor appointments to see their lawyer and banker regarding their end-of-life documents and plans. It was so affirming that they proudly introduced me to each of these professionals as their oldest daughter of three, an architect from Utah.

23

Spiritual Violence

As I transitioned, I felt the difference between how men and women perceived and treated me. With the exception of my bishop, Darrell Cotton, LDS men questioned why a priesthood-holding "male" would ever want to give that up to be a woman. Why would any right-minded man, moreover a church leader and high-ranking church employee, relinquish the male privilege found at every level of the church patriarchy? In contrast, most women in the church were welcoming and compassionate toward me.

Many women of the ward, some of whom I had assisted with gentleness as their bishop in their difficult life circumstances, showed me great kindness. Female ward leaders assumed particular responsibility for me from the start of my social transition. After I came out, one of the counselors in the Relief Society presidency, a professional makeup consultant, invited me to her home on a Saturday to tenderly give me tips on makeup and colors and tones to wear in my clothing. This helped me overcome the decades of female socialization I had missed. Her gift was one of the most affirming things that I experienced in the ward.

At that time, Sunday worship in the church consisted of a three-hour block of meetings, including a sacrament meeting held in the chapel for everyone, separate Sunday School classes for youth and adults, and finally, Aaronic Priesthood quorum meetings for adolescent boys, "Young Women" meetings for adolescent girls, Melchizedek Priesthood quorum meetings for men, and Relief Society meetings for women. The strictly gender-separated nature of these classes is often triggering for transgender youth and adult members, who don't feel welcome in *either* class.

Following my transition, my priesthood leaders invited me on several occasions to continue to attend the all-male adult priesthood quorum meeting. Although I appreciated the invitation and felt it was genuine, I could not bear to validate the church's formal denial of my gender identity. The idea of sitting in a circle of chairs with older men in suits while I wore a dress and women's shoes felt like nothing short of torture.

At this point, no official direction from church leaders was published in the church's handbook of instructions regarding transgender members' attendance of the gender-separated classes, leaving the matter to the judgment of local leaders. This meant that in some wards of the church, socially transitioned members were welcome to attend the class or quorum that aligned with their gender identity and presentation. But in other wards like mine, that was not the case.

So I followed the direction President Stillmann gave me, to hold off on attending Relief Society until he could determine how the women would receive me. I followed up regularly with him, but he continued to put me off. His preventing me from attending Relief Society classes and activities felt ironic. No one had a problem with me visiting these women's meetings when I was presenting as male and serving as a bishop and stake president. But now that I was presenting as a woman, I was no longer permitted to join those same women's meetings.

The ward Relief Society president at the time, Tracy Austin, appeared to yearn for me to attend with the other women. But she confided in me that her hands were tied and that she could not go around the stake president. Such are the ramifications for women who "lead" under the direction of the all-male priesthood.

When I served as stake president, I had assigned myself to work closely with the various Relief Societies in the stake, attending their meetings when it was appropriate for me as their priesthood leader to do so. Service with the sisters was a considerable balm to me and helped mitigate some of the dysphoria I struggled with while attempting to fulfill my responsibilities as stake president.

One evening before a General Relief Society Meeting broadcast, I attended a dinner for the sisters of the stake in my role as stake president. I could have felt quite the outsider in such a situation, yet it was perhaps the most comfortable social experience I could have had in a church setting. As we enjoyed our meal, seated around standard church-issue folding tables, I forgot myself. The women at my table, including Tracy, did too. The conversation drifted into topics women would never discuss before a priesthood leader. The relaxed environment left me feeling accepted by the women as one of their own despite my "authority" and male presentation. I talked with Tracy recently about that evening. To my surprise, she remembered it, too, and corroborated how I had been brought in and accepted among the women even back then.

But now that I was living full-time as a woman, I left the church meetings alone after Sunday School each week while everyone else moved into their third-hour classes divided by gender. Those Relief Society and Priesthood meetings were the most social of the three Sunday meetings. I was excluded from where I knew I could receive the best fellowship and joy with the other sisters at a time in my church membership when I needed it the most. The reality of some of my "ward family," whom I had served as their bishop and stake president for fourteen years, being unwilling to accept me for who I was—even though most of my biological family had—weighed on me as I walked the 384 steps from the church to my home. When I got into my house most Sundays, I sobbed from rejection.

One week, several months after beginning to attend church as Laurie, I chose to enter a Relief Society class. I was helping out in the ward library as usual when the elderly assistant librarian told me she felt weak from low blood sugar. Concerned, I asked if she needed me to accompany her down the hall to the Relief Society meeting. We arrived about ten minutes into the lesson.

I debated whether I should sit in the hall during the lesson, but knowing that her calling required her to be back in the library again in fifteen to twenty minutes, I went in and sat with her. When it came time to go, I accompanied her back to the library. I was surprised when President Stillmann called me within fifteen minutes of the end of the meeting, demanding my appearance in his office.

Unbeknownst to me, a few women who saw me sitting in the Relief Society room had fomented an uproar of angry Facebook posts, texts, and emails. Damage control required my immediate presence in the stake president's office. My explanation of the circumstances that led to my attending the Relief Society class only intensified President Stillman's visible angst. He told me he might need to convene a church disciplinary council due to my actions, which seemed to me like a total overreaction.

During this time of my ongoing meetings with President Stillmann, I learned that I was not the only transgender member being told not to attend the third-hour church class that aligned with my gender identity. I read multiple accounts in our TransActive LDS Support Group about priesthood leaders around the country suddenly and simultaneously informing transgender ward members, who had long been attending the third-hour meeting of their choice, that their attendance would no longer be allowed. We later had hints about this, too, when the January 8, 2016, Utah Area Council Meeting minutes leaked. In that meeting, an Area Seventy asked about a case brought to him by a stake president, in which a stake member wanted to "dress as a woman in church, sit by his wife, and go to Relief Society." The response was that this member should be counseled "not to disrupt the church or its members." Church members with "transgender desires" should "come to church dressed and acting like who God made them. They should understand that it is important to keep everyone else comfortable."

Significantly, Area Seventies in this meeting were also instructed to train stake presidents that "a disciplinary council is mandatory for a member who is in apostasy." Someone asked, "How do we help a stake president who is reluctant to step up and handle the situation?" By counseling with him and developing "possible approaches together," was the answer. Stake presidents should approach members requiring discipline in a methodical, deliberate manner, the meeting's minutes recorded. One solution was that "the member in question might ask for their name to be removed" from church records.[1]

In May 2017, I was back in President Stillmann's office yet again. Only this time, he took a new approach and requested that Marleen come with me. As usual, he was seated behind his desk, looking just like Mormon priesthood leaders are expected to look. He was wearing a white shirt, conservative tie, and dark suit, even though the afternoon and the room were too warm for a suit coat.

Marleen and I were dressed in modest blouses and skirts, with conservative makeup and accessories we deemed appropriate to our age and social position. At the time, I failed to realize I merely traded the look of the standard Mormon man for the look of the standard Mormon woman!

"You are instructed to de-transition back to male or write a letter and resign your membership in the church," President Stillman announced.

In all my years as a bishop and stake president, I had never spoken to anyone with the threatening tone my successor was now using with me. Quite the opposite, church leaders had taught me to never suggest, let alone *require,* that an individual resign their church membership. At that moment, I thought less about what I would say next and more about how contrary his request was to church protocol. I felt wounded by what this man—my current stake president, my former counselor when I was a stake president, and someone I had once considered a friend—was saying to me. But by then, I was not surprised.

His face showed tension as his eyes squinted more tightly than usual. His emotions seemed on the verge of crossing over to anger as he again accused me of going against his direct counsel to not attend Relief Society. In the past, I would not have hesitated to find a way to follow the direction of a priesthood leader, but that time was now gone.

Three years of hormone replacement therapy had changed me physically and emotionally so much, bringing calm and peace to my soul. There was no going back to that dark place in my past when I was tormented by the incongruity between my gender identity and my physical biology. The specter of suicidal ideation and the real possibility I might attempt to end my own life was far too great a risk to consider a return. It was dehumanizing for anyone to ask me to do so for the comfort of others around me who understood nothing of my struggle.

When it came to my church membership, although I had been forced from church employment and church service, I still retained a desire to strive within the church to encourage members and leaders to welcome transgender individuals who wanted to worship and contribute within the ward family.

My response to Stillmann's mandate was measured and deliberate. "President, as you are aware, I cannot safely medically de-transition at this point, nor is it in my heart to resign from the church."

His immediate response seemed pre-programmed. "Then I have no choice but to convene a disciplinary council."

Perhaps as a last effort to get me to change my mind, he turned to Marleen and said, "If you stay with him, we may have to discipline you as well." Marleen and I were aghast. Church leaders refused to accept me as a woman, so much so that they wanted to purge me from the church. But at the same time that Stillmann was insisting that I was a man, he was threatening Marleen for being in a "same-sex marriage" with me as a woman.

A few days later I would learn that a stake president elsewhere in Utah levied the same threat against the wife of a socially transitioned spouse who was also striving to remain active in the church. The church's November 2015 policy, that members in "same-sex marriages" were in apostasy and required church discipline, was still in effect. That couple is now divorced. Church leaders seemed to be looking for a way to sanitize its congregations of transgender members, using that official, published policy in the absence of one on transgender members.

Church protocol for holding a disciplinary council of a member requires prayerfully determining the verdict only after hearing all the relevant witnesses and issues of a case. But as we left Stillmann's office, I felt that someone had pre-determined the outcome in my circumstance and I would soon be put out of the church. I sensed this conclusion was not my stake president's alone but influenced by church headquarters, despite assurances from general church leadership that they left member discipline in the hands of local leaders. Even if President Stillmann felt any empathy for my situation, he had no real power to exercise it. He would risk his position as stake president if he disregarded the direction he was receiving from his file leaders. I soon received a letter from Stillmann, informing me that the date of my disciplinary council was set for June 4, 2017.

I began grieving what I was sure would be my excommunication from my faith community, a community which constituted every aspect of my adult life. Even so, the loss of my identity as a church member, which I highly valued, paled in comparison to the peace and joy I had found through finally living my true identity as a woman and a daughter of God.

I shared a description of my meeting with Stillmann and the pending disciplinary council in the TransActive LDS Support Group. One of my socially transitioned friends, who lived 1,500 miles away, had been in her stake president's office just the week before and received the same charge to "de-transition or resign." This was no coincidence but evidence of the headquarters' administration of the "transgender problem," described in the training received by the Area Seventies previously.

I began planning my response to my forthcoming disciplinary council. I had the option of not attending the council at all, or I could come to the meeting and offer my defense. I knew that church policy allowed members facing such a council to bring witnesses to speak on their behalf, as long as these witnesses were "worthy," temple-recommend-holding church members.

Not attending the council seemed out of the question. I wanted to bear witness one last time to why I had transitioned, hoping to soften some hearts toward me or future LGBTQ church members.

I was well versed in the procedures for such a council, having participated in several in the past as a clerk, bishop, and high councilor. Though stake presidents convene and preside over these "church courts," I had only called for one when I was in that role. I never wanted to convene such a council except in an egregious circumstance. Instead, I exhausted all other options to lift and support a member rather than consider expelling them punitively.

Women in the church facing discipline were almost always dealt with at the ward level instead of the stake level. This meant that the discussion of charges, alleged "sins," and all extenuating details, occurred just with the ward bishop and his two counselors, with minutes taken by a clerk, constituting a tribunal of four men with priesthood authority over one woman.

Even though I had legally changed my name and gender markers months before, my church records still showed, incorrectly, that I was male, and correctly that I had been ordained to the Melchizedek Priesthood. Thus, church policy required that my disciplinary council be held at the stake level. This meant my tribunal would include the entire stake presidency, clerk, and the twelve-member stake high council. Sixteen men with authority over one woman. Me. Although I had experience in such a setting as the presiding officer, it felt terrifying considering how damningly imbalanced it was.

Meanwhile that spring, the new Provo Missionary Training Center—the project I was working on when I was forced out of church employment—was nearing completion. My dear friend Richard Heaton, who had been the director of the MTC during the planning and design, had continued to meet me for lunch occasionally and kept me aware of the project's progress. He assured me I would be welcome at its VIP tour and open house when the project was completed. I didn't think much of it but thanked him for his kindness in never abandoning me.

True to his promise, Richard contacted me when the date was set for the new MTC's open house. It would take place on Tuesday evening, June 6, just forty-eight hours after my disciplinary council!

I wrote back to tell Richard about the pending council and the likelihood that I would no longer be a church member by the time the tour took place. I told him I fully understood if, for that or any other reason, I would not be welcome at the VIP open house. I would be okay with stepping aside and not attending to avoid being a distraction at the special evening. Richard responded quickly. Nonsense, he said, I must be present; he wouldn't have it any other way. I told him that as Laurie Lee, I would wear my Sunday best and look to the world like a senior missionary sister.

The goodness and support I found in Latter-day Saints like Richard Heaton, Darrell Cotton, Tracy Austin, my assistant Susan, and many others, bolstered my belief that a transgender person could belong in the Church of Jesus Christ of Latter-day Saints, worshiping and serving in peace.

Notes

1. Utah Areas, Area Council Meeting Minutes, January 8, 2016, mormonleaks.io.

24

In the House of My Friends

Sunday, June 4, 2017, was Utah's annual LGBTQ Pride Parade in Salt Lake City. It was also the day of my church disciplinary council.

That morning, I attended church services in our ward with my family. Since my social transition at church, we had slipped into the back of the meeting to sit on the folding chairs in the gym that served as the chapel's overflow under the basketball hoop. This put us behind the view of all others in attendance to avoid the stares and the realities of judgment.

To the surprise of the congregation, at the beginning of the meeting, one of Stake President Stillmann's two counselors released from service our bishop and my friend, Darrell Cotton. Bishop Cotton had only served for three of the typical five-or-more-year term for bishops, signifying his removal from service was deliberate. When the man who released him asked ward members to raise their right hands in the customary "show of thanks" for Bishop Cotton's service, I raised my hand high. This was the last formal show of thanks I would ever offer as a church member, and it was on behalf of this good man who repeatedly petitioned for my inclusion and equality within the ward and stake. Darrell told me that afternoon that his early release came because of his passionate support of me. It was just the beginning of the day's painful events.

At 7:00 P.M. that night, Marleen and I were invited into the stake high council room at our church building, where my disciplinary council was about to begin. I had conducted countless wonderful meetings with ward and stake members in this room, many with the men now assembled in attendance. I tried to smile at these men, my friends and neighbors, as Marleen and I took our seats to the right of the stake presidency as directed. As their former stake president, I had ordained most of them to priesthood offices and had called them to serve in various responsibilities at church. They looked back at me with pained and anxious faces.

I sensed Marleen's nervousness as she sat next to me. Her last-minute decision to attend the council with me may have been less about supporting me and more about defending herself if needed. She hadn't forgotten how, at our last meeting with President Stillmann, he had warned that if I did not "de-transition," he might need to discipline her as well for being a woman married to a woman. She was left feeling shocked and fearful, not one to stray from the centerline of the road of mainstream Mormonism.

"Brother David Bruce Hall Jr.," President Stillmann commenced, showing disrespect by using my "dead name," my former name that no longer existed, even legally. "You are charged with refusing to follow the council of priesthood leaders and with apostasy for your personal views of certain general church teachings." The disciplinary council format allowed me to respond to the charges and answer questions posed by the stake presidency and six of the twelve high councilors in the room who were assigned specific roles in the council. Three of these six were supposed to represent my interests and the other three the church's interests.

Responding to the charges, I explained that my alleged refusal to heed church leader council involved my brief appearance at a single Relief Society meeting. After I rehearsed why I had attended a portion of the meeting in support of another sister, I turned to the accusation of my so-called apostasy. I proclaimed my belief in the church's Family Proclamation statement that "gender is an essential characteristic of individual premortal, mortal, and eternal identity"—a statement that was true to my lived experience.

I explained the difference between the scientifically recognized categories of "gender" (which refers to how every individual perceives themselves) and "sex" (which refers to a person's biological attributes). I shared substantial scientific evidence demonstrating that some mortal bodies do not develop consistently with gender identity, thus causing conflict between gender identity and the physical body. I shared my personal, spiritual experiences that showed me that God knows me and who I have always been. I had accepted this personal truth, my eternal gender identity, and was trying to live consistently with this knowledge.

I had invited only one outside witness to speak on my behalf. When he came in, the emotions rose to a crescendo. It was my affirming and, as of that morning, *former* bishop, Darrell Cotton. He shared his loving, high opinion of me, the validity of my struggle, and the sacred nature of my journey to be true to myself. I felt joy for Darrell's goodness and hoped that if my testimony hadn't touched the council members' hearts, perhaps his would. He was then excused without comment.

The discussion during these first thirty minutes eliminated any notion of "apostate" behavior on my part, as apostasy never came up again during the council. I had testified of my lived experience to the best of my ability and was satisfied I had done what I came to do. Despite the spiritual gravity of this proceeding, I endured it in a calm, emotional state. I knew my truth and was already dedicated to living it, which spared me from being caught up in the moment's emotions. Then it was time for me to answer their questions. To my amazement, none of the high councilors asked me anything about what I had just shared. Nor were their inquiries empathetic or coming from a place of concern. Instead, each man came with a carefully prepared question to ask, as if scripted and assigned. One soft-spoken young man who had been my stake clerk asked if I intended to go to the press with my story. Why would he care? The whole thing felt rigid, calculated, and rehearsed. But it didn't matter. I knew the predetermined result of the proceedings. Nothing said or done in the council would change it.

The comments of the three high councilors whom President Stillmann designated to protect my interests were even more disappointing. One of them, Don Collard, was a neighbor whose family I home-taught for eight years before my transition. He described the moment in a Sunday School class when he claimed to "witness me losing the Spirit." It was the first and last time I taught Gospel Doctrine as Laurie, when Don had stood up, glared at me, and stormed out of the classroom.

After describing this incident, Don offered an emotion-filled plea to have his "old friend back." In hindsight, I wish I had said, "It's me, Don. I'm right here. This is who I always have been." Instead of fulfilling his assignment to safeguard my interests, he denounced me. He pleaded that I remake myself into an image that had been killing me but made him feel comfortable.

There was a time for Marleen to express her feelings. In an emotional voice louder than appropriate for the room, she gestured to me and said, "I do not have sex with this person!" The room full of conservative men shifted anxiously in their buy-one, get-two-at-fifty-percent-off-suits. As she defended herself, I felt sorry for her. She did not want the church to discipline her, too. She refused to be labeled as a same-sex couple or treated as such. It was true we had enjoyed no physical intimacy for several years. We were living like roommates, not lovers. She didn't have to say anything more.

Then the two counselors in the presidency took turns asking me the final questions, showing again how choreographed this whole exercise was. The first question concerned my attitude towards the priesthood and why I had offered to stop exercising my priesthood authority, thus preventing myself from using it to bless the lives of others as I had once done.

In response, I related my experience serving as an elder's quorum president in Albany, New York, in the early 1980s. Several men in our ward told me how the church had marginalized them by the pre-1978 policy that prohibited men of African descent from holding the priesthood. These men had joined the church, been ordained to the priesthood, and began researching their family history, only to discover they had African ancestry.

To manage these situations, the church's policy back then was to declare that priesthood ordinances these men had performed were still valid. But church leaders asked the men not to exercise the priesthood any longer. Sitting in the disciplinary council, I drew on that precedent. Since I now lived as a woman, and the church prohibited women from holding the priesthood, I should not exercise the priesthood any longer. I stopped short of expressing my hope that the church would someday extend priesthood ordination to women as it had to men of African descent. In retrospect, I wish I had said so.

The final question came from my dear friend Robert Adams, the other counselor in the stake presidency. He had been one of my counselors when I was a bishop, and I later called him to serve as a bishop after I became stake president. I had comforted and cried with him over the accidental death of his young son one Saturday afternoon at a ward activity.

Now sitting closest to me at the high council table, Robert leaned into me and asked what felt like the only sincere question of the night. "What do you want the outcome of this to be?"

Without hesitation, I answered. "I want to be allowed to worship God according to the dictates of my conscience, and my conscience confirms to me that I am a woman!"

President Stillmann instructed Marleen and me to wait in the foyer while council members deliberated their decision. Darrell Cotton kept vigil with us.

The disciplinary council decision is the sole responsibility of the presiding officer, in this case, President Stillmann. The expectation is that in a private discussion after interviewing the accused in the disciplinary council, the three members of the stake presidency will come to a united decision on whether to excommunicate or otherwise discipline the church member, then make their recommendation to the high council. The council only proceeds with an affirming vote of that decision if all concerns are satisfactorily resolved.

Because I felt my excommunication was a foregone conclusion, I was unprepared for how long that deliberation period went on. We sat and waited for two and a half hours. Although the General Authorities wanted me out of the church, friends and neighbors with whom I had served for years would not so quickly go along with that decision.

Finally, at about 11:00 P.M., Marleen and I were invited back in. We seated ourselves and listened while President Stillmann rattled off some hard-to-follow remarks. He then declared me excommunicated and announced that all my church ordinances—my baptism, my priesthood ordination, my temple endowment, and my eternal sealing to Marleen and our children—were nullified as though they never occurred. He told me to remove my temple garments after I returned home and not wear them again. Though I was welcome at sacrament meetings and Sunday School as long as I was not disruptive, I was not allowed to partake of the sacrament, speak, or pray out loud at these meetings.

Even though I had told Marleen many times that I knew this would be the outcome, the reality of our temple marriage sealing being canceled still overwhelmed her, and she could not contain her tears. I jumped to my feet and escorted her out, not wishing to remain in that room another minute. In the foyer, we shared the news with our waiting friend, who was crestfallen.

Though the spiritual trauma was heavy to bear, I knew I had shared the truth, and the truth would set me free. I had boldly told the tribunal that I wanted to be free to worship God according to the dictates of my conscience. I would come to understand that when they expelled me from the organized church, they did indeed grant my request.

25

The Sun Still Rises

The morning after my excommunication, as I lay in bed trying to awake from the sleep that still fogged my mind, I checked my phone and saw a text from Darrell Cotton: "On my way to work, I noticed the sun still rose again today."

It was true. The bright June sun was streaming into my bedroom window and warming my face. Despite what happened the night before, life would still go on and could be hopeful. I was grateful for his message. I rehearsed in my mind the knowledge that my excommunication was merely an institutional administrative action, and God wasn't in it. God hadn't excommunicated me from him. Nothing could separate me from God's love and acceptance—nor from the love and acceptance of people who cared about me.

Two days after my excommunication, my nerves were on edge as I pulled through the familiar gates of the Provo MTC and told the security officer that I was part of the VIP tour of the new buildings. My friend Richard Heaton soon set me at ease. Several church leaders, including Area Seventies, church department heads, and many of the MTC's senior staff were on the tour. Richard graciously introduced me to everyone he could as Sister Laurie Lee Hall, chief architect of the MTC expansion.

As I walked with those on the tour, some knew me from before as Brother Hall and kindly asked me how I was doing in my transition. I don't know whether they knew I was excommunicated, but there were only positive discussions.

The completed facilities and grounds, which began as an idea in response to the design guidelines I had written on my office whiteboard four years earlier, were beyond expectation in every way. As the sun set, groups of new missionaries were walking to their dormitories after their classes in the new classroom buildings. Richard stopped them on their path and quizzed them about their experiences in the new MTC. They shared their glowing answers, confirming that our design goals were making a difference for good. Richard introduced me to these groups of missionaries, too, as Sister Laurie Lee Hall, chief architect of the project. After the spiritual violence I was put through forty-eight hours before, how affirming and lovely it was to be recognized as the woman who led this magnificent work! It felt like I was experiencing two entirely different religions. That Tuesday night was a balm to my wounded soul.

According to church policy, the excommunicant has thirty days to appeal the disciplinary council's decision to the Office of the First Presidency. I prepared my appeal letter because my case did not warrant excommunication. Through my work on temples, I also knew First Presidency members Thomas S. Monson, Henry B. Eyring, and Dieter F. Uchtdorf, so I hoped their knowing the good person I was might at least shine more attention on the challenges faced by transgender people, and remind church leaders how the church could be more supportive and compassionate. I shared my history of gender dysphoria and how, by prayerfully following the medically recommended path to mitigate dysphoria, I had socially transitioned and eliminated its debilitating effects. I emphasized that, freed from this turmoil in my life, I could feel God's love for me more than ever before.

I detailed what took place during the meeting, then summarized that the root of the charges against me seemed to lie in my appearance after my social transition, which made some people at church uncomfortable. I argued that member discomfort should never be grounds for exclusion from the Church of Jesus Christ, particularly as the church seeks to value the diversity of its membership. Would the church ever return to excluding members whose race, ethnicity, language, appearance, hygiene, habits, or even cultural beliefs differ from the majority? I asked. I hoped they might agree they would not excommunicate faithful souls simply for being "different."

As I awaited the response to my appeal, I attended a political gathering where some mutual friends introduced me to John Dehlin, host of the popular Mormon Stories podcast. John was fascinated to learn of my story of being a former stake president, former church chief architect, and now excommunicated transgender woman. He asked if I would consider sharing my story on the podcast. Something deep inside me overcame my logic and fear to say yes.

I arranged with John to discuss the ground rules for my interview. High on my list was that I would not disclose confidential details regarding the church's building programs, pastoral experiences, or family. He agreed, and we planned to meet the following Monday for the interview, which he would broadcast on Facebook Live. John also proposed that I be interviewed by the *Salt Lake Tribune's* religion writer, Peggy Fletcher Stack, for a companion piece published concurrently with the release of the Mormon Stories episodes. I agreed to that as well.

I now realize why one of the scripted questions in the disciplinary council asked whether I would go to the media. Rather than being silenced as an excommunicant, my prominence as a former architect of LDS temples, my visibility as a former stake president and bishop, and my being a woman made people want to hear what I had to say. I decided it was my responsibility to use my voice to increase awareness of the transgender experience, tell the truth about how the church I loved was treating its transgender members, and thereby create positive change for the better. It was not my intent to disparage anyone.

On July 18, 2017, I arrived at John's house for our 9:00 A.M. interview and sank into a low, overstuffed chair while he set up a tripod in front of me with his phone set to video mode. Two spotlights bore down on me like the hot sun. The interview was supposed to last three hours, but we were halfway into my story at noon, so we kept going. Because it was a live broadcast, even the slightest movement of my legs would jostle the tripod and video feed, so I kept still for what ended up being a five-and-a-half-hour interview.

I was a wreck, or at least I felt like one. My feelings regarding my excommunication were raw, and my emotions spilled out through my tears. The heat in the room became unbearable, and I was sweating profusely. The interview wrung me out, yet I was also ecstatic to have a platform to talk about the transgender experience. I'd never had such an intense time reciting my whole life story in one conversation. Though exhausted and hungry, I did not want it to end. The production team edited it to four, one-hour segments, which I titled "Standing in My Truth, Walking in My Faith."

Tribune religion writer Peggy Fletcher Stack interviewed me in my little business coaching office the next day. Her article and my Mormon Stories interview were released concurrently as planned, receiving a total of nearly 60,000 views. I felt vindicated when my photo and Peggy's article appeared on the front page and "above the fold" of the printed newspaper. I chuckled when I thought of how the *Trib* was one of the daily papers sent to the General Authorities and department managing directors at church headquarters. My face would be smiling up at them from their desks when they arrived at work that morning.

But the news story's release also brought me some pain. Despite friends' warnings to "never read the comments" on the online version, sometimes I couldn't resist. One negative comment particularly stung: "He doesn't make a very attractive woman."

At that point, I had lived full-time as Laurie Lee for less than a year. I was still far from being comfortable in my new presentation, even though I rejoiced every day at finally walking in my authentic shoes. When transgender individuals socially transition, the anxiety of conforming to look like our sex assigned at birth gets traded for fear of whether we "pass" as we dress and groom according to our authentic gender identity. Many, particularly those who transition while still young, successfully pass. But this goal is elusive or impossible for the rest of us. Each of us must come to terms with what is physically possible through cosmetic, medical (HRT), and surgical means, as well as what we can afford to pay for. There is simply no one way to accomplish the transition of presentation.

Though the troll's comment about my appearance hurt back then, I have grown comfortable with middle-aged me today. I have chosen not to have any surgeries. I feel good about how I look compared with other women my age. I work from home and tend to be less active socially. My appearance is consistent with my lifestyle.

Far more hurtful than the commenter's putdown of my appearance was his pronoun usage. One of the most damaging things someone can do to a transgender person is to use incorrect pronouns intentionally. Referring to me as "he" after I had bared my soul about my gender conflict and dysphoria was equivalent to him saying, "I do not believe your life experience. You are a liar." His comment promulgated hate and the false worldview that gender identity is equal to or determined by biological sex alone.

The article and the podcast got the attention of all kinds of folks. Friends and LDS feminists started referring to me as "Madam Stake President." I received criticism for failing to condemn the church and for saying nothing supporting the Ordain Women movement. As I thought through such critical comments, I began to realize that, although I struggled internally as a suppressed woman, my outward male presentation had allowed me all the privileges of a white man, including priesthood authority. My perspective on this topic was unique, but it seemed inadequate compared to the perspective of the many women who had spoken about this topic before me. I had never fought on the same ground that other women had made sacred by their efforts and sacrifice.

One Sunday, I sat alone after a sacrament meeting when an older, quiet, and quirky couple in the ward approached me. They told me they had listened to every word of my Mormon Stories interview and were sorry for what had happened to me. They expressed their love, support, and outrage over my treatment. The woman said she would start a petition to get me reinstated if it would help but feared she might wind up right where I was if she did. I thanked them both for their kindness and embraced them. Evidently, our local leaders lost the confidence of others who saw their injustice. I found it ironic that I was charged with hurting testimonies and breaking hearts with my social transition, but our leaders' treatment of me had done precisely that.

At that time, I was also noticed by the new executive director of Affirmation, a support group for LGBTQ Mormons and their families and allies. He phoned me to ask about my well-being and my faith after my excommunication. Although I felt raw on many aspects of the church, I responded that my faith in the divine was intact. He invited me to speak at the Affirmation International

Conference that September, and I accepted. I silently wondered why Affirmation had previously ignored my requests to join the Affirmation Facebook group, but it felt nice to be needed now.

Other good things happened that summer. A good friend, the affirming dad to a transgender son, who I came to know through the TransActive LDS Facebook group, mentioned a building development he and his business partner were planning in the historic district on Main Street in Pleasant Grove, Utah. He had recently completed a smaller building in the same area and had used a residential designer to produce the plans. Although that had been successful, this next building would be larger and more complex. In chatting with him, I explained he would need the services of a licensed architect familiar with multi-use commercial projects. Soon, I was making myself available to look at his concepts. This interaction led me to start my own architectural practice, LLH Studio. I opened up an office in Salt Lake City, and my first project was to design my friend's new development. After a winter of rejection in my profession, the prospect of new projects to practice my craft as my authentic self thrilled me and renewed the confidence I had lost.

I soon experienced firsthand what it is like to work as a woman in a male-dominated field. In one of my early project meetings in Utah County, I met with my friend, the project owner, and one of his contractors. The contractor completely unsettled me when he had no respect for my input. I was so accustomed to making knowledgeable contributions to any meeting, but in this one, I felt entirely stonewalled. This man told us all he knew, some of which I knew to be wrong, but I held my peace. Afterward, I shared with my friend my perception of what happened and how sexist and hostile it felt. Fortunately, he valued my insight and did not invite that contractor to work on the project.

Having now lived and presented as both male and female, I have gained a unique perspective on the difference between how men and women are perceived and treated. I do not believe that limitations should be placed on women in any way, including in the church. When I needed to make leadership decisions as a bishop and stake president, I consulted the guidance of the Spirit, not my genitalia. Nothing in my male biology or XY chromosomes informed my

In front of her new office in Salt Lake City, June 2017. Courtesy Laurie Lee Hall.

service as a priesthood holder. Limiting the priesthood and church leadership to men only is based on cultural and social traditions and patriarchal control bias, not on God's will. I successfully served as a priesthood leader with my woman's heart, might, mind, and strength.

At the end of July 2017, the First Presidency mailed my stake president its ruling on my appeal to overturn my excommunication. Protocol required President Stillmann to notify me in person of the First Presidency's decision. Stillmann's executive secretary tried to get me to come to the stake offices to meet with him, but by then I was no longer willing to go. Dressing in Sunday clothes and meeting him on his turf meant I still acknowledged his authority over me. I had reached the point where I was convinced that no one with priesthood authority was willing to accept anything I said about why I lived as a woman. I'd had enough of the manipulation and ecclesiastical abuse Marleen and I both experienced in the stake offices. President Stillmann agreed to come by our home instead. I just wanted to know the First Presidency's response to my appeal. I knew their three options were to ask the stake president to reconvene the council, uphold its decision, or overturn it. Both of these latter two would finish the matter.

Several days later, Marleen and I were enjoying the pool with our grandkids in our backyard when Stillmann unexpectedly appeared at our back door. When no one answered the front door, he walked through our home and came onto the back deck, where he had heard us playing outside. He asked me to go inside to meet him, and I obliged. He wore his full priesthood uniform—dark suit, white shirt, and tie. Wearing my one-piece bathing suit and hot-pink lace coverup, I sat across from him on our living room loveseat. Smiling and squinting nervously, he informed me that the response came from the First Presidency, upholding his decision to excommunicate me. I stood, thanked him, and showed him the door. Those were the last words we ever exchanged.

26

A Wedding and a Separation

The LDS Church forbids excommunicated members from wearing the sacred undergarments that LDS adults wear after receiving a religious rite called the "endowment" in the temple. I had worn the garment since I first attended the temple thirty-five years earlier. Symbolic of covenants made with God, the garment fostered a sense of belonging to which I had grown accustomed. It was also part of my identity. Several years earlier, as part of my initial transitioning, I had begun wearing garments for women, which was very affirming for me as a Latter-day Saint woman.

Though it was emotionally challenging to stop wearing the garment as a condition of my excommunication, I did not realize the impact it would have on Marleen. After I started wearing regular women's underwear, Marleen came across it while folding laundry. The panties were a physical reminder that my excommunication had canceled our temple marriage sealing through no fault of her own, placing her at risk of losing her place in the afterlife's highest heaven according to Mormon doctrine. All because of my choices.

Though I continued to attend the first two hours of church each Sunday with her, the weight of my loss of membership and the end of our "eternal marriage" sealing became extraordinarily heavy for Marleen to bear. Living for years together as I progressively transitioned was a journey we had learned to navigate, but no longer being able to share in church membership and temple covenants became more than she could endure. Life together under the same roof became increasingly conflicted. Living in a way that brought me joy and peace was causing her deep wounds and pain. We both felt unloved and disrespected.

As we got ready for bed each night in the weeks following my excommunication, conversations in our tired and anxious state often turned into angry, emotional outbursts. One night, I entered our primary bathroom wearing the dark brown, lace-trimmed nightgown Marleen had bought me after I came out to her five years earlier. She was at the vanity washing up for the night. Hoping to mitigate our frequent nightly conflicts, I suggested we sleep in separate bedrooms.

I was wholly unprepared for what happened next. Marleen pivoted from the vanity and slapped me back and forth across my face. I did nothing to defend myself but took the beating while she screamed indictments against me.

My suggestion that we no longer share a bed reinforced how far apart we had grown in her mind. She lashed out in frustration for all she had lost, and I was the target. She hated the realization that our marriage had dissolved into nothing more than two middle-aged, female roommates. My proposal that we use separate rooms cemented that.

After the physical abuse of that horrible night, I realized I no longer loved Marleen. I quietly began hoping we would separate, but I determined that I would not be the one to initiate it. I did not want the narrative of our story to be that I abandoned her and our special-needs daughter to pursue my so-called "deviant lifestyle." I would remain committed. Marleen would have to make such a decision.

When news got around that I had been excommunicated, even ward members who had been kind to me through the months of my transition seemed negatively affected. Church members don't seem to know how to befriend an excommunicant. One exception was Darrell Cotton. He decided the best use of his third-hour class time, rather than attending priesthood meeting, was to meet with me under the pavilion behind our church meetinghouse. There we conducted wonderful and insightful gospel discussions by the Spirit, where only two were gathered.

During this time, the day came for our daughter Elizabeth and her sweetheart's sealing in the Bountiful Utah Temple, with their reception north of there in Ogden. It was a wonderful day to celebrate this idyllic young couple. Marleen poured herself into every aspect of the planning and execution for the two months leading up to the date, which provided her with a distraction from our challenges at home. Their wedding day was all about the couple, so I kept to myself the painful experience it was for me as Liz's excommunicated parent.

She had met her future husband when I was living full-time as Laurie, and by the time they sent out their wedding announcements, I was excommunicated. We all knew well, with sadness all around, that I would not be allowed inside the temple for their marriage ceremony because I was no longer a church member. So instead, I offered to handle the logistics of the family luncheon and evening reception. I hauled all the food and decorations an hour from our home in Tooele to the two separate venues in Ogden. All the while, our family and friends attended the wedding ceremony at the Bountiful temple.

By midday, I was worn out. The emotional toll of it all drained me as well. I sobbed after Marleen left our home for the temple. I cried again when I thought of how Marleen would be doing all that moms do to help their daughters look beautiful in the bride's room of the temple, knowing I'd never share in that experience.

After setting up the luncheon, I was supposed to go to the temple grounds for pictures after the ceremony. I was running late and missed seeing the newlyweds emerge from the temple and taking the family photos. The photographer reassembled some of the basic poses I had missed, but my not being there for many of them further highlighted that I had not been at my daughter's wedding ceremony.

I wasn't emotionally prepared for how many people there would see me as Laurie for the first time. I felt incredibly awkward, as my very presence seemed to scream, "Here I am, unworthy because I dress and groom as a woman!" Extended family, former bishopric counselors, and others barely spoke to me. Some couldn't even look at me. The judgment felt thick as fog. In such an uncomfortable situation, I was thrust next to the happy couple to smile for the camera as if this Camelot was something I was part of. Feelings of hypocrisy filled me for being at the temple and being photographed looking all happy. I felt uncomfortable as if I were pretending to belong when I knew I was no longer welcome. I did it for Liz and my new son-in-law. But it was so much more complicated than I expected. Where was the loving inclusiveness that should have prevailed at such a happy event?

By the evening reception, I was doing better emotionally. I had been terrified that there would be a receiving line that night, but fortunately, the couple chose to greet their guests without their parents and siblings having to endure the process. Not having a reception line allowed me to sit at a table in a corner, where guests who wished to chat with me could come over and stay as long as they wanted. Some did, and it was lovely. Old friends embraced me and asked sincerely how I was doing over the past year. One senior couple, who served as missionaries with Liz in Los Angeles, introduced themselves. We chatted about Liz's wonderfulness, and they asked if I was the bride's mother. I said no, just one of her parents. They left confused but still friendly.

Those who couldn't stand to be near me, including some men who had been part of the disciplinary council that excommunicated me, could easily avoid me in the corner. Marleen had invited them because their wives were her friends. Just like at the temple grounds, I saw many give me a quick, uncomfortable glance before turning away.

Participating in such a social, religious event as someone who is "off script" was painfully revealing and, in ways I will not forget, deeply informative of the lack of inclusion and humanity that should exist among people of faith. Where should someone such as myself find greater love and acceptance than among family and lifelong friends? At times during the evening, I felt the stinging loneliness and heartache of being alone in a room filled with hundreds of loved ones.

Excommunication means isolation, a forced loss of one's community. A formal meeting of those in authority, acting under the teachings of those with higher authority, had rescinded my sacred ordinances. Then, scores of everyday saints implemented that administrative action through hundreds of microaggressions. Excommunication wasn't just about the things I could no longer do, such as receiving the sacrament or attending the temple. Many who knew me before as a friend and priesthood leader accepted that I had been declared a spiritual and social pariah, as though I represented a danger to themselves and their family to be shunned. I had never experienced anything so unchristian as this.

After the wedding, Marleen took a trip to the city of St. George in southern Utah, where her sisters and their aging parents now lived. While there, she called me to inform me of a plan she and her family had devised. We would sell our house in Tooele, Marleen would take Tatyana and move near her parents, and I could get an apartment in Salt Lake City near my new office and architectural practice. She told me she had fasted and prayed on the subject and felt spiritual confirmation that this plan was right. I had seen this coming since that horrible night in the bathroom, so I accepted her idea without question. As soon as I hung up, I went online to find an apartment.

After we put our house on the market, I overheard some ward members' comments to her in the hallways at church. They didn't know how or why she had stayed with me so long. They wouldn't put up with what I'd put her through. Getting away from me was a foregone conclusion. Comments like these reconfirmed that she was doing the "right thing" and that she should no longer associate with someone living below the church's standards. These members seemed to believe they were right in encouraging our separation, honoring her as the righteous victim and painting me as the evil villain.

Marleen later explained to me that her need to leave wasn't because I transitioned and lived full-time as my authentic self. She had years to prepare for that eventuality. My transition had changed our relationship, but it left her without a sense of *her* identity. The priesthood, which she highly valued but could not hold as a woman, was no longer held by anyone (namely, me) in her home. Her temple sealing to me was pronounced null and void, leaving her badly broken and her testimony shattered. Having lost her spiritual mooring to me, she hoped to find it with her parents and sisters. She explained these circumstances to me and asked for my forgiveness, especially for hitting me and, more broadly, for not being strong enough to support me through the difficulty of my journey. I extended my forgiveness, appreciation for where she was coming from, and encouragement for her life ahead.

I knew it wasn't Marleen's fault for how she felt. For years, she had fixated on the priority that there would be "no empty chairs" around her "table in heaven" as long as she remained faithful. Nothing in her church participation prepared Marleen to consider alternatives to the gospel plan or how to view the world should anyone in her circle fail to live up to the ideal it proscribed. She once trusted me to guide her life spiritually. Who could she turn to since the church said my spiritual witness regarding my gender identity was wrong and contrary to current church teachings? What would happen to her when the stake president threatened her with church discipline if she continued to stay with me and we were to attend church as a same-sex, married couple?

The results of my disciplinary council often ran through my mind that summer, too, though they ultimately had a different impact on me. On my way to my office one morning, I thought about my newfound liberty to think clearly and explore new ideas. When my friend on the stake disciplinary council had asked me what I hoped the outcome of that meeting would be, I responded that I wanted "to be able to worship God according to the dictates of my conscience." It struck me that they had granted my request! They had relieved me from obedience to the dogma and often incorrect teachings of the institutional church. I was now truly free to follow the dictates of my conscience. With this also came a greater responsibility to self-determine what those dictates were. My ongoing experiences with the church as a released former leader, forced-out employee, and now excommunicant had led me to center my faith in my relationship with God and the Holy Ghost. Though I continued to want to participate in the church, I no longer saw it as the only way to happiness and eternal life.

Looking back, it seems strange to swap what my identity was—a Latter-day Saint—for a definition of what I now *wasn't*. The notion of being pushed out of something lingered with me for a while but served as a needed transition to affirming who I was. Church members often asked me what my leaders identified as grounds to excommunicate me. I testified that I had committed no grievous sin appropriate to the penalty levied other than to commit the "audacity of living authentically" as Laurie Lee. I had been willing to follow personal revelation and live according to the light I received, regardless of how that sat with the institutional church.

I often said that though I did not choose to be an excommunicant, it is where I found myself. I felt an obligation to observe what it was like and share my experience—to tell the tale of the excommunicant's journey.

Though I felt profoundly grateful for my newfound personal freedom, the social ramifications of my excommunication were still painful. They were driven home on Halloween night less than five months later. Marleen took our grandkids out trick-or-treating while I stayed in our well-lit and decorated house, ready to hand out candy to all the kids we expected to come. Previous Halloweens at this address had been wonderfully busy. Living in a neighborhood and ward with many children, we had an almost constant flow of cute, costumed kids at our door. But not so on this last occasion. I sat on the loveseat across the room from the door, candy-filled bucket by my knee, looking out the picture window as family after family walked past without stopping.

Occasionally, a group would come to the door. As I handed out their candy, I realized they weren't kids from our ward, so they didn't know to avoid the Halls' house. As this went on the entire night, I felt so grateful we had just sold our house. It was the right thing to do. I could no longer live amongst these saints I once called my friends. Tooele Valley, where I had felt inspired to move our family and where I had lived and served my community for two decades, was no longer home. Within six months of my excommunication, Marleen and Tatyana moved to southern Utah, and I lived in a tiny apartment in South Salt Lake City.

27

Finally Finding Liberty Amongst the Saints

Moving into my apartment near my office in South Salt Lake brought relief to me. Good things started happening. I spoke at the Affirmation: LGBTQ Mormons, Families & Friends annual conference, sharing my story in an address titled, "Each According to the Dictates of Their Own Conscience." It was the first time I'd been asked to publicly speak anywhere since my release as stake president five years before. People must have appreciated what I had to say because Affirmation asked me to join its board of directors a few weeks later. I happily accepted and felt like I had found a place where I could serve in leadership again, mainly through sharing my experience as the only transgender member of the board.

Settling into my new neighborhood, I again attempted to find my place in the church. I wasted no time contacting my new stake president, President Dunwiddie, to see what I would experience here. He seemed delighted to meet me. Before we met, he researched me on Facebook and listened to some of my Mormon Stories interviews. He told me I was loved and welcome in their stake. I started sobbing and could not speak for several minutes. It was very tender. I felt his words in a way I hadn't for years at church.

We shared each other's stories, and I felt comfortable being open with him. The spirit in the conversation was strong and palpable until he insisted that church headquarters doesn't get involved in local church discipline. I felt the good feeling withdraw, and he seemed to as well, so he backpedaled a bit. He said our next step would be to invite my new bishop into the conversation. President Dunwiddie suggested I might want to be involved with a service calling somehow, which I confirmed. He felt there should be some way for me to do so.

I learned that there were two refugee congregations in the stake. After losing my home and my community, I felt like a refugee in my own way. Even more poetically, the name of my new congregation was the Haven Ward, which also felt welcoming.

That same week, I had lunch with Richard Heaton, my friend and former colleague. He reassured me that we would always remain friends. He got that I'm still me—just my best version. It was a very affirming conversation.

Richard asked if I still felt the gift of the Holy Ghost, which church members are blessed to receive when they are confirmed members of the church. Members are taught that they will lose this blessing if they are excommunicated. My response surprised us both. I told him I had never felt the loss of the Holy Spirit. We talked about what the "gift" must mean. I offered that the gift to me was an invitation to cultivate a relationship with the Holy Ghost, which invitation I accepted thirty-seven years earlier. I had always continued to nurture my relationship with the Holy Ghost, so I presumed that my "receiving the Holy Ghost" had been fulfilled. I had not offended the Spirit by anything I had done. God continued to honor with power the relationship I had fostered with the Holy Ghost, which was as active and vibrant as ever.

On November 5, 2017, the second anniversary of the "Policy of Exclusion," I read online that some declared it a day of self-care, perhaps to be spent away from church meetings, a day to do an act of service or to mourn with those who had cause to mourn this harmful policy of the institutional church. That day happened to fall on the first Sunday that I would be able to attend my new ward, where only the stake presidency knew my past. After suffering so much turmoil at the hands of the church over the past year and a half, the thought of joining the protest by withdrawing from church that day was intriguing. But the hope that I might go amongst this new congregation and find kindness and welcome was stronger. I attended all three hours of the Sunday meetings, something I had never been allowed to do as my authentic self. I was welcomed at Relief Society and made to feel that I belonged. When the meeting ended, a cadre of close, happy sisters asked me to sit up front with them the following week. They wanted to get to know me better and invited me to their upcoming Relief Society activities.

"Pinch me," I thought, "Is this for real?" Will this last when they learn I don't have a membership record? Would they still welcome me when they knew my story? I wondered. But I knew that on this day, at least, I belonged. I was Sister Hall. I was Laurie Lee, the new sister in the ward. I felt love. I felt like I belonged. I cried with relief and happiness.

The next Saturday evening, President Dunwiddie asked me to meet him in his office during the ward Relief Society meeting the next day. When I told him I did not want to miss Relief Society, he told me he needed to see me immediately. I saw the writing on the wall.

When I met with him that night, he told me he had read my disciplinary council proceedings and talked with President Stillmann. He then informed me I was not permitted to attend Relief Society and, oddly, cautioned me against speaking to the media. The love I'd seen before in his eyes had turned to fear. Something that either President Stillmann or someone at church headquarters had said seemed to have poisoned him and convinced him I should not be accepted as the woman I was.

My heart was broken again. Through sobs, I told my new stake president that if I were not permitted to go to Relief Society, I would not go at all. After experiencing that kind of othering and marginalization for the past eighteen months, I could not put myself through that again. I expressed that there was no reason he would ever say to another woman within his jurisdiction that they were not allowed in Relief Society. He responded that he was not seeking his will for me but God's. I testified that he did not know God's will for me, then, because I knew that God regarded me as his beloved daughter.

I was so tired of crying myself to sleep over the treatment I received from church leaders, especially when many ward members, especially women, were ready with open arms to accept me. I had tried to come through the front door to this new ward and stake, being open and sincere about my desire to participate in church as the woman I was, but that course again failed.

People often told me to walk away from the LDS Church and find a more accepting faith community. Despite the treatment I continued to receive, it still was not in my heart to look elsewhere. The Latter-day Saints were my people, my faith community. They were the people I loved and wanted to serve. I still yearned to prove that someone like me, a modern Esther, could break down barriers and help the church become a safe place for transgender members.

I posted to a Facebook group for nuanced church members called "A Thoughtful Faith." I asked if there was a sister or sisters I could attend the three-hour block of Sunday meetings with, including Relief Society. Several male friends offered to sit with me at church, which I appreciated, but I hoped everyone understood this was a job for a woman.

Someone referred me to a kind bishop from a nearby stake where I might find a safe, spiritual place to worship. This bishop talked with me for forty minutes, seeking to understand my situation, but then prepared me for a let-down. He would speak with his stake president to learn if there was any direction or policy regarding my attendance at Relief Society as a visiting, transgender, non-member. When he got back to me after talking with his stake president (a senior attorney at Kirton McConkie) and President Dunwiddie, it didn't go well. Once again, I was told I could only attend sacrament meetings and Sunday School. I politely declined his offer and told him I would continue to look elsewhere.

A breakthrough finally came when I met a delightful couple at a cottage meeting for an informal study group called "Faith Again." George and Joan told me they had a young, affirming bishop and that Joan was the Relief Society president. They invited me to attend their ward with them.

This ward felt almost too good to be true. I sat with my new friends, who introduced me as their friend Laurie Lee. I talked with many sisters throughout the morning. One of Joan's counselors in the Relief Society presidency invited me to Relief Society, where I was introduced to all the other women in the class. It was all perfect and normal, as it should be. As the young priesthood boys prepared and blessed the sacrament that day, the Spirit prompted me to receive the bread and water again, symbols of Jesus Christ, because it was right to do so. My new congregation was the Liberty Ward, Salt Lake Liberty Stake. I felt liberty amongst these saints, affirmed and rooted in a ward where I felt God's presence.

The following week was the first time in two months that I felt welcome to return to a ward for a second set of Sunday meetings. Finding acceptance in an LDS faith community that affirmed me as worthy of love was still something I needed in my life. I put forth my best effort to find my way into the hearts of my new fellow ward members.

I found my way onto the "kitchen committee" for the ward Christmas party. I arrived at the ward building two hours early, dressed in my holiday best, and went to work with a handful of others in the kitchen. Some of these folks were meeting me for the first time, but they trusted me to dive right in. We served 200 dinner plates that night. I worked my tail off for three hours, then ate after everyone else. I walked around serving each of the twenty tables cream puffs for dessert, cleared the tables, bagged up leftover food for people in need, and stayed with the Relief Society presidency doing dishes and clean-up till near the very end. The whole ward saw me serving them, and no one refused to take a cream puff from me because of who I was.

The ward's bishop, Hunter Gustafson, and others thanked me repeatedly and said it wouldn't have been possible without me. Of course, it would have, but it felt good to be appreciated. My feet were sore, but my heart was full. I had missed being able to serve fellow ward members in the six months since my excommunication, and I couldn't wait to see everyone again at 9:00 A.M. the next day.

This was my third week attending church at this ward. My friend Joan was home sick, so I ventured to Sunday School and Relief Society on my own, with increased confidence after having cooked for and served the ward at the previous night's celebration.

It was all natural and comfortable. I enjoyed many greetings and pleasant conversations between meetings. A woman sitting in front of me in Relief Society mentioned during the lesson that she worked in the Church Office Building. I recognized her from my past life. As soon as class ended, she got up, sat beside me, looked into my eyes, and said deliberately, "I have something to tell you. Welcome to Relief Society." Her greeting was so much more than just a welcome to class. It was a welcome to the sisterhood of the Liberty Ward.

While trying to place her, she reminded me that we often sat in Church Purchasing Department meetings, discussing temple furnishings and other issues. Then she told me about her journey to understand my transgender experience, beginning when she read the article about me in the *Salt Lake Tribune*. Though she could not "wrap her mind" around it, she didn't give up trying. She watched my Mormon Stories interview and became so engrossed in it that she lost all track of time. To her surprise, she had watched all four hours of it into the wee hours of the morning. She told me she understood my situation and wanted me to know I was welcome as her sister.

I also discovered that the two women I stayed late washing dishes with the night before were not only the two counselors to Joan in the Relief Society presidency but also the wives of the bishop and the stake president. After church, the stake president entered our Relief Society room to wait for his wife. Wary of stake presidents after my past two years of negative experiences with them, I made eye contact with him from across the room and smiled nervously. He simply smiled back. Fine, let's keep it that way. I arrived home that day, elated that I had enjoyed a typical Sunday morning as a Latter-day Saint woman.

I woke up thinking one morning about an upcoming council meeting of ward Relief Society class members that Joan was conducting. Our ward met in a 1908 chapel with an odd, "L" shaped Relief Society room in the basement. Joan couldn't envision setting up the room so the class could sit in council together and make eye contact while talking together. I wasn't in the Relief Society presidency or a church member, but had not stopped receiving God's inspiration. I lay in bed for a while, thinking about how I could best help Joan achieve a positive experience leading the sisters in a council setting on Sunday. I reread the material on the church's website on the subject of councils, and though I had many ideas, I decided it would be best to start simple. I led the design of meetinghouses worldwide for five years, so I certainly could help Joan set up the chairs in the room for a council meeting instead of a class.

Bishop Gustafson came in as Joan and I were arranging the chairs in one leg of the "L" into an oval. He had been outside shoveling the snow-covered walks when he saw the light on and found us inside.

He greeted me warmly. He still hadn't gotten over how much I had done to help at the ward Christmas party the previous month. We talked for a while about the potential of the next day's council meetings. Then he turned his attention to me and asked if I was a church member. He wanted to request that my church records be sent to the ward so he could give me a church calling. I told him I was not a church member.

"Okay, that's fine," he said. He could offer me several other service opportunities anyway.

"Yes, of course, I'd like that," I answered.

When Joan mentioned how helpful I had been to her, the bishop smiled and quipped, "Great, Laurie. You're already the third counselor in the Relief Society presidency."

Perfect, I thought. That works for me.

The following day, Joan told me the bishop hoped to be able to talk to me again sometime. To be obliging, I stayed after church, waited by his office until all his other interviews were done, and offered to meet with him right then. It was a lovely talk. I learned that he, too, was an architect. He expressed gratitude for how I had already contributed to their ward. I bit my tongue and tried not to chuckle when he said, "You can't imagine how much that means to a bishop."

He said what made me unique was that I came to the ward prepared to love everyone first, and the ward couldn't help but respond in kind. The bishop relayed that the ward Sunday School president had submitted my name to be a teacher. I reminded the bishop that I had been excommunicated, which didn't seem to phase him in the least. He replied, "We want you to teach the Gospel Principles class for new and returning members." I said I'd absolutely love to. Joan and I had been attending the class and enjoyed it, and loved the people in it.

"Wonderful," he said. He just needed to figure out how to make that happen. He wasn't sure if everyone in the ward would support an excommunicant teaching Sunday School.

No offering of a church calling had ever been more exciting to me. To be so accepted that they wanted me to teach a class felt unbelievable. Joan told me it was because of who I am, because God loves me, and because this bishop is listening to the spiritual promptings he is feeling, unencumbered by the "garbage" that surrounded me in the past. I marveled at how much things had changed in the ten weeks since I began looking for a ward to accept me.

Bishop Gustafson devised a creative way to involve me in teaching the Gospel Principles class. Regular class attendees included a couple just returning to church after many years away. They were turning their lives around after recovering from drug addiction and preparing to attend the temple for the first time. The bishop called them to teach the class, something they had never done before, but reassured them that I would be their team teacher, sitting in the front row. The bishop publicly announced their new calling in sacrament meeting, as was the custom, but I served unofficially. No one besides Joan and these teachers knew. From the front row, I supported them as they led the discussions, reinforcing what they were teaching by volunteering a scripture verse, telling a personal experience, or sharing anything else to enrich the class discussions. We continued like this for eight months, and they became confident teachers. I had a great time contributing again while watching their growth.

One Sunday, Joan and I sat near the chapel's center during sacrament meeting. In front of us was the bishop's wife, Sister Gustafson, struggling to manage three young children while balancing her fourth, a four-month-old baby, on her leg. Bishop Gustafson could only watch his wife's scuffle from the rostrum, where church protocol requires bishops to sit while presiding over church meetings.

I was surprised but thrilled by what Sister Gustafson did next. Needing help, she turned around to her left and handed her baby into my arms. She could have turned to her right and given her child to Joan, the Relief Society president, but instead, she gave her baby to me while everyone in the ward watched. Delighted, I kept the baby entertained for the remainder of the meeting. I never asked her about it, but I believe that she, as a leader and the bishop's wife, wanted to show the ward by example that I was worthy of trust and acceptance in the community. And that's precisely what happened in my Liberty Ward.

When my teenage daughter Tatyana spent her break with me the following summer, our ward was just as accepting of her. She enjoyed attending church with me, and though she has special needs, she fit right in and received so much love from the ward's leaders for young women. It was a wonderful summer for her and one more demonstration of how the church functioned well in this location.

A group of women in the ward asked me why I continued attending after being judged and rejected in other church settings. I responded that I continued attending church to claim my seat on the bus they thought they'd thrown me off. I was claiming my seat for closeted people who wanted to remain LDS. I was claiming my seat for those excluded or driven out for any reason. I was claiming my seat to normalize what it means to be a faithful queer person amid the congregation. Someday, I hoped anyone who wanted a seat on the bus would be welcomed without having to fight for it like I was. I identified with Rosa Parks. I would not give up my seat on the bus.

28

Two Houses

As 2018 began, I looked forward to all the opportunities the new year would bring. I was happily living in my second-floor apartment in South Salt Lake, just a few blocks from my thriving architectural practice. I was fully settled into a loving ward and enjoyed opportunities to serve there. I was forming new friendships with scores of people attracted to—rather than repulsed by—my story and my association.

One such group of friends was a lunch bunch of several progressive male Mormon thinkers who called themselves the "Latter-day Latitudinarians." Included in the august group was Darius Gray, who helped found the Genesis Group of Black Latter-day Saints in 1971, before Black church members were allowed to enter the temple or hold the priesthood. The nine men around the table listened intently to my story, particularly interested in the events surrounding the loss of my temple recommend and priesthood. After our meal, Darius embraced me and whispered, "Dear sister, you are walking where I once walked."

I also enjoyed participating on Affirmation's board of directors. When we met as a board in January, I was ready to make a mark, bringing to the organization the structuring skills I had gained through years of church leadership and managing church departments. I volunteered to lead Affirmation's governance committee, which was responsible for modernizing the organization's charter and bylaws. These documents had been floundering in various states of drafts for months, but our committee got them updated and approved by the board and membership at the next annual conference in July.

Professionally, my architectural practice was growing so much that I needed a larger office. When a more spacious one opened just three doors down from mine, I took the plunge, signed the lease, bought equipment and furniture, and hired a couple of young interns to assist with my growing workload.

Marleen and I used the equity from the sale of our Tooele home to construct a comfortable new house for her and Tatyana outside St. George, Utah. Though I never planned to live in that house with them, I helped Marleen make the material choices.

All seemed to be going well until one morning in late January when I received an emotionally charged phone call from Marleen asking for a divorce. In all we had been through together, including separation, we had never raised the specter of divorce. In fact, at the start of our marriage, Marleen had made it clear that she did not believe in divorce. I took that as gospel until this day. I don't remember if I agreed with her on that phone call, though I probably did. We were past the point of being able to live together or even work together.

A few days later, as I ate supper at the same little table where I had once designed the Provo City Center Temple, I read a blog post in which Josh and Lolly Weed announced their impending divorce. The Weeds, a Latter-day Saint couple, had been quite public about how they, as a gay man and straight woman, were successfully navigating a loving, mixed-orientation marriage and raising a family. I had seen their story published many times in various pro-Mormon places as exemplars of the success of gay men marrying straight women, mitigating so-called "same-sex attraction."

I had seen many close friends who had followed that church counsel go through painful divorces, often after decades of giving their all to make it work. Yet I had still chosen to emulate the Weeds in hopes of proving that marriages could also survive the gender transitioning of a spouse. But that had become impossible in my case, and now I read that it was no longer possible in theirs, either. "We're sorry to any LGBTQIA person who was given false hope by our story," they wrote in their blog post. They realized that their platonic love could not substitute for romantic love, "and that is what human beings need to be healthy—all of us. Romantic attachment. It's one of the main purposes of life!"

I went into my bedroom, where our one-time marriage bed now filled the tiny room, and cried. I mourned for the loss of my marriage, for the loss of the Weeds's marriage, and for everyone else who had the best of intentions in trying to live as someone we were not. I was inconsolable.

I became so distraught that I knew I needed to leave my apartment to find a friend to sit with me through my grief. I knew that being alone at times like that put me at risk of spiraling into depression and even suicidal ideation, and that scared me. Fortunately, Joan answered my phone call. She let me come immediately to her home to receive the consolation and support I needed.

Though I'd been thriving in other areas of my life, the reality of divorce and the end of my dream that our marriage could survive my gender transitioning sent me into a funk. It struck me that I had never lived alone and that no one had ever romantically loved me as my authentic self. Marleen only loved the man I had pretended to be and the benefits of that "normal"-appearing union. It had been years since I had experienced physical intimacy. I sorely missed human touch. If I were ever to be well, safe, and entirely whole, I needed to find someone who could love me profoundly and romantically for who I was. But insecurity overcame me as I wrestled with what I thought was the reality that no one would want a relationship with a middle-aged, transgender, pansexual woman with little to offer in terms of financial security. I did not feel good about my appearance and felt sorry for myself.

In March, I went to St. George to close on the new house and help Marleen and our daughter move in. While there, I felt impressed to tell Marleen I hoped she would find someone new. I knew how important it was to her to be sealed to a worthy priesthood holder.

"That will never happen," she told me. I felt sorry to hear her response. I didn't know whether it represented her lack of self-confidence or her fleeting hope that someday I would "detransition," be rebaptized, and return to her, but I replied that I hoped to find someone who would love me for who I was.

Around this time, I was approached by the leadership of Encircle House in Provo, Utah. Encircle was just beginning to set up a safe house for LGBTQ youth ages twelve to twenty-five who needed a supportive community. Encircle's leadership wanted to discuss my previous work on the Families and Gender Variance Project, providing transgender youth and their families with tools to navigate their journey successfully. They hoped I might create similar programs for Encircle. The result was a series of presentations called "Becoming," which I directed as a volunteer. Together, we envisioned it as a place to bring youth and family members together to safely discuss issues of coming out, coping with change in families, and showing respect as everyone in the home experienced transition. The weekly Tuesday evening program featured great presenters, and attendance was strong.

One spring evening, I was alone in the main sitting room of the Encircle House before the meeting. I looked out the window and saw the beautiful Provo City Center Temple. I thought of how the fire had burned out that tabernacle to nothing but its shell, but I had redesigned it and transformed it into something even better, a holy temple, the House of the Lord. Countless families would be sealed together for eternity within its walls.

As I stepped towards the sunlit window to gaze more closely at the idyllic scene, the light illuminated my face, and my reflection appeared in the glass. The window reflected the face of a gracious woman, also whole and transformed, now serving in another house whose work she considered sacred—serving those not permitted to enter the temple because of who they were. Tears reflecting simultaneous joy and pain ran down her cheeks.

29

Love Is Love

In March of 2018, not long after I told Marleen I hoped to find someone who loved me as I am, my phone pinged with a Facebook notification that would change my life. A Nancy LaVange Beaman of Crestwood, Kentucky, had liked my cover photo. The photo was of the Nubble Lighthouse down the road from my grandparents' cottage, symbolizing the happy part of my childhood.

Nancy's last name was familiar to me. I had distant cousins with the last name Beaman, whom I discovered were members of the congregation I attended nearly forty years earlier in Massachusetts when I spent summers at my parents' house. After checking out Nancy's profile, I felt certain she was part of that same family, so I took a chance, messaged her, and asked the question. Her quick reply was yes, she was married to the oldest son of that family—Ernie, my distant cousin.

As we began messaging, Nancy revealed to me that Ernie, who had been previously diagnosed with digestive cancer, had just been told he had two to three months left to live. She needed someone to talk with about this, and she found it easy to unburden her feelings with me, a stranger. I mourned with my new friend in her grief. At one point, I asked her how her ward was supporting her and Ernie through his illness. She said he had received a few visits from priesthood leaders but that she had not received care from the women of the ward.

"Would you let me be your virtual visiting teacher?" I blurted out. Offering to serve her as she walked the lonely journey ahead of her was as natural as any service I had given over my many years in the church. She said yes, and with that we formed a bond. She later told me my offer to be her virtual visiting teacher deeply touched her heart.

As we talked, we discovered astonishing coincidences. Ernie first became ill from the cancer and saw a doctor on September 9, 2016, the same day I retired from church employment and began my life as Laurie Lee full-time. I reflected to Nancy with heavy feelings, "The day he began to die was the day I began to live."

I also learned how Nancy came across my lighthouse picture. A Beaman family member who had known me in the 1980s and introduced me to Nancy once had watched part of my Mormon Stories podcast interview. She told Nancy to watch it too, saying, "You'll never believe who is transgender." Nancy did watch it, but had an entirely different reaction. Partway through the four segments, she found herself in tears over how the church had treated me and felt deeply touched by the person I was. After that, she did a little "Facebook stalking" of me and "liked" my lighthouse cover photo. When I, in turn, "stalked" her right back, a photo of Nancy and Ernie from a few years earlier jumped out at me. In it, she was looking up at him in the most adoring way. I longed to someday find someone who would look at me as Laurie Lee and love me the way that Nancy so obviously loved Ernie.

I texted Marleen on Sunday evening, April 1. Though she had previously asked for a divorce, I asked her if there was any hope of us reconciling and being together. She replied that this could happen if I "returned to the covenant path," doing whatever it took for me to submit to my church leaders and be rebaptized. She had just spent the weekend watching general conference, and her answer reflected it.

Marleen then said something unimaginable: she had discussed my situation with her family and others, and they had concluded that a "female devil who only wanted my body" had possessed me. As soon as she made these comments, I knew there would never be a chance for us to reconcile. I proceeded to file for divorce in liberal-leaning Salt Lake City. I believed I would have a better chance of being treated fairly in front of a judge there than in conservative Washington County, Utah, where Marleen now lived.

Nancy and I began texting or talking by phone every day. On the morning of May 15, she called to tell me of a traumatic experience.

She had been at her neighbor's pool with her granddaughters and several others when an accident occurred. While everyone took a lunch break from swimming, Nancy's three-year-old granddaughter, Sarah, had somehow gotten back inside the secured gate and was found face down and lifeless in the pool. After pulling her out and performing CPR on Sarah with no response, Nancy described crying out to God for help. She was losing her husband of thirty-eight years, and she couldn't bear to lose this beloved granddaughter, too. An unmistakable impression came to her, "Pick her up, move her around, and squeeze her." Nancy did so, then started CPR again. By the time the paramedics arrived, Sarah had begun labored breathing. They attributed Sarah's survival to Nancy's self-control and clear-mindedness under incredible duress. They rushed Sarah to a downtown hospital, where doctors induced her into a coma and placed her on a ventilator.

After notifying Sarah's parents of this traumatic event, I was the next person Nancy called—someone she'd never met in person and had known for less than two months. I marveled at the path our supportive friendship had taken and the powerful connection we had formed. Three days later, Nancy sent me a picture of a lively and vibrant Sarah, playing on a slide in her backyard. Nancy has said that the experience helped restore her confidence that there is a loving power beyond what we can see, a fact she sorely needed as she faced the nearing death of her husband.

Sometime over the next several days, I asked Nancy if she and Ernie were prepared with all the typical end-of-life paperwork and decisions. I had learned about such matters the year before when I'd helped my parents as my dad experienced a serious health scare. Even though Dad's health improved, it was an invaluable learning experience. Nancy responded that, amidst the trauma of terminal illness and hope that Ernie would still somehow survive this, they had done little to prepare for his passing. Nancy asked if I could come to Kentucky "for a week or two" to help her and Ernie as I had helped my parents. I booked a ticket for a two-week stay. Nancy later admitted that she was nervous to meet me, whereas I was a little excited to get to know her better. I had grown attached to her through our long-distance connections and wanted to get together, even under these circumstances. Upon my arrival, our first hug in her driveway felt beautiful and, at the same time, awkward.

Over the next two weeks, Nancy, Ernie, and I visited quite a bit. All three of us were originally from Massachusetts, and we reminisced about our families and growing up there. Sometimes, our discussions became quite tender. I learned that although Ernie regularly attended the temple just down the street from their house when he was healthy, he had only rented the ceremonial temple clothes, and had never owned his own. Since Latter-day Saints are buried wearing these ceremonial robes, Nancy would have to buy them for Ernie to be buried in. The three of us shared tears when I explained that I still had my male temple clothes and would be honored to send them to Ernie in preparation for his burial. Since I could not use them to enter the temple anymore, I could not think of a more hallowed way for them to be used.

Nancy was impressed that her politically conservative, Mormon husband seemed so comfortable with this odd, new person in his home. I covered many end-of-life issues with them, updated their essential documents, and ensured their files with insurance policies, bank accounts, passwords, and so forth, were organized. I fixed several things around the house that had gone unattended and helped Nancy with a few updating projects.

Nancy told me more about her experiences watching my podcast interviews. "I totally accepted you for who you are," she said. "I came to love you as a person while watching you share your story." One evening towards the end of my stay, Nancy and I were upstairs lying on opposite ends of her bed talking. I saw an expression of emotion come over her face, so I asked about it. She told me that the connection we shared amazed her. I told her I felt that connection, too.

When it was time to leave, Nancy drove me to the airport in a somber mood. I cried after she dropped me off, and she cried all the way home. The next several days found me very distracted. My friend's big project that led me to expand my architectural practice had lost its funding source and was on hold. I had completed some other smaller projects, but now I had no new projects or leads to follow. Clients had promised me work that they subsequently shuffled to others. Doors were closing all around me. What had seemed so promising over the first year now seemed to have evaporated.

In our long-distance conversations, Nancy told me she did not want to live alone in her house after Ernie died. I in turn shared with her how my work had dried up, my in-person volunteer service at Encircle had ended, and there was nothing keeping me in Salt Lake anymore. We talked about how we both felt our coming together was a "God thing." Nancy asked me if I would consider moving to Kentucky and sharing expenses and her home after Ernie died. It was not hard for me to say yes.

On July 9, I was lying on my bed in a reflective mood when I got the overwhelming urge to write to Ernie. I resisted for a while, not knowing what I would say. Finally, I got up and wrote to him on Facebook Messenger the words that flowed into my heart and mind. When I finished, I reread what I had written and was astonished at what I had said. I didn't dare send it to him. I had no business sharing the things I did. I turned off my phone and put it down without sending the message. I shut out the light and went to bed.

But I didn't sleep. The same force that drove me to write a message to Ernie pushed me to send it. A little after midnight, my mind tired and my resistance lower, I turned the phone back on, reread my letter, and hit send. I turned out the light and finally fell into a deep and peaceful sleep.

In it, I described to Ernie how my marriage had failed despite six years of trying to make it work as I transitioned to living full-time as Laurie. I told him that my architectural business, though busy at times the previous winter, had wholly stagnated due to projects being put on hold. I shared how I felt the Spirit guiding me again through my challenges, just as it always had.

I emphasized that meeting Nancy and then Ernie and their family did not feel coincidental. I explained how I had felt moved to say and do things that my rational side resisted. Though I fought the impressions, they still compelled me forward. God was in it. I became thoroughly convinced of that during my visit to his home. I explained a couplet I had shared with Nancy the night before, "Wherever you are, there I will call home." Though it seemed ridiculously presumptuous of me to write these things to him, I wrote, I found myself compelled to do so by the Spirit. I assured Ernie that Nancy would never be alone, afraid, or have reason to lose hope in his absence—all I wanted to offer Ernie was peace of mind.

When I awoke in the morning, I saw that Ernie had already responded. I clicked on his message and read, "Wow, what a beautiful letter. I want you to feel welcome here. We love the spiritual insights you bring. You make this burden lighter, and I thank you for that."

I felt deeply humbled that by following a prompting, I had made his journey lighter.

Those were the last words Ernie ever expressed to me. He went downhill the next day and passed away three days later. That night, with the hospice worker and her daughter Allison in the room with Ernie, Nancy took a break from their vigil to call me. We talked for a while as I sought to listen and help comfort her. She then ended the call to return to her husband's side. Nancy called me back a while later to describe his passing and how, at her request in the middle of the night, men from church had come and dressed Ernie in my temple robes before the mortuary caretakers took his remains away.

Nancy wanted me to attend the memorial service. I told her I would be there and bought my plane ticket. As soon as my flight landed in Atlanta for a layover, my phone blew up with caustic messages from some members of Ernie's family. They were voicing their disapproval of my being around during the memorial and staying at Nancy's house, where they planned to stay. They said that someone would pick me up at the airport and drop me at a hotel because Nancy was too distraught to have to deal with me. I was shocked.

When I arrived in Louisville, I was relieved that Nancy was there awaiting me. As we drove back to her house, she told me she had found out what others had texted me and "put them in their place." She could have anyone she wanted in her home, she told them, and they could stay elsewhere if they chose, so some did. The following day, Nancy's oldest daughter, Allison, approached me and said, "I don't know what kind of power you have over my mom, but from the time daddy died Saturday night until you got here, she was a complete basket case. Since you arrived, she's been completely calm again. We're so glad you're here for her."

After the Saturday memorial service and family gathering in Nancy's home, the relatives and guests traveled home, leaving Nancy and me alone by Sunday evening. Late that night, she climbed into my guest room bed, sobbing. For the first time in years, I put my arms around someone as we drifted off to sleep. The next day, we planned for me to return again, this time with all my belongings.

Nancy and I began our life together in August 2018. Within a few weeks, it was evident that we were falling in love. We initially downplayed our relationship with Nancy's friends and extended family. When we went to church, I was just "Ernie's cousin from Utah." Nancy did not want news of our relationship to become an irritant in the minds of ward leaders. "It was none of their business," she said. Over time, as friends and family got to know me, it simply became apparent and accepted that Nancy and Laurie Lee were a couple.

In telling our love story, I offer hope to all LGBTQ readers that they *can* find lasting love and that such love is God-given and valid. In this love story, I recognize the influence of God, whom I trust guided my life to this relationship by his Holy Spirit. That same God affirms loving, healthy relationships of every type and description. If it can happen to me, it can happen to all of us.

30

Denial and Affirmation

While packing up for my move to Kentucky, I received a phone call from my friend and fellow Affirmation board member, Nathan Kitchen. After we talked at length about the organization's need for robust and visionary leadership, he told me that I should be the president of Affirmation. I said I needed time to think about it. When I called him back a few days later, I told him *he* needed to be president, and I would support him as his senior vice president. He agreed, and with another board member, Jairo Fernando Gonzalez Dias, we began our campaign to become the new executive committee of Affirmation. We won the election and started our first two-year term in January 2019.

One of our most significant contributions was establishing Affirmation as the go-to source for media statements on all things at the intersection of LGBTQ issues and Mormonism. We added an "immediate response team" to our communications committee. We met at least annually with the LDS Church's Public Affairs Department—including the managing director and his staff members assigned to LGBTQ issues—to keep the dialogue between the church and ourselves in the community open and informative. Both entities acknowledged that Affirmation and the church were responsible for the same families, whether they were families with queer members who were still on the rolls of the church or those who had stepped away. We postured that we at Affirmation knew how to provide pastoral care to these families and were willing to help the church do better.

In these meetings, we shared our personal stories of how we and our families had been mistreated at church. I shared the story of my unnecessary and unprovoked excommunication, including how our stake president explicitly threatened Marleen. I asked the church public affairs representatives if "protecting the church's good name" was worth the collateral damage to marriages and families like mine. Once again, I felt like Esther advocating for her people before the king. A member of the Public Affairs Department, himself the father of a gay son, cried as he listened to our stories.

On April 4, 2019, at a training session for General Authorities during the church's general conference, First Presidency counselor Dallin H. Oaks announced that the First Presidency was effectively rescinding its exclusionary policies for LGB parents and their children, issued in November 2015. The First Presidency's official statement called the abrupt change a reflection of "the continuing revelation that has been part of the modern Church" since its beginning. Just like that, the policy that church president Russell M. Nelson had called the "prophetically declared will of the Lord" in 2016 was tossed aside.

In announcing the changes, President Oaks said the new and "very positive policies" should help affected families. Married LGB couples were no longer considered "apostates" requiring church discipline, Oaks said, though he cautioned that the change did not represent a shift in church doctrine. Also, "children of parents who identify themselves as lesbian, gay, bisexual, or transgender may be baptized if the custodial parents give permission for the baptism."[1] This statement struck me as odd since the original policy never mentioned bisexual or transgender members, only parents in same-sex relationships. I reflected on the impact on affected families, including my own, which was driven apart.

I hoped that Affirmation's leadership had been instrumental in that significant turnabout. At the time, I was serving on the immediate response team of our communications committee. We released a public statement stating that "Affirmation ha[d] been a firsthand witness to the damage caused to families within and beyond membership in the church affected by this policy over the past three and a half years."[2] Same-sex couples had been brought before church disciplinary councils. Mixed-orientation couples who divorced became embroiled in intense custody battles, fueled by the straight spouse's

The Executive Committee of Affirmation at the 2019 International Conference in Provo, Utah. Nathan R. Kitchen, Jairo Fernando Gonzalez Dias, and Laurie Lee Hall. Courtesy Affirmation: LGBTQ Mormons, Families & Friends.

anxiety for their children's acceptance at church. Children of same-sex couples were treated differently from their peers at church. Families had felt forced to choose between supporting their LGB loved ones and obeying their church leaders.

Although we applauded the removal of restrictions on children in same-sex families, allowing them to again receive the ordinances of the church like their peers, and that the church had removed the accusation of apostasy for same-sex couples, we grieved that legally married, same-sex couples were still considered to be in serious transgression. We also noted that the announcement did not address hurtful and unresolved issues surrounding transgender church members, who experience alienation, anxiety and uncertainty over their future in the church. We didn't know it then, but that shoe would drop at the next general conference that fall.

On October 2, 2019, once again at the leadership training session of general conference, President Dallin H. Oaks laid out the church's stance on gender identity and biological sex assigned at birth. In spite of medical evidence and lived experiences proving the contrary, Oaks

Speaking at the 2019 International Conference of Affirmation, Provo, Utah. Courtesy Affirmation: LGBTQ Mormons, Families & Friends.

cited the church's Family Proclamation as evidence that gender identity and "biological sex at birth" are the same, and that "binary creation is essential to the plan of salvation."[3]

Oaks's statement dramatically changed the conversation with transgender Latter-day Saints. Representing Affirmation, I told the *Salt Lake Tribune* that it would "send shock waves through our transgender community. They are going to be traumatized and damaged by this statement."[4]

On October 8, six days after this First Presidency statement, the United States Supreme Court heard the related case of *R.G. & G.R. Harris Funeral Homes Inc. v. Equal Employment Opportunity Commission*. In this landmark case, the Equal Employment Opportunity

Commission argued that a funeral home where a transgender woman worked could not fire her as a result of her surgical and social transition. Lawyers contended that Title VII of the 1964 Civil Rights Act included sexual orientation and gender identity in its list of classes protected from employment discrimination.

News broke that the LDS Church's legal counsel at Kirton McConkie filed an amicus brief on the case on behalf of the church and several other religious organizations. The brief stated that construing Title VII to include sexual orientation and gender identity in its protected classes would conflict with the rights of religious organizations to have workplaces that advance their religious missions. One "hypothetical" example given of a possible scenario was "a transgender woman sue[ing] when not hired as a chapel architect at a denominational headquarters."[5] I was shocked when a friend alerted me that the brief contained this hypothetical scenario that closely mirrored my situation. Were church lawyers concerned I might sue? Ultimately, the court ruled in a 6-3 decision that Title VII did protect LGB and transgender people from employment discrimination.

In February 2020, the First Presidency's new teaching that gender identity and biological sex at birth are the same was quietly added to the church's online general handbook: "Gender is an essential characteristic of Heavenly Father's plan of happiness. *The intended meaning of gender in the family proclamation is biological sex at birth.* Some people experience feelings of incongruence between their biological sex and their gender identity. As a result, they may identify as transgender. The Church does not take a position on the causes of people identifying as transgender."[6]

Although this statement may seem benign on its face, for gender-variant persons like myself, it states unequivocally that their gender identity, or who they know themselves to be, is invalid per the authority of the church. The church encourages members to seek personal revelation from God to guide their lives, yet when an individual feels spiritual confirmation of their gender identity that runs contrary to church dogma, the institution seeks to negate those sacred impressions.

We at Affirmation quickly issued a response to the handbook changes, titled, "New Church handbook provides some clarity but minimizes LGBTQ identities." In it, we stated that "while applauding the increase in transparency and clarity the new handbook provides, Affirmation remains concerned that Church policy diminishes the lived experience of LGBTQ individuals." I wrote, "Identity is a sense of self that is in the mind, in the heart, and in the soul. [It] transcends physical biology, whatever that may be. Ultimately, many individuals reach the point where they must live authentically [with] how they feel internally, in their mind and heart."[7]

I am proud of the amount and quality of communications we released during our tenure at Affirmation. I appreciated the chance I always had to ensure that transgender and non-binary people were seen and included in all of Affirmation's statements and interviews. During our service together, Nathan often compared my role in the executive committee to that of the queen on a chess board, able to move anywhere to protect him as the president of Affirmation whose success, like the king on a chessboard, is key to the survival of the organization. We liked the analogy, and I rejoiced in doing whatever I could to help him lead. Nathan has written much more about our time together in the leadership of Affirmation in his memoir, *The Boughs of Love: Navigating the Queer Latter-day Saint Experience During an Ongoing Restoration.* To this day, I continue to assist Affirmation's executive committees as a volunteer member of its oversight committee.

Notes

1. "First Presidency Shares Messages from General Conference Leadership Session," Church Newsroom, April 4, 2019, lds.org.
2. "Affirmation Applauds Reversal of the November 2015 Policy on Gay Families, Acknowledges Continuing Pain," Affirmation: LGBTQ Mormons, Families & Friends, April 4, 2019, affirmation.org.
3. "General Conference Leadership Meetings Begin," Church Newsroom, October 2, 2019, lds.org.
4. Peggy Fletcher Stack, "In 'dark day' for transgender Latter-day Saints, Oaks defines gender as 'biological sex at birth,'" *Salt Lake Tribune,* October 2, 2019.
5. Supreme Court of the United States, "R.G. & G.R. Harris Funeral Homes, Inc., Petitioner v. Equal Employment Opportunity Commission, et al.," No. 18-107, August 22, 2019
6. "A Look Inside the New General Handbook for Church Leaders and Members," Church Newsroom, February 19, 2020, lds.org, emphasis added.
7. "New Church handbook provides some clarity but minimizes LGBTQ identities," Affirmation: LGBTQ Mormons, Families & Friends, February 19, 2020, affirmation.org.

31

My Dreams Come True

Early in 2020, Nancy and I spotted a vacant, older home we liked near ours in Kentucky. It was an intriguing, mid-century modern house reminiscent of the "Brady Bunch" house from the 1970s TV show. When a "for sale" sign appeared in its yard, we bought it and decided to make it our first "flip" house project. I transferred my architectural practice to Kentucky, obtained my realtor's license, and set Nancy up as president of her own construction company. Nancy had surprised me when she told me she had been a property manager in the past and maintained a lively relationship with a long list of tradespeople. I was amazed to observe her skills in negotiation and procurement of materials on smaller projects we had done. We were ready to tackle a big one.

When Nancy's second daughter, Kristen, and her family walked through the house with us, Kristen was enamored with it and told us it was her favorite style. She was also looking to move her kids into a better school district, and this house was just over a mile from us. Nancy and I decided we would forego making a profit on this rebuild, customize it for our Kristen's family's needs, and sell it to them at our cost. This would allow them to upgrade into a home big enough to raise their family of four girls.

The project turned out beautifully. More importantly, Nancy and I learned much about working together, and Kristen and her family came to love me as they felt my generosity through the hard work I did on their behalf. Stories of the project for the family were shared with all of Nancy's children and others, which improved how everyone perceived me.

In June 2020, not long after completing the house remodel, I went to the historic Oldham County Courthouse to get my Kentucky driver's license. While waiting, I became intrigued by architectural renderings on the hallway walls outside the clerk's office. They depicted a concept design for a new, much larger county courthouse complex to be built on the same site, replacing the old building where I now stood. The more I looked at the renderings, the worse I felt about the quality of the design and the loss of the historic building. When I got home, I described my experience to Nancy, who encouraged me to write a letter to the county officials and tell them they were making a mistake. I did so and offered to help them improve their project as an interested citizen and architect.

I wasn't surprised when I received a "thank you for your interest" form letter from the Judge Executive's office a few weeks later. I figured that was the end of it, so I *was* surprised when I received a call from the Judge Executive's assistant. "He wants to meet you," she said.

Nancy and I were thrilled by the invitation and decided to go to the meeting together as business partners and a couple. If they couldn't deal with who we were, there would be no point in trying to work with them. Our county is very conservative Republican, so much so that in county races there are often no Democratic challengers for any position. We weren't sure how the judge would receive a transgender woman and a same-sex couple.

I went prepared with a letter, ideas, and my resume. Impressed, our Judge Executive ended our meeting by telling me he would seek approval from the fiscal court to hire me as the county's architectural consultant. The timing couldn't have been better. Not long after I was approved to work for the county, a heritage watchdog group called Preservation Kentucky raised a considerable challenge to the current court project, fighting at the state capitol to incorporate the historic courthouse building into the expansion project rather than demolishing it.

I was thrilled by this turn of events. Historic preservation is my specialty. Knowing the project team needed help determining how

With Nancy Beaman, standing on Dover Cliff overlooking Long Sands, York Beach, Maine (Laurie's grandparents' former cottage site), July 17, 2022. Courtesy Laurie Lee Hall.

to proceed, I showed the Judge Executive files and a video of how we had saved the shell of the historic Provo Tabernacle, suspending it in the air as we completed a new temple in and around it. He was astounded by the project and grateful to have someone with my experience in historic building preservation available to the county's Project Development Board.

With my help, the lead architectural firm and construction manager developed a plan to lift the historic courthouse off its foundation, move it to the center of the courthouse project site, and make the landmark building the centerpiece and two-story public lobby of the new court facility. Later, I traveled to the chief architect's offices in Lexington and conducted a focused design meeting to establish the appropriate scale and details of the lobby within the historic building. The Oldham County Judicial Center was under construction at the time of this writing and will be unique and beautiful.

Just as I used to do in my work for the church, in my work for the county I have made presentations before all kinds of leaders— project committees made up of circuit court judges, county attorneys, and magistrates, all of them conservatives. Except in this case, without exception I was accepted and appreciated by them as an architect and a female professional. I was not once misgendered nor ever made to feel uncomfortable for who I was or how I appeared. I've seen my dream come true to be able to practice my craft and find success and acceptance as my authentic self.

For a time, Nancy and I were supported and accepted in our Mormon congregation in Kentucky, too. Unfortunately, that changed after some negative experiences at the end of 2022. Our ward building, located on the same site as the Louisville Kentucky Temple, also houses the offices for the Louisville Kentucky Mission. In one sacrament meeting, the new mission president and his wife, who recently came to Kentucky from their home in Idaho, sat across the aisle from us to our left. The young sister missionaries in the mission, who had always been friendly to us, sat next to me on my right.

Early in the meeting, Nancy and I became aware that the mission president was staring at us. We tried to ignore him, but he would not stop staring at us. We tried returning his glare, and at one point, Nancy even tried smiling at him, but neither tactic was effective. Meanwhile, I shared a hymnbook with one of the young sister missionaries.

When sacrament meeting ended, the mission president sat like a stone while his wife simpered over to us. She said loudly enough to be overheard, "I just had to come over to meet these lovely *ladies.*" Her words did not feel loving. Trying to be friendly, I mentioned how much we enjoyed having the young sister missionaries to dinner occasionally in our home. She then returned to her husband's side, where he stood and led her out, now no longer looking at us. I considered the irony in how these mission leaders treated us, knowing that the church's mission is to "invite all to come unto Christ." Experiencing such hostility in a place of worship from yet another church leader was a painful ordeal.

Things worsened when our bishop called a new Relief Society president. Although she had been friendly to Nancy in the past, this new president could not hide her homophobia and transphobia and had withheld her friendship from Nancy since my arrival. Nancy noticed that visits from ward members abruptly stopped. Once, Nancy saw this new Relief Society president in a store and called her name. This sister blurted out a nervous "hi," then turned and hurried away.

Deeply saddened, Nancy discussed this new turn of events that night. We wondered if an overriding decision on the part of the central or local church was leading to our isolation. Nancy decided to write a letter to the bishop describing her experiences and asking if the church had implemented a hostile position toward her because of her relationship with me. Though I didn't think it was anyone else's business, Nancy also explained that although she loves me deeply, we have separate rooms and are not physically intimate. Finally, Nancy wrote that she did not feel safe attending church meetings.

The bishop responded quickly, visiting us on the following Sunday at noon. He was loving, genuine, and sincere, as we had always known him to be. Nancy encouraged me to talk, but I felt at a loss for words to describe the conflict that was raging within me regarding my relationship with the church. On the one hand, I love associating with kind, loving folk like this good bishop and my former bishops, Darrell Cotton and Hunter Gustafson. I missed the community of Saints, which I once was an integral part of every day of my life. On the other hand, I had experienced enormous dissonance regarding the general church, its stances and statements concerning itself, and its damaging policies toward traditionally oppressed groups, whether by sex, race, gender identity, or sexual orientation. We explained to the bishop how I had gone from being the center of the community's love and admiration to being its pariah in a very short period.

After he left, I sat down to write a thank-you note to the bishop, and the words flowed more freely than I imagined they would. "For me, there is a vast difference between our local ward, many of whom are just like you, kind and loving, and that of the general church," I wrote. "The general church feels less and less safe to me, where I am often marginalized. Still, I do feel the kindness and love of our ward in general, and you are a great example."

This good bishop was another example of the paradigm I have witnessed repeatedly over the past twelve years. Local church members are generally very warm and accepting towards me, but the leadership of the general church sees people like me, who don't fit into the typical box, as threats. Top church leaders then train subordinate leaders, down to the stake presidents, to see and treat us accordingly at the local level—marginalizing, excluding, and sometimes even purging people like me.

These experiences were the last straw of my challenges in the church. Nancy and I decided not to return to Sunday services, though we cherished the friendship and love we had received from many local members. We continued hosting parties and activities in our backyard and attending other ward activities, showing our resilience in adversity. Though I had fought for years to keep my seat on the bus, I finally decided that I no longer wanted to be on that bus. It just wasn't bound for where I wanted to go.

Though I am saddened by the loss of my lifelong faith community, I marvel at the goodness and happiness I have found in my new life. I am free to go about in the world as I choose, in a supportive home and community. Though my retirement health insurance through the LDS Church is affordable, it refuses to fund gender-affirming care. I am fortunate enough to be able to pay out-of-pocket for any medical procedures I choose. I live and love in peace within myself and my circles. Although I am deeply concerned about misinformation, anti-transgender legislation, and hatred spreading throughout the country against gender non-conforming people, I move about without fear, violence, and few, if any, moments of discrimination. I recognize that much of this is because I have the privilege of being a white, middle-class professional. Though I have borne and worked through difficulties and challenges for a season, I have never experienced the violence, evil, depravity, and pain that others have known. Some have survived, and others have not. I honor them all and hold a place for their pain. Sometimes I wonder if I should feel guilty, knowing overflowing queer joy and only a limited amount of queer sorrow or pain?

In July 2023, Affirmation: LGBTQ Mormons, Families & Friends presented me with its annual Mortensen Award, recognizing my years of leadership and service to this community. I was the first transgender recipient, a landmark for the gender-divergent community I represent within an organization that had traditionally only supported only gays and lesbians.[1]

Receiving Affirmation's 2023 Mortensen Award. Past recipients Olin Thomas and Francisco Ruiz flank Laurie Lee on her left and right. Photo courtesy Affirmation: LGBTQ Mormons, Families & Friends.

I remember often and appreciate that I reap where others have sowed. I live in a lovely, large home on a rural acre fully paid for because of Nancy and her late husband Ernie's hard work. His life opened the door to many of the blessings I now enjoy. He died before he retired—his family filed his retirement notice the day he died. In the luxury of semi-retirement, I work when I want to and am selective with the clients and projects I choose to take on. I enjoy Nancy's daily love and kind touch in his place and his absence. I am grateful that I have inherited the love of his children and grandchildren as though they were my own, although it saddens me that most of these little ones will only remember me and not him. Nancy's children have accepted me as their stepparent and love me in ways some of my family have chosen not to, at least for now. I am always hoping and ready for change.

Every year since 2021, after the pandemic eased, Nancy and I have visited my children and their families in Utah. Tatyana has spent several months with us in our home each year. My oldest son and his wife still won't have anything to do with me, but the others—Alissa, Liz, Wade, and their families—bask in Nancy's generosity and love for them. We arrive in Utah on each trip with big duffle bags filled with presents and clothes that Nancy thoughtfully picks up for each family member. Nancy and I now have a combined total of nine adult children, seven children-in-law, and twenty-two grandchildren—the youngest seventeen of whom are girls.

Of course, I experienced loss, too. Transitioning to live as my authentic self required me to lay on the altar of sacrifice all that was precious to me and nearly everything that defined who I was—my marriage, my family, my friends, my home, my dream job as an architect, my priesthood, and my opportunities to serve as an ecclesiastical leader. Though I lost many of these things, now I lack for nothing, and I am profoundly grateful that I have retained many of my most precious relationships and now enjoy many new ones.

Does what I have lost and gained back represent some universal economy? In some ways, I relate to the experience of Job in the Old Testament, who, after losing all in an unjust test of character, ultimately proves himself and is rewarded with more than he ever lost. I recently marked twenty-eight years since gender dysphoria pushed me near the edge of ending my life, a life filled with the pain of pretense. I survived it and many subsequent battles with my demons since. Yet I still live, and so much more abundantly. I recognize so many others who do not live to reach this point in life, and I mourn them.

The love, peace, and acceptance I now find in my life have given me a chance to heal and reflect during my time here in Kentucky with Nancy. I have experienced recovery from the trauma I experienced. Time and space have been available to reflect on the triumphs and injustices that have made up my story. Through writing my story, I have uncovered essential memories that I had lost, made connections, and found patterns that have given me a greater understanding of the events of my life. The unique nature of my story and the privilege I have enjoyed imbue me with the responsibility to use my voice to give this story and my insights to benefit others, provide understanding, and witness arriving at personal authenticity despite significant odds.

I am deeply grateful to Nancy for her abiding love, without which I would not have been able to write my story.

It all came down to the point of my ordeal when I could no longer bear the thought of watching the man in the mirror grow old. Time has taught me that I rose to the challenge and chose correctly to watch the woman in the mirror grow old instead.

I only recently discovered that when I was young, I bore a remarkable physical resemblance to a biological grandmother, whom, due to a sad turn of fate, I never had the chance to meet. I found her by connecting a census record with a DNA relative after using 23andMe. Not only did I look like her, but from what I have learned about her, I have a disposition similar to hers compared to others in my family. I don't take after those I lived with. I take after the lady I never knew.

As I watch the woman in the mirror age, I feel I'm also seeing my grandmother age. Though we never met, I think I know her much better every night as I look in the mirror and see the woman I am looking back. She is me and always has been.

"When looking back at your life," American comparative religion author Joseph Campbell wrote, "you will see that the moments which seemed to be great failures followed by wreckage were the incidents that shaped the life you have now. You'll see that this is really true. Nothing can happen to you that is not positive. Even though it looks and feels at the moment like a negative crisis, it is not. The crisis throws you back, and when you are required to exhibit strength, it comes."[2]

In writing this memoir, I have shared many experiences that appeared to be wreckage but, over time, became beautiful triumphs. Often in my career, I studied architectural problems and the distinct design solution became clear in my mind. The same has happened during key moments of my life. Faced at times with conditions that appeared impossible, I studied until I could see the outcome clearly. This spiritual vision has empowered me to be unrelenting and achieve what I have already seen for myself. Each time, my life advanced for the better. Like Campbell, I have learned to love my fate, even to anticipate it and desire to meet it.

I willingly share my life's journey in hopes that the world will become a kinder, more accepting place for rising generations of LGBTQ people, particularly those in high-demand religions.

Notes

1. "Laurie Lee Hall named the 2023 Mortensen Award winner," July 31, 2023, affirmation.org.

2. Joseph Campbell, "A Joseph Campbell Collection: Reflections on the Art of Living," *Harper*, March 3, 1992.

Afterword

Even though I stopped attending the LDS Church in 2022, the organization's policies still matter to me because of the people I care about—including transgender individuals—who participate in it. I want it to be a better and safer place for them. I have continued to track policies and changes proceeding from church headquarters.

In June 2023, through Affirmation's executive committee, I heard that the First Presidency was considering publishing more restrictive policies against its transgender members. Then, on August 19, 2024, the church released these policies in its online handbook of instructions for local leaders as I was finalizing this memoir for publication.[1]

The new policies apply to any individual who pursues "surgical, medical, or social transition away from their biological sex at birth" and reaffirm the First Presidency's statement that gender is the same as "biological sex at birth." The policies instruct local leaders to discourage church members from transitioning in any way and prohibit the baptism of transgender people into the church unless they receive First Presidency approval.

The new restrictions prohibit people from attending the gendered classes and activities that do not align with one's "biological sex at birth," with any "rare" exceptions requiring Area Presidency approval. Those who have pursued transition may not participate in overnight church activities, such as ward campouts or youth camps. Transitioned members may no longer be teachers in any church capacity, serve in any position working with children or youth, or have gendered responsibilities such as serving in the Relief Society or a priesthood quorum. This prohibition eliminates nearly all church callings. The result will significantly reduce transitioned members' ability to serve and be socially involved in the church.

Finally, transgender individuals are required to use a single-occupancy restroom while at church. If no such all-gender restroom exists, they must either use the bathroom that aligns with their biological sex at birth or use one that corresponds with their "feeling of their inner sense of gender, with a trusted person ensuring that others are not using the restroom at the same time." This policy echoes the church's 2017 amicus brief on restroom restrictions.

When viewed as a whole, these policies and restrictions reinforce the false perception that transgender persons present a danger to others, cautioning church leaders to treat them in the same ways that leaders are instructed to treat physical or emotional abusers, sex offenders, and those who steal from the church. I believe these restrictions will foster a surveillance culture singling out anyone, particularly youth who appear to vary from strict gender-binary actions, dress, or habits. The church has taken a giant step backward, marginalizing and excluding innocent people, including transgender individuals, their families, and many others who might only *appear* to be gender-variant. Formalizing these policies leaves little common ground for transitioned people to dialog with their local church leaders about what is best for them, their families, and their local congregations. This policy has made a church that should provide a loving, inclusive refuge into an unwelcoming and unsafe place.

Many observers have drawn a parallel between the new restrictions on transgender members and the November 2015 "policy of exclusion" that targeted members based on minority sexual orientation. This new exclusion now focuses on members with atypical gender identity. Before 1978, a minority race was the basis of priesthood and temple exclusions. Any exclusion, whether based on race, gender, orientation, or identity, is cruel, unchristian, and untenable. Church leaders are again on the wrong side of history to the detriment of church members.

The critical question concerning gender is this: Is gender, by definition, equivalent to biological sex assigned at birth, as many conservative political and religious groups demand, or is gender the self-determined, inherent, and immutable identity of each individual? Defining gender as biological sex at birth fails even to acknowledge the existence of nonbinary and intersex persons. Social, medical, and even surgical transition is the proven standard for the treatment of individuals who experience long-term gender dysphoria. Transgender individuals often, as I did, require transition to survive, overcome dysphoria and the anxiety and depression that frequently accompany it, and eventually thrive. The insistence that biological sex at birth determines one's gender identity demonstrates the church's denying the bodily autonomy of its members, much in the same fashion that conservative governments have sought to intrude between patients, their families, and their doctors.

Suppose, as my memoir has demonstrated, gender is self-determined, irrespective of assigned birth sex. In that case, within free societies and organizations, freedom of full individual gender expression, right to equity of resources, and equality before the law for all gender-variant persons must exist. Gender rights and gender freedoms are human rights. Attempts to force gender identity to fit the imperfect definition of "biological sex at birth" demonstrate ignorance of the issue.

Still, today, in the United States and many other presumably free democracies, gender-variant people are denied equity to resources, do not enjoy equality before the law, and, in too many cases, are the targets of discrimination, violence, and even the threat of death.

During the three years that I have been writing this memoir (2022 through 2024), state legislatures have seen a significant increase in anti-LGBTQ legislation. For the 2024 state legislative sessions, the ACLU tracked a record 527 (a count that continues to rise) anti-LGBTQ bills in state legislatures across the nation. A growing majority of such bills specifically target the transgender community. These include bills limiting or eliminating access to medically necessary healthcare, particularly for minors, preventing the appropriate decision-making that should be extended to youth, their parents, and their physicians. The wording of such bills often targets transgender persons while exempting cisgender individuals (meaning those whose internal sense of gender aligns with their assigned sex at birth) for the same procedure or treatment. In some places, laws target providers or parents for criminal penalties for providing access to needed treatment.

Some measures curtail fundamental rights, including restricting or preventing the ability to change gender information on identity documents and vital records. Transgender, intersex, and non-binary people need IDs that accurately reflect their name and gender to travel, apply for jobs, and enter public establishments without risk of harassment or harm. Other bills seek to prohibit transgender people from using public bathrooms and locker rooms. Everyone should have access to these spaces, regardless of gender identity or expression. If you can't use the restroom, you can't fully participate in work, school, and public life. At our schools, laws have prevented trans students from participating in school activities like sports, required teachers to "out" students to their parents, class members, or school administrators, and censored in-school discussion of LGBTQ people and issues. Instead of limiting resources, education, and opportunities, our schools should protect and support *all* students to learn and thrive. While not all of these bills will become law, they all cause harm to LGBTQ people.[2]

Why is this happening? According to recent articles from the *New York Times*, "efforts to restrict what is known as gender-affirming care have thrust [transgender people] into one of the nation's most pitched political battles."[3] And, "the increase in state legislation is also part of a long-term campaign by national conservative organizations that see transgender rights as an issue around which they can harness some voters' anger and raise money."[4]

As these cruel, manipulative, and self-serving attacks on the transgender community have continued to escalate, thankfully, seventeen states and several major cities have enacted laws establishing them as transgender sanctuaries. These states have enacted protection for transgender people, their families, and their healthcare providers from prosecution by other states with laws against gender-affirming care.

The LGBTQ community and their families are now subject to forced migration within the United States. These fellow Americans, writes *New York Times* columnist Charles M. Blow, are in danger of becoming a "new class of political refugees." Given their forebears' history of being refugees and displaced people after being driven from Missouri and Illinois in the 1830s and 40s, Latter-day Saints should resonate with this dilemma. "When you have to take a look at history and what other authoritarians have done when seeking power," explained a transgender former aide in the Florida legislature, "you have to make a decision of: At what point is it too dangerous to stay?"[5]

Nationwide polling data suggests the most significant domestic migration since the Dust Bowl upheaval of the 1930s is occurring. Eight percent of all transgender Americans have already relocated to safer states, and an additional forty-three percent are considering doing likewise. This equates to between 130,000–260,000 transgender people and their families who have left their homes. As many as a million more, "themselves contemplating relocation in the coming months, remain in a state of apprehensive vigilance, awaiting the potential signal that they too must bid farewell to their homes," said one observer. "The current tendency doesn't just underline a social trend, it underscores a profound human rights issue unfolding on our soil."[6] For many of these American gender refugees, the harsh reality is employment challenges, economic factors, ties to their community or extended family, care for aging parents, and so on make moving impossible. Leaving their homes to avoid political persecution is a privileged option that is not available to everyone.

Fortunately, there have been signs of relief from this destructive legislation. Federal judges have now blocked at least six states from enforcing bans and anti-trans statutes, noting violations of the constitutional rights to equal protection under the law, unlawful discrimination based on sex, and the harm that enforcement would cause to transgender youth. One of the most notable actions came on June 20, 2023, in which a federal district judge in Arkansas permanently blocked the state's ban on gender-affirming health care for transgender youth.[7]

Another of these injunctions is notable for the federal judge's language. On June 6, 2023, Tallahassee's Federal District Court Judge Robert L. Hinkle issued a preliminary injunction, presenting "a constitutional challenge" against the Florida statute and rules banning gender-affirming care to youth in the state. The arguments made by Judge Hinkle provided an immediate sense of relief to me after I had struggled for months under the weight of the proliferation of anti-transgender legislation across conservative American states.

The injunction provides ample legal precedent to challenge similar state bans in as many as nineteen other states. It might represent the day the legislative tide turned on the anti-transgender agenda. I hope that soon, there will be many similar rulings built on the work of Judge Hinkle and his associates.

Hinkle's most significant assertion, established as a legal given, is that "gender identity is real. The record makes this clear. There are those who believe that cisgender individuals properly adhere to their natal sex and that transgender individuals have inappropriately *chosen* a contrary gender identity, male or female, just as one might choose whether to read Shakespeare or Grisham. Many people with this view tend to disapprove all things transgender and so oppose medical care that supports a person's transgender existence."[8]

Just that plainly, the judge acknowledged what many of us have always known with a mixture of dysphoria and euphoria: the gender identity we recognize and have always felt *is* real. More than a decade ago, the American Psychiatric Association stopped classifying as a mental disorder the sense of one's gender identity being incongruent with their assigned sex at birth. Today, the DSM-V uses the more accurate definition of gender dysphoria as a mental health issue requiring care and treatment. Before this ruling, gender identity had rarely benefitted from the broad legal support deserving of comprehensive legal protections now asserted by this court. Living according to my self-determined truth is legitimized if gender identity is socially accepted *and* legally recognized as real. I am not a sinner or someone maintaining a "charade" or "delusion."

Judge Hinkle continued his injunction by confirming the well-established standards for the treatment of gender dysphoria, "including biopsychosocial assessment, which could lead to three possible medical interventions for adolescents or adults, but never younger children: first puberty blockers, second cross-sex hormones, third for some patients, surgeries."

I am one of those who did not receive transgender healthcare until I was in my early fifties. As a result, many aspects of my body bear the unresolvable impact of masculine maturation as a youth and adult. These characteristics, including unwanted facial hair, male skeletal and muscular development, and voice tone and pitch, put me at a higher risk of being visible publicly as transgender and, therefore, targeted for discrimination and even violence.

Furthermore, Judge Hinkle found that Florida's decision to ban treatment is not "rationally related to a legitimate state interest." Often, conservatives disguise proposed anti-transgender laws to somehow "safeguard parents' rights," while in reality, a parent's right to guide their children's healthcare has been misappropriated by the state. Judge Hinkle concluded by ruling Florida's gender healthcare ban as unconstitutional, reiterating that "gender identity is real. Those whose gender identity does not match their natal sex often suffer gender dysphoria. The widely accepted standard of care calls for evaluation and treatment by a multidisciplinary team. Proper treatment begins with mental health therapy and is followed in appropriate cases by [puberty blockers] and cross-sex hormones."[8] We must continue to hope that such clarity and logic become pervasive, stem the anti-transgender affront now occurring, and give potential sanctuary states the courage to declare their position for the sake of those who continue to live under oppression.

In the LDS Church, members frequently hear messaging that says, "It's okay to identify as trans, as long as you don't act on it." Those who accept this mandate, like those who are LGB but choose to live celibate lives, may participate fully in all outward aspects of the church but never be loved or accepted for who they *truly* are. That is conditional acceptance and not representative of the love of the God I worship.

The solution for the church concerning its transgender members is ironically straightforward. As harmful as the oft-weaponized Proclamation on the Family can be, it has always contained a resolution that the church may hold up as revelatory one day. Just as Judge Robert Hinkle declared that "gender identity is real," the church can do the same using its own practically canonized words of the Proclamation: "Gender is an essential characteristic of individual premortal, mortal, and eternal identity and purpose."

Accepting this assertion would open up the fullness of the gospel of Jesus Christ to my LDS transgender siblings, eliminating any perceived need for membership restrictions. This is my hope for all generations of transgender and gender-variant people, wherever they are and whatever their dictates of conscience.

Notes

1. Tamarra Kemsley, "New LDS Church policies relegate trans members to 'second-class' status, scholars warn," *Salt Lake Tribune,* August 19, 2024.

2. Mapping Attacks on LGBTQ Rights in U.S. State Legislatures, *ACLU.org,* June 28, 2024; "Transgender People and Discrimination," ACLU.org.

3. Francesca Paris, "Bans on Transition Care for Young People Spread Across U.S.," *New York Times,* April 17, 2023.

4. Adam Nagourney and Jeremy W. Peters, "How a Campaign Against Transgender Rights Mobilized Conservatives," *New York Times,* April 17, 2023.

5. Charles M. Blow, "L.G.B.T.Q. Americans Could Become a 'New Class of Political Refugees,'" *New York Times,* June 14, 2023.

6. Erin Reed, "US Internal Refugee Crisis: 130–260K Trans People Have Already Fled," *Erin in the Morning,* June 14, 2023.

7. Ryan Thoreson, "US Courts Block Anti-Trans Legislation, New Rulings Condemn Anti-Trans Discrimination," *Human Rights Watch,* June 22, 2023.

8. Judge Robert L. Hinkle, "Doe v. Ladapo, United States District Court for the Northern District of Florida, Tallahassee Division," June 6, 2023.

My Inner Voice

The innocence of a child,
Found my inner voice,
Yearning to be seen.

The uncertainty of youth,
Longed to live my truth,
Not allowed to be seen.

My inner voice buried.

The resolve of a scholar,
Trained to follow my craft,
Fought to be recognized.

The pragmatism of submission,
Discovered my faith,
Gave myself over.

My inner voice chafed.

Subject to safety and conformity,
Identities of profession, religion, success,
Concealed my truth.

The confinement of a prison cell,
Life's choices make fast the door,
And impenetrable the walls.

Incarcerating my inner voice.

Refusing to go unheeded,
Dogma demanded obedience,
My inner voice grew firm.

Against the constraints affixed,
Stripped of friends, family, and appearance,
Penalties were imposed.

My inner voice found expression.

With the blessing of healing,
My inner voice triumphant,
Openly, she loves and lives in joy.

—Laurie Lee Hall

Appendix A

Laurie Lee Hall's Projects for the Church of Jesus Christ of Latter-day Saints

KEY

C	Director of Construction
D	Director of Design
D, C	Director of Design and Construction
d, c	Manager of Design and Construction
*	Denotes original design not used
**	Denotes concept design of site only

TEMPLES

The number refers to the order of each temple's dedication.

115	Brisbane Australia Temple	C
116	Redlands California Temple	C
117	Accra Ghana Temple	C
118	Copenhagen Denmark Temple	C
119	Manhattan New York Temple	C
120	San Antonio Texas Temple	C
121	Aba Nigeria Temple	C
122	Newport Beach California Temple	C
123	Sacramento California Temple	C
124	Helsinki Finland Temple	C
125	Rexburg Idaho Temple	D, C
126	Curitiba Brazil Temple	C
127	Panama City Panama Temple	C
128	Twin Falls Idaho Temple	C
129	Draper Utah Temple	C
130	Oquirrh Mountain Utah Temple	C
131	Vancouver British Columbia Temple	C

132	Gila Valley Arizona Temple	D, C
133	Cebu City Philippines Temple	D, C
134	Kyiv Ukraine Temple	C
135	San Salvador El Salvador Temple	D, C
136	Quetzaltenango Guatemala Temple	D, C
137	Kansas City Missouri Temple	D, C
138	Manaus Brazil Temple	D, C
139	Brigham City Utah Temple	D, C
140	Calgary Alberta Temple	D, C
141	Tegucigalpa Honduras Temple	D, C
142	Gilbert Arizona Temple	D, C
143	Fort Lauderdale Florida Temple	D, C
144	Phoenix Arizona Temple	D, C
145	Córdoba Argentina Temple	D, C
146	Payson Utah Temple	D, C
147	Trujillo Peru Temple	D, C
148	Indianapolis Indiana Temple	D, C
149	Tijuana Mexico Temple	D, C
150	Provo City Center Temple	D
151	Sapporo Japan Temple	D
152	Philadelphia Pennsylvania Temple	D
153	Fort Collins Colorado Temple	D
154	Star Valley Wyoming Temple	D*
155	Hartford Connecticut Temple	D
156	Paris France Temple	D
157	Tucson Arizona Temple	D*
158	Meridian Idaho Temple	D
159	Cedar City Utah Temple	D*
160	Concepción Chile Temple	D
161	Barranquilla Colombia Temple	D
162	Rome Italy Temple	D
163	Kinshasa DRC Temple	D*
164	Fortaleza Brazil Temple	D
166	Lisbon Portugal Temple	D*
167	Arequipa Peru Temple	D**
168	Durban South Africa Temple	D**
169	Winnipeg Manitoba Temple	D**

MAJOR TEMPLE RENOVATIONS

Sao Paulo Brazil Temple	C
Anchorage Alaska Temple	C
Apia Samoa Temple	C
Santiago Chile Temple	C
Papeete Tahiti Temple	C
Nuku'alofa Tonga Temple	C
Laie Hawaii Temple	D, C
Boise Idaho Temple	D, C
Buenos Aires Argentina Temple	D, C
Ogden Utah Temple	D, C
Mexico City Mexico Temple	D, C
Montreal Quebec Temple	D
Suva Fiji Temple	D
Freiberg Germany Temple	D
Jordan River Utah Temple	D
Frankfurt Germany Temple	D
Oakland California Temple	D
Hamilton New Zealand Temple	D

SPECIAL PROJECTS

Provo Deseret Industries Store	d, c
Welfare Square Master Plan	d, c
Deseret Dairy Products	d, c
Welfare Square Cannery	d, c
Sacramento Deseret Industries Store	d, c
Ulaanbaatar Special Purpose Building	D
Phnom Penh Special Purpose Building	D
Tema Ghana MTC	D
Salt Lake Tabernacle Renovation	D, C
Church History Library	D, C
LDS Business College (Ensign College)	D, C
BYU Salt Lake Center	D, C
LDS Philanthropies Offices	D, C
Mormon Battalion Center	D, C
Accra Ghana MTC	D, C
The Alexander Residential Tower	D, C

Philadelphia Pennsylvania Stake Center	D, C
St. George Family Search Center	D, C
Mexico City MTC	D, C
FamilySearch Office Building	D, C
Provo MTC Expansion	D, C

MEETINGHOUSES

North America Standard Plan Program	D
Worldwide Standard Plan Program	D

Appendix B

General Authority Correspondence

(Please note that the following several letters and meeting discussions took place before the release of the DSM-V, which changed "gender identity disorder" to "gender dysphoria," no longer a mental disorder).

EXCERPT OF MY LETTER TO ELDER DON R. CLARKE, OCTOBER 28, 2012:

I wish to take a moment to articulate my situation. I answered all your questions truthfully as I understand the issues, but I was less prepared to explain myself fully. Considering my circumstances, I pray this information will help you and the brethren.

I have had strong feelings of gender incongruence throughout my life, as early as age five. I have not always understood these feelings, and only for a little more than a year have I been able to identify what they are and talk about them with others.

I have what is currently referred to as gender identity disorder (GID), which, as defined by psychologists and physicians, is a condition in which a person has been assigned one gender, usually based on their sex at birth, but identifies as belonging to another gender, and feels significant discomfort or being unable to deal with this condition.

The clinical criterion for GID includes the following three conditions:

1. Long-standing and strong identification with another gender.
2. Long-standing disquiet about the sex assigned or a sense of contradiction in the gender-assigned role of that sex.
3. Significant clinical discomfort or impairment at work, social situations, or other important life areas.

I have documented more than one hundred instances from my life at all ages which fit this criterion. The best-accepted standard for determining this condition's existence is to interview the patient.

This condition is a real medical, emotional, social, and physiological condition, the cause of which is not well understood. However, the painful dysphoria associated with it is very real. It manifests in anxiety, panic attacks, depression, and suicidal ideation. Accepted medical treatment for substantial GID includes administering hormone replacement therapy (HRT) and sexual reassignment surgery (SRS).

I fully understand that the Church counsels against "elective transsexual surgery." Still, out of respect for my wife and our covenant sealing, I have determined that surgery is not an option for me. Instead, I am working very hard at mitigating the effects of my dysphoria using a three-point approach, as follows:

1. Medication (Celexa for depression, Xanax for panic disorder, and Wellbutrin for anxiety)
2. Psychotherapy and Support Group Interaction (Terri A. Busch, LCSW in Murray, Utah, is my therapist and is an expert in treating individuals with GID, and I am a member of the North Star International Gender Identity online support group. I also interface online with other covenant-keeping Latter-day Saints who suffer the effects of GID)
3. Mild Cross-Gender Expression (I have adopted some feminine grooming practices and have a wardrobe of casual women's clothes, including tops, blouses, and jeans that I wear when not at work or Church.)

I have found that all three are essential to support my ability to cope and live a functional life. I hope these measures will suffice and that more invasive steps will not be necessary to maintain my health.

EXCERPT OF MY LETTER TO BISHOP GARY E. STEVENSON, JANUARY 3, 2013:

Thank you for meeting with me on Tuesday, November 20, 2012, and for your kind and thorough explanation of the meetings regarding my employment status in the eyes of the First Presidency, the Presiding Bishopric, and the Human Resources Department. You characterized the response as one of love, support, and empathy, and I am deeply grateful for those feelings on my behalf.

After outlining certain conditions, I understood I must follow to remain in positive standing regarding my employment with the

Church, you asked me if I would adhere to those conditions. I told you I would try, but there could be impacts upon me, and I might not be able to do so thoroughly. As we meet in the future, you asked me to please be open about the impacts I experienced, and I agreed I certainly would. This is the reason for this letter: to describe more fully my response to the things that have been asked of me as conditions of remaining a Church employee.

First, I must say I value my employment as a great privilege. It is an honor to work in the design of temples and to have the interface with the Senior Brethren who direct this work, including the First Presidency. I have worked my entire adult life since joining the Church in building up the Kingdom of God and establishing Zion.

There are many people, both within and outside the Church, who experience what is referred to in the current Diagnostic and Statistical Manual of Mental Disorders (DSM-IV) as gender identity disorder (GID), which, as defined by psychologists and physicians, is a condition in which a person has been assigned one gender, usually based on their sex at birth, but identifies as belonging to another gender, and feels significant discomfort or being unable to deal with this condition.

Given I have a diagnosable and actual medical, physiological, and emotional condition, I formally request the accommodation necessary to mitigate its effects on my life and to allow me to continue to function effectively as an employee in my current job assignment.

In our interview, you confirmed that I am still considered temple-worthy on behalf of the brethren. However, you outlined specific conditions I must meet to remain an employee, and I was responsible for setting up regular accountability interviews with you to report on my actions. I want to review each of those conditions and provide my response.

1. You directed me to cease all participation in online transgender therapy forums and cease to post to my blog. I understand your explanation of the potential risk of embarrassment to the Church through my involvement.

Although I found both the forums and my blog beneficial, I confirm I immediately unsubscribed from the therapy forums and discontinued reading their postings. I have ceased to use the associated email addresses. I have not posted to my blog since mid-October and have now deactivated it so any outside reader cannot see it.

2. You directed me I must not wear any article of women's clothing, whether visible or otherwise, and said if I were to do so, it could be construed as a breach of the "highest standard of behavior" expected of Church employees. While I certainly recognize the need to ensure no embarrassment comes upon the Church through any behavior on my part, given my condition, I must request accommodation on this condition as follows:

I have thoroughly proven that wearing some androgynous women's clothing significantly mitigates the painful dysphoria I experience daily due to GID. I do not consider doing so as a matter of "inappropriate behavior" but as an actual coping practice to maintain my mental and emotional well-being. I must request that I continue to do so away from work.

A symptom of GID is the need to express the self-identified gender. I have found when I do so in this simple and non-offensive way, my situation is considerably improved; when I cannot do so, I suffer anxiety and depression to the point of becoming non-functioning.

Since we last met, my anxiety and panic symptoms have significantly increased due to trying to conform to your demands in this area.

To deny this coping practice altogether could be considered a cruel and unusual requirement and could negatively impact my ability to perform as an employee. However, I commit I will not use any article of women's clothing at work or in work circumstances out of respect for the need to protect the Church.

3. I furthermore confirm I will be diligent to ensure no discussion of these matters will occur with anyone else in the workplace. I will take great care to avoid any situation that would cause a sexual harassment concern for the Church. I appreciate this is a private matter between me and selected General Authorities.

I reiterate my interest and desire to continue as a Church employee and my commitment to strive for the same high level of performance characteristic of my previous seventeen years of service. You and the senior brethren have my sustaining and loyalty.

OFFICE OF THE PRESIDING BISHOPRIC,
BISHOP GARY E. STEVENSON LETTER, DATED FEBRUARY 19, 2013,
AND RECEIVED MARCH 1, 2013:

Dear Brother Hall:

It was my pleasure to meet with you recently, and I thank you for arranging the meeting and for your letter to me on January 3, 2013, which we discussed. I look forward to meeting with you again to review your efforts to follow the counsel you have received and to meet the conditions of continued employment we discussed. I was pleased to confirm your commitment to your temple design work and desire to live the gospel and build the kingdom.

Through our conversation and reviewing your letter, some points would benefit from clarification in writing. For that purpose, I follow up with this letter. First, let me summarize my recollection of the conditions you accepted as you met with Ben Porter and me.

1. You would not wear any women's clothing, visibly or otherwise, at any time, whether at work, at home, in public, or elsewhere, nor would you groom as a woman;
2. You would discontinue participation in online gender identification therapy or discussion forums and email discussions;
3. You would terminate your blog about the topic;
4. You would not discuss your feelings about the topic at work, and
5. You would continue to be temple-worthy.

You mentioned in your letter that you would try to adhere to these conditions, but because of their impacts, you might not be able to do so thoroughly. I hope our periodic visits will help you in that effort as those conditions continue to apply, and your continued employment will depend on your successful adherence to them.

You asked in your letter to wear androgynous women's clothing while away from work as an accommodation to enable you to function effectively in your job. However, as we discussed this in our meeting, you explained you have successfully avoided wearing any women's clothing and have been able to do so because you have found clothing in men's stores or departments that are brighter in color or have other attributes that reduce your anxiety. I understand from this you have found a way to follow the condition to which you agreed without the need for accommodation as requested in your letter. Therefore, the accommodation request is moot.

Furthermore, you stated in your letter you commit never to wear any article of women's clothing at work or in work circumstances. Please remember our understanding is you will not wear any women's clothing at any time.

You also indicated in our discussion you would find and begin meeting with an LDS therapist and you would give me his or her name once you've begun. I look forward to receiving that name from you. In the meantime, I can recommend Brother Justin McPheters, a counselor for LDS Family Services, who has some experience that may be helpful to you. I invite you to contact Brother McPheters and visit with him. If you don't find him to be a good fit, he will be able to recommend other LDS therapists.

Brother Hall, I have the sense this issue has become a dominant concern in your life and may be displacing other concerns of greater eternal consequence. I would advise you look more beyond yourself and work toward identities that are more Christ-centered such as your identity as a husband and a father, a priesthood holder, a child of God, and as a fellow Saint. I believe as you increase in your desires and efforts in those areas and fill your time with service in those roles, you will find a more fulfilling balance in your life, and the anxieties you are experiencing that you relate to gender issues will temper.

EXCERPT OF MY LETTER TO BISHOP GARY E. STEVENSON, AUGUST 6, 2013:

I received your letter dated February 19, 2013, at my office on March 1, 2013. I admit the tenor of the letter surprised me in that I did not feel the loving understanding in its words that I felt from you as we met on January 29th in your office. I find it unacceptable that my sincere request for accommodation was dismissed as moot. I understood the opposite when I explained I was looking for ways to reduce my genuine and ongoing dysphoria through various aspects of my wardrobe, including using some androgynous women's clothing; I understood you felt comfortable granting me some flexibility. I wrote in my notes from the meeting, "(Bishop) hand wrote a sentence on his copy of my letter, and said, "It is OK, we will accept where you're at with this exception," which I understood to mean granted me some latitude in wardrobe so I could maintain myself as a healthy, effective employee. You referred to this exception as the "amendment on clothing."

Please know I have sincerely tried to adhere to the conditions you have placed upon me and find I cannot do so and maintain a functional level of mental and emotional well-being. This is not a matter of faithlessness, disloyalty, or disobedience; it is directly related to my health.

Since receiving your letter, I have taken some additional time to sort out my feelings and needs on this matter, and I find my need for accommodation far exceeds clothing alone. I have attached a copy of my Treatment Summary prepared by my therapist, Terri Busch, an experienced mental health therapist trained in gender issues. The Summary includes her diagnosis of my gender identity disorder (now Gender Dysphoria) and Terri's summary of appropriate treatment steps for those with my condition as outlined in the World Professional Association for Transgender Health Standards of Care (WPATH-SOC).

These treatment steps, defined in the WPATH-SOC as "a medically necessary intervention for ... individuals with gender dysphoria," include hormone therapy and other physical changes to one's body and appearance to align it with one's immutable gender identity. In my case, I intend to proceed with recommended hormone therapy and facial electrolysis. These steps, I feel, are essential to my mental and emotional health. As my employer, you need to know there may be visible changes in my appearance over time due to this treatment.

Therefore, I respectfully request your accommodation in that you grant me the support I need as an employee to take these steps necessary to my well-being, and you will permit me to continue to perform the work assignments given to me without further threat of termination.

Over time, I plan to live and work full-time as a woman, including making the necessary legal changes commensurate with my gender (change of name, gender markers, and so forth). I sincerely desire to continue to serve in my employment responsibilities and realize I can only best do so with my whole health (spiritual, physical, intellectual, emotional, and social) in its best overall condition.

Appendix C

EXCERPT OF THE LETTER I WROTE TO THE FIRST PRESIDENCY, APPEALING MY EXCOMMUNICATION, JULY 2, 2017:

I am writing to appeal the proceedings and decision of the stake disciplinary council held this past June 4th under the direction of President Gregg Stillmann. The grounds for my appeal are: 1. The presiding officer and council members assigned to speak were known to be biased against me before the council; 2. During the council, their statements showed their inability to overcome personal feelings, preventing them from responding with sensitivity or compassion toward me; and 3. The council failed to identify any specific wrongdoing on my part, making their decision to excommunicate appear capricious and emotionally motivated. I understand the content of my appeal must focus on the actual proceedings of the council, but some background may be helpful. With informed consent and significant personal prayer, I have gradually transitioned my gender presentation to live full-time as my authentic female self. Doing so has eliminated from my life the debilitating effects of dysphoria and the associated depression, anxiety, panic disorder, and suicidal ideation. Relieved of the suffering I experienced for decades, I have found greater joy and the ability to serve others compassionately. I continue to receive manifestations of the Father's love for me and the guidance of the Holy Ghost throughout this complex journey.

Unfortunately, some local members and leaders, have been visibly and vocally opposed to my presentation transition to female. Their aggressive and vicious treatment of me has hurt many other ward and stake members, causing many to question their confidence in our local leadership. These feelings have been exacerbated by the council's recent decision to excommunicate me.

I attended the disciplinary council, sensing I might not be heard and the likely result would be a negative response toward me. But I was stunned by the anger and malice I felt during the council. It was palpable, not only in the spirit present but in the faces and body language, particularly those high council members selected to speak. Although many expressed their "love," there was no love conveyed. I will focus my concern with the proceedings, representative of the imbalance of the council, upon two of the three high council members who were selected "to stand up on behalf of the accused and prevent insult and injustice" (Sec 102:17).

The first spoke with great pain about how he "just wanted his old friend back." He, this man who is a near neighbor, has completely shunned me and made every attempt to avoid speaking to me for the past eleven months. The second told how he "tried to avoid me" every time he was present in our ward the past year. Their comments were entirely about themselves, so they failed in their assignment on the council to protect me. Despite trying to explain my witness and history with this issue and the genuine health risks, no one present expressed any level of understanding or compassion for my circumstances. This confirmed that a fair hearing in this stake was impossible for me, and this appeal was entirely justified.

The fact that I "refused to follow counsel" by attending Relief Society on a single occasion figured prominently in the charges brought against me. I know many active transgender Latter-day Saints are welcomed by their leaders to attend the third-hour meeting consistent with their gender identity. Yet, doing so just once, even while caring for another's needs, represented grounds for discipline and seemed very punitive. I was also charged with apostasy, allegedly believing contrary to the teaching that "God assigns our gender before birth, and it is unchangeable." I clearly explained to the council my sincere belief in that principle, and when no mention of apostasy was made in the concluding remarks, I assumed I had resolved that concern. However, apostasy (without any explanation) was mentioned in the letter given to me as grounds for my ex-communication.

The letter also says I was "excommunicated for conduct contrary to the laws and order of the Church." It was never made clear to me what "laws and orders" I violated. I can only assume the "order" referred to is their personal opinion of how things should look, which seemed to be what they focused on in the council.

Brethren, in truth, the behavior or appearance of one person that makes particular people "uncomfortable" should not be considered grounds for ex-communication from the Church of Jesus Christ. Particularly in this day when the global Church values the diversity of its membership, as well taught recently by President Dieter F. Uchtdorf and Elder Jeffery R. Holland, among others. Are we to excommunicate those whose race, ethnicity, speech, appearance, hygiene, habits, or even personal beliefs differ from the majority? No, certainly not.

Being transgender and presenting myself according to my personal, deeply held experience and identity is not contrary to any laws of the Church I am aware of. I have no intent to injure or deliberately disturb the worship of others; I wish to worship and live according to the dictates of my conscience, to enjoy fellowship with the Saints, and to feel loved for the woman of worth that I am, not only as the person others thought I was.

I have a deep and abiding testimony of the love of God the Father, the Atonement of his Son, my redeemer, Jesus Christ, and the continual ministry of the Holy Ghost, whose presence I still enjoy daily. I study the Book of Mormon in my family and have prayer daily, personally and with my spouse. Guided by the Spirit, I have learned compassion for the marginalized and injured. I have helped many who suffer real health risks to continue to live, have hope, find faith, and come unto Christ. I will continue to do so.

We are taught that there is no law or punishment, and I am unaware of any law I have broken. I consider the feelings of "personal injury" felt by those who sat on this disciplinary council rendered them unable to act fairly and justly. I do not think God's will was accomplished in these proceedings, and I humbly ask that this appeal be carefully considered. Thank you in advance for your time, attention, and leadership regarding the needs of all transgender members of the Church.

About the Author

Laurie Lee Hall was raised in New England and trained in architecture at Rensselaer Polytechnic Institute. Her career included managing design and construction programs for the Church of Jesus Christ of Latter-day Saints as its chief architect. She simultaneously served in several ecclesiastical leadership capacities until her church excommunicated her following her gender transition. Since then she has served on the executive committee of Affirmation: LGBTQ Mormons, Families & Friends. In 2023, she became the first transgender recipient of Affirmation's Paul Mortensen Award for leadership within the LGBTQ/Mormon-adjacent community. She and her partner, Nancy Beaman, live in Kentucky and have nine children and twenty-four grandchildren.